Critical Criminology

Editorial Group

John Clarke, Mike Fitzgerald, Victoria Greenwood, Jock Young

Contributing Editors: Rosa del Olmo (University of Caracas), Tamar Pitch (University of Perugia), Herman Schwendinger (State University of New York), Annika Snare (University of Oslo), Boaventura de Sousa Santos (University of Coimbra, Portugal), Ian Taylor (University of Sheffield), Anthony Platt (Institute for the Study of Labour and Economic Crisis, San Francisco).

This new series aims to publish work within the radical criminology perspective. It is international in its scope, providing a rallying point for work in this rapidly growing field. The substantive areas covered are the sociology of crime, deviance, social problems, law and sexual deviance. It includes work in ethnography, historical criminology and the practice of social work and law as it relates to radical criminology. The series is two-tiered, publishing both monographs of interest to scholars in the field and more popular books suitable for students and practitioners. One of its aims is to publish the work of radical organisations in the area, particularly that of the National Deviancy Conference, the European Group for the Study of Deviance and Social Control, the Crime and Social Justice Collective and La Questione Criminale.

Titles in the Critical Criminology series

Published

Peter Archard: *Vagrancy, Alcoholism and Social Control*
Michael Ignatieff: *A Just Measure of Pain*
National Deviancy Conference (ed.): *Permissiveness and Control*

Forthcoming

Steven Box: *The Medicalisation of Social Problems*
Crime and Social Justice Collective (ed.): *Crime and Social Justice in America*
Dario Melossi and Massimo Pavarini: *The Prison and the Factory*
Ian Taylor: *Crime at the End of the Welfare State*

Permissiveness and Control

The fate of the sixties legislation

Edited by

National Deviancy Conference

First published 1980 by
THE MACMILLAN PRESS LTD
London and Basingstoke
Associated companies in Delhi Dublin
Hong Kong Johannesburg Lagos Melbourne
New York Singapore and Tokyo

Printed in Great Britain by
Unwin Brothers Limited, The Gresham Press,
Old Woking, Surrey GU22 9LH

British Library Cataloguing in Publication Data

National Deviancy Conference, *Sheffield, 1977*
   Permissiveness and control. – (Critical
   criminology).
   1. Law reform – Great Britain – History –
   Congresses
   2. Sociological jurisprudence – Congresses
   I. Title   II. Series
   344′.41   KD654.A75

   ISBN 0–333–26680–3
   ISBN 0–333–26681–1 Pbk

Contents

Contributors   vi

Introduction   vii

1. **Reformism and the Legislation of Consent**   1
   Stuart Hall

2. **The Conservatism of the Cannabis Debate**   44
   Its place in the reproduction of the 'drug problem'
   Nick Dorn

3. **Social Democratic Delinquents and Fabian Families**   72
   A background to the 1969 Children and Young Persons Act
   John Clarke

4. **Where Have All the Naughty Children Gone?**   96
   Steven Box

5. **The Contradictions of the Sixties Race Relations Legislation**   122
   John Lea

6. **Ghettos of Freedom**   149
   An examination of permissiveness
   Victoria Greenwood and Jock Young

   Notes on Organisations   175

   Notes   176

   Bibliography   186

   Index   196

Contributors

Steven Box, Senior Lecturer, Department of Sociology, University of Kent.

John Clarke, Lecturer, Department of Sociology, North East London Polytechnic.

Nick Dorn, Research Officer, Institute for Study of Drug Dependency, London.

Victoria Greenwood, PhD student, Department of Sociology, University of Kent.

Stuart Hall, Professor of Sociology, Open University.

John Lea, Lecturer, Department of Sociology, Middlesex Polytechnic.

Jock Young, Principal Lecturer, Department of Sociology, Middlesex Polytechnic.

The NDC wishes to thank Carol Johns for help in preparation of the manuscript.

Introduction

The papers in this volume were first presented at the National Deviancy Conference in Sheffield, Easter 1977. The Conference, organised around the theme of permissiveness and control, and posing the question 'Whatever Happened to the Sixties Legislation?', was the latest organised by a group of radical criminologists in this country.

Its aim was to look at the image of this era of progressive reform, examining critically how liberal the sixties actually were and tracing the controversies and problems which arose over the implementation of such legislation. The NDC, an organisation which arose in the sixties, has paralleled the period examined: from the heady liberalism of the sixties to the critical re-examination of theory and practice necessary in the austere seventies. The first NDC was held in York in 1968, and since then conferences have taken place once or twice a year. In 1972 the European Group for the Study of Deviance and Social Control held its first meetings in Florence, Italy. It has close links with the NDC and organises an annual conference. Details of both organisations can be found at the back of this book.

There have been two previous NDC books, *Images of Deviance* and *Politics and Deviance*, both published by Penguin. The papers in these books reflected the theoretical and research concern of NDC members in the late sixties and early seventies. *Permissiveness and Control* marks the significant shift in these concerns in the mid-seventies. The papers in this volume have moved beyond the labelling and social reaction perspectives which dominated the earlier conferences, and which embraced Marxism as the most important tradition in which to develop a *critical* criminology. This corresponds not only to a shift in perspective in this country but internationally to the European Group, mentioned above, to La

Questione Criminale in Italy and to the Crime and Social Justice Collective in the United States.

One of the consequences of this movement has been that the NDC increasingly attracts radical practitioners in the field of social welfare, particularly social workers and probation officers. Over half the papers and workshops at recent conferences have been organised around issues and controversies in the systems of criminal justice and welfare. This fundamental shift in the NDC has reinforced political debates at the conference. The NDC was set up in opposition to the arid, criminological conferences of the Institute of Criminology at Cambridge, sponsored by the Home Office, and will continue to provide a 'space' for radical thought and discussion of the nature of the state and its welfare and criminal justice systems.

1
Reformism and the Legislation of Consent

Stuart Hall

The term 'legislation of consent' is used, in the first instance, indicatively: to refer to two active periods of legislation affecting the spheres of sexual and social conduct and freedom of expression.[1] These periods coincided with the tenure of the office by two notable reforming Home Secretaries, drawn from each of the two major parties: R. A. Butler and Roy Jenkins. These two men influenced both the pace and direction of the legislation, though the initiative cannot be attributed exclusively to their influence. Many other figures of note made a contribution to what was accomplished. More significantly, broader social trends were assisted to their conclusion by the reformist process. Of even greater significance is the fact that the two reforming periods were supported by Parliaments in which the two opposing political parties held majorities. The first period – the 'Butler reforms' – included the limitation of the death penalty (the Homicide Act 1957), the Street Offences Act 1959 (dealing with prostitution), the Obscene Publications Act 1959, the Suicide Act 1961, and legislation affecting licensing, betting and gambling. Above all, it included the *Wolfenden Report* (1956–8), which enunciated the fundamental principles and doctrines that shaped legislation for the whole decade (HMSO, 1957). The second – largely coincident with the tenure of Roy Jenkins – included the Murder (Abolition) Act 1965, the second Obscene Publications Act in 1964, the Sexual Offences Act 1967 (dealing with homosexuality), the Family Planning Act 1967, the Abortion Act 1967, legislation on divorce (1969), theatre censorship (1968) and the law governing Sunday entertainments (1968). Strictly speaking, the *Wootton Report* on drugs also belongs to this phase, though the Misuse of Drugs Act 1971 abandoned entirely the Wootton approach, legislated in a thoroughly reactionary direction, and may well be regarded as bringing the period of Home Office 'reformism' to an end.[2]

In a purely descriptive sense, the liberalising thrust of these measures can hardly be doubted – especially when contrasted with the return to moral orthodoxy, rectitude and 'right-thinking' which has characterised the seventies.[3] Yet, in a deeper sense, the question remains as to what precisely was the character – the main tendencies and limits – of this 'reformism'? With what wider social, political and economic tendencies did it connect? Is the listing *merely* aggregative and descriptive?

There are different ways of answering these questions. All the issues involved arose as the initiatives of Private Members' Bills, piloted through the House without the aid of the Whips, on a 'free vote', with members voting 'according to conscience'.[4] Some studies have concentrated on this aspect – the party system (cf. Walkland, 1968), the influence of 'backbench opinion' and the role of the lobbies and pressure groups (see, *inter alia*, Finer, 1958; Moodie and Studdert Kennedy, 1969; Roberts, 1970; Pym, 1974). Another approach has stressed the 'enforcement of morals' aspect. Wolfenden did spark off such a debate, to which Lord Devlin and Professor H. L. A. Hart were only the two best-known contributors.[5] This aspect will be dealt with below, though not in its more narrowly legal–philosophical dimension. Yet another approach has stressed the connection between this legislation and 'permissiveness'. In a vigorous, knockabout, irritating study, *Permissive Britain*, Christie Davies (1975) argued that the legislation marked a shift in such matters from a 'moralist' to a 'causalist' perspective. This particular argument is not pursued here. But the link with 'permissiveness' is clearly present and cannot be avoided. The term itself is, however, difficult to define. Descriptively, we may agree that the tendency of the legislation was to shift things in the general direction of a less rigid, looser, more 'permissive' moral code. But the term has a stronger connotative value. Did the legislation also *express* a society where moral standards and values were being eroded? Did it, perhaps, even promote such a trend? Here we are no longer in the realm of pure description, but have entered that terrain where the term 'permissiveness.' performs the role of a powerful ideological counter. Our aim must be to probe – not simply to accept and adopt – such characterisations. Rather than assuming that the legislation was 'permissive' in all these senses, we pose the question: what was it about the shifts in the modality of moral regulation which enabled this legislation, plausibly, to be described as 'permissive'?

The organisation of legislation

Something further needs to be said about the legislative process, and about periodisation. The technical aspects of legislative enactment do not concern us in detail here. We are more concerned about the shaping up of two periods of intense legislation relating to the moral and sexual aspects of social conduct. For this purpose, the size of particular majorities on particular days is less significant than the broader fact that Parliamentary majorities *could* be secured, for legislation of a certain kind, on *these* kinds of issue, during these *particular* periods.[6] The organisation of such majorities is treated principally in terms of what it tells us about the wider political and ideological formations of the period. The fact that the first period of legislation (1957–61) coincides with a Conservative government, the second (1965–8) with a Labour government, suggests that the reformist impulse, crucially, cut across formal party alignments – a more important fact, for our purposes, than the precise details of how many of which party voted for which particular measure.

In many instances the legislation was preceded by an elaborate review of the 'problem' – in the classic form of the Royal Commission or Joint Select or Departmental Committee: the Wolfenden Committee on prostitution and homosexuality (cf. Wolfenden, 1976), the Morton Commission on divorce (see McGregor, 1958), the Royal Commission on the Death Penalty, the Joint Select Committee on Theatre Censorship, the Wootton Committee (drugs), etc. Again, the slow, cautious Parliamentary procedures involved – following the 19th-century precedent – are less significant for us than the implication they suggest of a quite extensive public concern about issues affecting the moral tone and 'health' of society.

Two other features of the 'legislative moment' can be dealt with quickly at this point. The first concerns the active lobby organisation and activities which accompanied it. The failure of Sidney Silverman's first attempt to abolish the death penalty in 1945 and the formation of the Royal Commission was followed by the fusion of the two most active pressure groups in this field – the National Campaign against the Death Penalty and the Howard League (cf. Tuttle, 1961; and Christoph, 1962). The Censorship Reform Committee (on which Roy Jenkins, Wayland Young, and Lord Annan – later a member of the Joint Select Committee – were active) was created in 1958. The Divorce Law Reform Union was established in 1966; the Homosexual Law Reform Society in 1958.[7] These lobby organisations go some way to explaining why the reform movements were successful at this time, and why reform took the form that it did. They cannot explain why these issues became socially pertinent in the first place. The 'lobbies' were pressure groups of a very specific and familiar kind. They were not the outcome of a wide, popular agitation; they were not involved in mobilising their relevant constituencies to stand up and take action for themselves; they did not engage in the kinds of politics designed to create a popular thrust towards reform to which Parliament was obliged to respond.[8] In an important sense Parliament 'led' – and the lobbies served and serviced sympathetic Parliamentarians. These pressure groups were 'Fabian' in spirit and practice, if not in direct origin. Their aim was to influence the influentials, to assist in giving moral concern a practical and effective legislative expression. They provide review committees with the sort of 'hard', practical evidence, with the accredited witnesses and persuasive arguments, designed to sway 'responsible opinion'. They, on the whole, studiously avoided the more controversial aspects or the more radical arguments, for fear of giving offence. They were formed, so to speak, in the margins of, and steadfastly oriented towards, Parliament. Their purpose was 'piecemeal moral engineering'.

Another, often neglected, feature is the role of religious opinion and of religious organisation in creating a climate favourable to reform. Some of the offences 'decriminalised' in the course of this legislation had, at one time, been ecclesiastical offences, before they were secular ones: divorce, for example, and homosexuality. Long after their full appropriation into the framework of the secular law, religion continued to exercise a critical influence in giving these offences, proscribed by law, a moral content and gloss. We have only to think of the deeply rooted religious attitudes towards, for example, such questions as the 'sanctity of human life' (abortion), the 'just' taking of life (capital punishment), the 'spiritual' basis of the marital union (divorce), the pollution attributed to extra-marital and 'perverse' sexuality (prostitution and homosexuality), the prevention of blasphemy (censorship), and the preservation of the 'separate and distinct' character of the Lord's Day (Sunday Observance) to appreciate the powerful influence of religion in the articulation of both official legal and popular moral ideologies. In so far as existing legislation did retain – in however confused a form – some relationship between illegality and immorality, it was the religious trace which provided the bridge between the two, securing their intimate correspondence (cf. Delvin, 1965, p. 23).

Shifts in religious attitudes were bound to have an influence on such matters: if not in positively enabling reform to proceed, then in undermining the moral certainty and conviction of its opponents. Such a shift is indeed to be observed, although it was not all moving in a single direction. At no time is religious opinion to be found uniformly swinging over to the reformist cause. On two issues in particular religious forces and teaching were not only influential in sustaining the opposition to reform, but provided that opposition with its moral backbone. This is true of the Catholic and fundamentalist churches with respect to abortion, and the nonconformist fundamentalist sects with respect to Sunday Observance. On other issues the shift in the reformist direction is significant. Commentators now agree on the influence for reformism exercised by, *inter alia*, the survey by the Church Information Board on *Sexual Offenders and Social Punishment* (1958), on which its powerful evidence to Wolfenden was based; the Church of England's pamphlet on divorce, *Putting Asunder* (1964); the publication of the Church Assembly's Board for Social Responsibility on *Abortion: an Ethical Discussion* (1965); and *Towards a Quaker View of Sex* (1966). How far these and other similar publications were impelled by a profound change of heart, a response to social forces and change too powerful to resist, or a convenient adaptation to an inhospitable secular climate is, of course, not recorded.

The general point to note is the vital and continuing force of religion in the articulation of moral ideologies and the regulation of moral practice, even in our so-called 'materialist' society – and at a period of their manifest institutional decline. We would argue that no significant shift in the moral economy by which such social behaviour in our society is regulated can occur without a corresponding movement in religious ideology – however marginal religious observance and practice may appear to have become. In this sense Lord Devlin was certainly correct to say that, as a matter of fact, the 'right-thinking man' had nowhere else to turn to for the foundations of his 'practical morality', based as it was 'not on theological or philosophical foundations' but 'in the mass of continuous experience half-consciously or unconsciously accumulated and embodied in the morality of common sense' (Devlin, 1965, p. 15).[9]

More pertinent is the evidence of a growing split and polarisation in religious ideology concerning questions of moral conduct –

recapitulating the polarisation into two distinctive 'moral climates', which can be evidenced elsewhere (and to which we shall return). In some areas religious opinion dug its heels in. Thus the teaching of the Roman Catholic Church on the 'sanctity of life' was an ideological force powerful enough to pull so impeccable a reformist as Mrs Shirley Williams, and even so potential a recruit as Mr St John-Stevas[10] – likely doyens of the 'liberal' majorities of the Parliaments of the sixties – into the orthodox camp on the issue of abortion. Elsewhere, the polarisation in religious ideology is clear. The more established churches, and the sectors of informed opinion influenced by them in terms of conventional moral ideology, responded to the changing climate and turned in the direction of reformism. More fundamentalist and orthodox tendencies swung – gradually at first, then more vigorously – in the opposite direction. In the backlash which followed the peak of the 'consenting legislation' of the sixties, fundamentalist religious ideologies provided the philosophic rationale and often the organisational base for a vigorous rearguard action (cf. the influence of the Lord's Day Observance Society, SPUC, the 'Clean-Up TV' Campaign, the National Viewers and Listeners Association, the 'Festival of Light' movement, etc.[11]) If the trend towards reformism was facilitated by a liberalisation of religious opinion, then the return to moral orthodoxy was powerfully fuelled by religious fundamentalism. In general, however, the role of religion in the formation of practical morality and in the construction of ideological common sense retains its centrality, even in a period characterised by so-called hedonism and secularism. Without making too immediate or direct a correlation, it seemed to be the more 'established' religious affiliations – those closely interwoven with the state and the law, with middle-class or 'gentry' society – which moved with the times. It was the more fundamentalist sects, with their hold over the moral ideologies of sections of the 'respectable' working class and the old petty-bourgeoisie, which increasingly stood with their backs to the defences. There is a clue here which, without falling for a crude class reductionism, we would be wise not to neglect.

What of the legislation itself? Clearly, no comprehensive review of its details is possible here. The key question for us must be: can one identify a general *tendency* which – given significant differences in timing and point of application – is common to the 'consenting legislation' of the period? If so, how is that tendency to be characterised? We have shown already how difficult it would be to accept the simple characterisation 'permissive'. It would be more accurate to ask how the balance between liberalisation and control was struck. Was the legislation, in sum, a sort of restructuring of the moral sphere, which, under the veneer of permissiveness and liberalisation, actually tightened the control by the state and the law over moral conduct – regulating and tuning it more finely? Or was the logic of its tendency a more contradictory one? Above all, what is the relation between the dominant tendency of this legislation and the wider aspects of reformism in the same period?

Here we must enter a warning. In the 'legislation of consent' no single, uncontradictory tendency is to be discovered. Even where, in retrospect, we may identify a general pattern to this reformism, we must attend fully to the variety of specific circumstances operating in each particular example. Their 'unity' is necessarily a *complex* one – the unity of this historical conjuncture only emerges through a series of diverse origins, contradictory forces, with different modalities and temporalities of development (cf. Althusser, 1969). Difference and specificity must not be elided under a convenient set of neat correspondences. Indeed, some correspondences may be highly misleading. For example, Sidney Silverman was a redoubtable Parliamentary fighter for libertarian causes – as vigorous, later, on homosexual reform as he was, earlier, on the death penalty. Yet the abolition of the death penalty and the legislation on homosexuality had profoundly different roots – different histories, belonging to different historical *dureés* – than this coincidence might suggest. Within the Labour Movement there was a long-standing opposition to the exercise of the death penalty, opposed to the traditional 'hanging lobby' in the Conservative Party – so much so that Silverman was genuinely surprised that abolition did not naturally follow the 1945 Labour victory.[12] Legislation on homosexuality was not a traditional Labour demand; and when, in 1957, the move to abolish hanging secured a majority, none could be found for altering by a line the legislation on homosexual offences. The two things 'happened' roughly in the same period, but they can only be said to belong to the same conjuncture or tendency in a highly *uneven* way.

To take another obvious point. Anyone who read Roy Jenkins' Penguin Special *The Labour Case* could have discerned from his final chapter, Is Britain Civilized?, a clear commitment to initiate legislation which would limit the state's restriction on personal freedom, and 'create a climate of opinion which is favourable to gaiety, tolerance and beauty and unfavourable to puritanical restriction, to petty-minded disapproval, to hypocrisy, and to a dreary, ugly pattern of life' (Jenkins, 1959, p. 135). There is, however, all the difference in the world between this thrust and that which had led, a decade earlier, to the formation of the Wolfenden Committee. Recent commentators appear to have neglected the fact that the Wolfenden Committee was formèd in direct response, not to a 'climate . . . favourable to gaiety, tolerance and beauty', but to a growing moral panic about the rise of prostitution and street-walking and the spread of homosexuality.[13] What the *Wolfenden Report* said, and how its recommendations were legislated on, must be referred to a context different in important respects from that which framed the second phase of reform.

We say 'moral panic' advisedly. When it came to examine the statistics more closely, the Wolfenden Committee was hard put to it to discover a factual basis for the widespread impression that both prostitution and homosexuality were increasing at a rapid and intolerable rate. It knew, and admitted, the shaky basis for this impression in the statistics on arrest, which, it recognised, were as much a product of police vigilance as an index of actual incidence.[14] However, it could not gainsay the general public *impression* that these offences *were* on the increase. With respect to homosexuality, it remained, to the end, agnostic about any significant increase: with respect to prostitution, it acknowledged the greater visibility of solicitor street-walking and kerb-crawling in the West End. Butler spoke subsequently of 'the condition of the streets around Mayfair and Piccadilly, which were literally crowded out with girls touting for clients . . . which gave a very unhealthy look to the centre of our capital city' (Butler, 1971, p. 204), and of the penetration of prostitution into hitherto respectable residential areas. (The Labour MP for Stepney was also most vehement on this point, extending it to Paddington, Notting Hill, and other parts of London, in the Commons debate on Wolfenden.[15]) The 'panic' about homosexuality was partly precipitated by the various spy scandals of the early fifties – Burgess, Maclean, Vassall – and the much-publicised trial of Lord Montague and Peter Wildeblood[16] in 1953 (cf. *inter alia*, Weeks, 1977; Butler, 1971; Wolfenden, 1976). The impact of the *Wolfenden Report*, which took even its chairman by surprise,[17] must be 'read' against a moral climate directed not towards the liberalisation but towards the tightening up of the legal regulation of moral conduct.[18] The contradictions within Wolfenden – the orthodox and restrictive proposals on prostitution, implemented at once; the liberal attitude to homosexuality, delayed for a decade – must be referred to a context significantly different from that of the 'swinging sixties', and the element of 'permissiveness' in its doctrine (which we shall discuss further below) interpreted accordingly. We must resist, here, any effort at a simple homogenisation.

Wolfenden and moral regulation

This said, Wolfenden nevertheless remains a necessary starting point. This is not because it was the cause and 'origin' of everything that followed, because a straight line of 'influence' can be traced in evolutionary fashion through to the end of the sixties, or because every feature of the legislation of consent in the two decades can be traced back to it. Rather, we must begin with Wolfenden because it initiated *a process*. It set out to articulate the field of moral ideology and practice which defines the dominant tendency in the 'legislation of consent'. This is also the factor which helps us to define both the specific character and the limits of that reformism which produced these legislative measures as one of its complex effects.

In certain respects, what is striking about the *Wolfenden Report* is its impeccable orthodoxy, both in many of its arguments and in its immediate consequences. Lord Wolfenden has subsequently confessed to (Wolfenden, 1971, p. 145) some wry amusement that his Committee, 'who were thought by many to be so outrageous in 1957, should now be regarded as Victorian.' It certainly was not. The attitudes of moral disapprobation, spiritual rectitude and moral rescue which scar so much of Victorian reformist writing on prostitution is altogether absent from the pages of the *Report*. It was indeed Wolfenden's practicality, its moral agnosticism, which constituted its 'scandal'. But the *Report* was undoubtedly socially orthodox.

On prostitution it proposed a substantial increase in the maximum penalty for persistent soliciting, progressively higher fines for repeated offences, with an ultimate maximum of 3 months' imprisonment, increased from 14 days. Wolfenden suggests that a possible spell in prison was designed to persuade the persistent soliciting offender to be more willing 'to listen to a probation officer' (Wolfenden, 1971, p. 139). There is, both here and in the sections on homosexuality, more than a hint in the *Report* of the trend towards the 'welfare-statisation' of criminal problems – the tendency to shift the 'treatment' of moral deviance more towards the 'social problem' paradigm, or to 'medicalise' it.[19] These, coupled with its other recommendations on street-walking and poncing, served the impeccably orthodox purpose for which the Committee had been established: to 'clear the streets of prostitution'. The *Wolfenden Report* based its reasoning squarely on the orthodox legal grounds of affronts to public decency and offences against public sector. The law, it said:

> . . . should confine itself to those activities which offend against public order and decency or expose the ordinary citizen to what is offensive and injurious; and the simple fact is that prostitutes do parade themselves more habitually and openly than their prospective customers, and do by their continual presence affront the sense of decency of the ordinary citizen. In doing so they create a nuisance which, in our view, the law is entitled to recognize and deal with (HMSO, 1957, p. 87).

The *Report* did not probe behind the public anxiety and sense of panic about the rising tide of vice. It took the *visibility* of prostitution as its principal object (cf. Bland, McCabe and Mort, 1978). It measured this against the sense of decency of the ordinary citizen 'who should be able to go about his business without the constant affront to his sense of decency which the presence of these women affords' (HMSO, 1957). The key interpellative structure of this discourse, the 'subject' it recruits, is '*respectable man*', that fictional centre-point of the turning world of the law – Lord Devlin's 'right-thinking man', 'on the Clapham omnibus' (Devlin, 1965, p. 15). If, finally, there is a Victorian touch, it is in the way Wolfenden sticks fast to the façade of respectable morality, sustaining that hypocrisy with which the law has, typically, dealt with prostitution: on which it morally frowns, which it legally harasses but which it refuses to make a criminal offence, and which it tacitly excuses on the grounds of the unstated licence to men to satisfy their 'natural appetites', provided the means to that satisfaction is kept out of sight. The *Report* is rich on why prostitutes, but not their male clients, should fall within the ambit of the law: 'the fact is that prostitutes do parade themselves more habitually and openly than their prospective customers' (HMSO, 1957, p. 79).

It was this flouting and flaunting of the hypocritical façade of respectable morality – the 'parading' – upon which the *Wolfenden Report* operated. It bypassed with little more than a glance the deep

[margin annotation: Is this really hypocrisy]

exploitation of female sexuality inscribed in the social relations of commercialised prostitutes, who may have been driven to it through poverty; in the 'affluent society', they were more likely to be 'women whose psychological make-up is such that they choose this life because they find in it a style of living which is to them freer, more profitable than would be provided by any other occupation' (cf. Greenwood and Young, in this volume). Still, as Wolfenden tersely observed, 'there were some things which were better swept under the carpet than lying about on top of it' (HMSO, 1957, p. 42).

The contradiction in Wolfenden arises from the apparent discrepancy between the orthodoxy of the proposals on prostitution and the 'liberal' thrust of the recommendations on homosexuality. Even here, when legislation finally came, there was no runaway libertarianism. The sanctions against soliciting and male importuning were strengthened. By failing to define 'in private' the Act left a loophole which some police forces exploited to the hilt (cf. Greenwood and Young, 1976; Weeks, 1977). The penalty against 'gross indecency' between a man over 21 and a youth below the age of consent was stiffened, and the *Report* had also been acutely sensitive to the problem of the 'seduction of the innocent'. Its liberalism stopped short of the merchant navy and the armed forces, presumably on grounds similar to those advanced by Lord Devlin, when he remarked: 'A nation of debauchees would not in 1940 have responded satisfactorily to Winston Churchill's call to blood and toil and sweat and tears' (Devlin, 1965, p. 111). Minors, who could presumably 'consent' to Churchill's call at 18 but not to anyone else's until they were 21, were protected against the 'hardcore minority'. So was Scotland and Northern Ireland. Nevertheless, the Act's principal recommendation based on the earlier *Report* – to withdraw from legal punishment consenting homosexual relations between two adults in private – was sufficiently 'permissive' to make the nation draw a deep breath.

This contradiction was more apparent than real. There was an underlying philosophy within Wolfenden which gave the *Report* and its proposals an underpinning unity – a philosophy. This involved a new principle for articulating the field of moral ideology. Wolfenden identified and separated more sharply two areas of legal and moral practice – those of sin and crime, of immorality and illegality. In creating a firmer opposition between these two domains, Wolfenden clearly staked out a new relation between the two modes of moral regulation – the modalities of legal compulsion and of self-regulation. This set of distinctions constituted a new, if temporary, 'moral economy'. It marked a shift, however small and imperceptible at first, in what Foucault (1978) has called the 'micro-physics of power'. This is the power of disposition, in this instance over sexual conduct. Such a power of disposition, Foucault argues, is 'not . . . a property but a strategy', not a set of fixed attributions but 'a network of relations, constantly in tension, in activity . . .' It is a power 'exercised rather than possessed – not the privilege acquired or preserved of the dominant class, but the overall effect of its strategic positions' (Foucault, 1978, p. 26). Wolfenden signified precisely such a shift in the disposition of moral regulation.

This 'revised doctrine' was no idle, passing speculation. It is boldly signalled at the opening, in Chapter II, 'Our Approach To The Problem'. It recurs at each of the critical turning points in the reasoning, it was the key element around which the learned debate turned, and it is the clue to Wolfenden's 'logic', his strategy:

> We clearly recognize that the laws of any society must be acceptable to the general moral sense of the community. But we are not charged to enter into matters of private moral conduct, except in so far as they directly affect the public good. In this field, its [the law's] function, as we see it, is to preserve public order and decency, to protect the citizen from what is offensive and injurious, and to provide sufficient safeguards against exploitation and corruption of others . . . It is not, in our view, the function of the law to intervene in the private lives of citizens or to seek to enforce any particular pattern of behaviour . . . Unless a deliberate attempt is to be made by society, acting through the agency of the law, to equate the sphere of crime with that of sin, there must remain a realm of private morality and immorality which is, in brief and crude terms, not the law's business (HMSO, 1957, pp. 9–10 and 24).

Privatisation and regulation

The application of this doctrine had clearly contradictory effects. It placed both homosexual relations between consenting adults in private and prostitution on the quiet, indoors, out of sight of 'the man on the Clapham omnibus', equally beyond the reach of the law. It transposed both from the regulation of the state to the regulation of private contract – the sphere of 'civil society'. The means by which this transposition was to be accomplished was by privatising both. Where prostitution was concerned, the application of this rule strengthened and confirmed existing practice. Prostitution 'in itself is not, in this country, an offence against the criminal law' (HMSO, 1957, p. 79). Where homosexuality was concerned, the application of the rule aimed to alter existing legal practice – for, until legislated for in the Sexual Offences Act 1967, homosexuality itself (unlike prostitution), whether in private or public, was a criminal offence.[20] Wolfenden thus equalised the application of its rule to both spheres. So far as homosexuality was concerned, this had the effect of 'decriminalising' sexual relations between adult men in private. So far as prostitution was concerned, its real practical effect was to drive prostitution from the streets into a vast expansion of the commercial prostitution agencies and the organised, commercial business-companion, 'hostess' and call-girl rackets.[21] Wolfenden had the unintended consequence of 'liberating' private prostitution for an increased rate of commercial exploitation, stimulating the re-organisation of the 'trade' on more modern, business-like and professional lines, so that it fitted in well with the new business moralities of the period, with their go-getting, commercial ethic, of which call-girl prostitution rapidly became an informal but in-stitutionalised support. In effect, the *Wolfenden Report* sanctioned, through its strict application of the key distinction between 'public good' and 'private morality', the emergence of a double morality. If the judgement of 'respectable man' was the standard against which the public conduct of commercial sexual relations were to be measured, the *Report*, in effect, sanctioned in private a more up-to-date, modern, 'liberalised' moral ethic and standard.

The key to the *Wolfenden Report*'s 'permissiveness', and the real index as to the specific character and the limits of its reformism, is thus the tendency it exhibited towards the *privatisation* of *selective* aspects of sexual conduct. The philosophical rationale which it employed was the distinction between crime and sin, illegality and immorality – a blurred and indistinct boundary within the English criminal law which, by selective reiteration, Wolfenden im-measurably strengthened. But the mechanism by which this distin-ction was practically implemented was the drawing of a sharper distinction between 'public' and 'private' – between the spheres of the *state* and *civil society*. The fact that such a distinction is a legal one, within the juridical framework of bourgeois society, does not rob it of pertinent effects.[22] This limited transformation in the regulation of moral conduct – both form and practice – does not, of course, equal that far-reaching, epistemic shift in the 'economy of punishment' constituted through the 18th-century reform of the criminal law, which has recently been the subject of such extensive and penetrating study (Foucault, 1978; Thompson, 1975; Hay, Linebaugh and Thompson, 1975).[23] Here we have the re-accenting of a field of disposition: there, the replacement of one paradigm and practice of punishment by another. Nevertheless, the differences acknowledged, the similarities are striking; for in its own way the *Wolfenden Report*, too, was supported by a surprising and unpredicted 'return' to certain classical utilitarian principles – an astonishing revival of legal *laissez-faire*, adapted, of course, to a more modern discourse and (here is the aspect requiring explanation) reappearing in a period normally characterised as marked by an unprecedented expansion of state intervention (though, on this question, as recent historians have shown, Benthamism was always more ambiguous than was once thought). The reprise, in the succeeding controversy, of the ghosts of Bentham and Mill by Lord Devlin was not fortuitous; where, in recent times, had the principle of self-regulating morality been so formidably invoked? Differences in context and language notwithstanding, Wolfenden represented a selective resurrection of legal utilitarianism.

More significantly, Wolfenden sought to articulate the two principles of legal regulation in a new relation – that is how he restructured the field as a whole, not merely through what he 'expected'. This was Wolfenden's 'double taxonomy': towards stricter penalty and control, towards greater freedom and leniency, together the 'two elements . . . in a single strategy'. Foucault noted something similar about his own period of reform. 'The reform of the criminal law must be read as a strategy for the rearrangement of the power to punish, according to modalities that render it more regular, more effective, more constant and more detailed in its effects' (Foucault, 1978, p. 80). What we must ask is 'how are the two elements, which are everywhere present in demands for a more lenient penal system, "measure" and "humanity", to be articulated upon one another, in a single strategy?' (Foucault, 1978, p. 74). Such questions, he acknowledges (perhaps to the consternation of his *epigoni*), 'cannot be separated from underlying processes' (Foucault, 1978, p. 80).[24]

No neat parallels can be drawn between Wolfenden's doctrine and the subsequent 'legislation of consent'. But our thesis is that, given the pertinent differences earlier remarked, something of the same tendency is exhibited in their diverse strategies. We can trace this more succinctly in the series of measures in the second period of reformism, dealing with sexuality, marriage and the family (the Family Planning Act 1967, the Abortion Act 1967, the legislation on divorce of 1969, and, negatively, that on homosexuality of 1967).

Again, each has its specific origin and point of application. The necessity for reform arose from a variety of particular causes: sometimes the law was simply archaic (divorce) or inconsistently applied (homosexuality); or practice had simply outstripped the terms of existing legislation (abortion), or new elements had affected its terms of reference (the availability of the contraceptive pill in the early sixties). The strategy was applied in a distinctive way in each area, through mechanisms specific to each domain. Yet each was also a domain *within* a single field of practices or formation – the regulation of sexual conduct – touching the same matrix of practices (sexuality, the family, marriage, reproduction). In each, the dominant tendency appears in a new articulation.[25]

With respect to homosexuality, Wolfenden's 'double taxonomy' was clearly exemplified, both in the strengthening of many controls and also in the major exception (consenting sexual relations between adult male partners in private), for the latter was to be governed by a different moral economy – that of the private contract between equal parties. Here the restructuring of the field of moral ideology was accomplished by *excluding* this aspect *from* regulation by the state. The same mechanism had been employed with respect to privatised prostitution. Divorce and abortion were re-articulated by the same taxonomy, but employing a different mechanism. Again, some aspects were more finely regulated. But also, again, private and consensual criteria were, this time, *included* – drawn *into* the orbit of the legal framework, in order to modify it in a consenting direction. In each case, the formal boundary was shifted in a different direction; but the taxonomy employed, and the pertinent tendency and effect, were similar.

Of the two, divorce is the clearer case. Previous to the 1967 Act, grounds for divorce – adultery, cruelty, desertion – were defined as 'matrimonial offences'. Divorce required 'proof' as to the commission of a moral offence; the legal and moral elements in this instance were inseparable. The offences concerned were committed against the sanctity of marriage and sexual monogamy, institutions whose inviolability were doubly sealed by religion and the law. Divorce proceedings were accusatory in form, involving the identification of 'guilty' and 'innocent' parties. The attachment of moral blame was an integral part of the legislative procedure. The legislation enacted in the 1967 Act did not shift an inch from the orthodox defence of the institutional basis of marriage and the regulation of sexuality by marriage. Its first and principal aim was 'to buttress the stability of marriage'. Yet, in embracing a second, and contradictory, aim – 'to enable the empty shell to be destroyed with maximum fairness and minimum bitterness, distress and humiliation' – it, in effect, dismantled the whole architecture of moral blame. In this respect it confirmed in its detailed application the clear separation of illegality from immorality which Wolfenden had enunciated, by abandoning the whole accusatory framework. Though matrimonial offences were not, in the event, wholly abandoned, they now became important principally as evidence for the 'irretrievable breakdown of the marriage', which now constituted the principal grounds for divorce. Though what was described as 'divorce by consent' was publicly denounced, in effect, once both parties had 'consented' to this definition of marital breakdown, divorce was more or less guaranteed. The single adulterous act no longer provided in itself sufficient grounds, the petitioner being required to show that, for reasons of persistent adultery, the marital relationship was no longer sustainable. Devlin, Denning and others insisted that this should not be understood as giving divorce over entirely to 'consent'. Marriage remained by definition a social and legal institution, in which the community retained some compelling interest.[26] But in practice the marriage became, as a consequence, much more like a private contract, the sustaining or abrogation of which depended overwhelmingly on the definition of the contract given by the 'consenting parties'.[27]

Abortion is a harder case. Homosexuality between consenting equal partners had no visible 'victim'. In divorce the 'victim' was a figurative one, the marriage itself. It was strongly argued – a clear exercise in the legal utilitarianism of 'the greater good' – that, to preserve the shell of marriage once the substance had departed was in effect to encourage extra-marital sexuality, thereby evading the law and ultimately undermining the foundations of the marriage institution. The legislators made, in effect, a pragmatic tactical accommodation, in the interests of saving the institution itself. But abortion had a clear 'victim' – the 'unborn child'. Since the legislators could not envisage respectable married women wishing to deny their 'natural' role and function by choosing abortion, the activity was clearly associated with illegitimate sexuality, and with the 'feckless and promiscuous woman'. Yet the anomalies remained: the rising curve of demand, the dangers of back-street abortions, the discrepancies between 'one law for the rich, another for the poor'. In this instance, however, the degree of 'permissiveness' was a good deal more circumscribed.

The attempts at reform were stubbornly resisted. The legislation was patchily and unevenly implemented in practice. The immediate jump in the demand – from respectable married women, rather than feckless and irresponsible unmarried ones – was so striking that the reluctant reformers entered the lists again almost at once to police its provisions more strictly. The legislation was hardly on the statute books before the widespread and virulent backlash began (cf. Greenwood and Young, 1976). Abortion remained within the keeping of the experts: to the expertise of the law was now added the expertise of the medical profession. A strong and restrictive public control over both the criteria and the practice of abortion was retained. No structural revolution in the rights of women to regulate their own sexual reproduction was initiated. Yet a small and ambiguous space was opened up through the admission of the so-called 'social clause' – admittedly in a reduced and amended form. This 'permitted' doctors to take into account, alongside the traditional criteria, the additional element of the mental health of the expectant mother and her 'actual and reasonably foreseeable environment'. It was this ambiguous formulation which was immediately exploited; and it was through this ambiguous opening that a 'consenting' element was introduced into an otherwise limited and restrictive piece of reformism. Here the law was obliged to recognise the force of criteria that were social and personal in nature rather than strictly legal or medical. In effect, this was the limited extent to which the restructuring of this field through legislation admitted a private and consensual element.

On the basis of this limited review, it is now possible to define a tentative answer to the question, was there a dominant tendency in the 'legislation of consent'? There *was*, it seems, an identifiable strategy. Essentially this consisted of setting into practise a 'double taxonomy' in the field of moral regulation. In each domain there is an increased regulation by the state, a greater intervention in the field of moral conduct – sometimes making more refined distinctions, and often taking a more punitive and repressive form then previously existing mechanisms of regulation and control. At the same time, other areas of conduct are exempted from legal regulation – and, so to speak, from the gaze of public morality, the yardstick of respectable, 'right-thinking' man – and shifted to a different domain, to be regulated by a different modality of control: that of the freely contracting private individuals.[28] This is the core of the tendency: increased regulation coupled with selective privatization through contract or consent, both in a new disposition.

How then is the tendency to be assessed? Was the legislation liberalising and 'permissive' in its general effect, or was there a tightening of control under a liberalising veneer?

These seem to us inadequate terms for a proper assessment. They pose the issue in too simple and binary a form. Clearly, *some* gains of a generally progressive kind were made, as adult homosexuals, divorced couples and women with large families facing another pregnancy could testify. These pointed in the direction of a more relaxed, less puritanical moral regime. In this broad evolutionary sense the 'legislation of consent' might be seen as one phase in that long, secular historical trend, initiated towards the latter half of the 19th century, towards a gradual relaxation of moral codes and a greater openness in the acknowledgement of sexuality.[29] Equally clearly, the gains were extremely limited – patchy and uneven in application, falling far short of any 'sexual revolution'. But this balancing out of 'gains' and 'losses' is not itself an adequate way of measuring social transformations. Rather than disaggregating gains and losses, ascribing each to its appropriate column in the grand historical balance sheet, we must attempt to grasp the contradictory nature of the reformism which had the 'legislation of consent' as one of its contradictory outcomes. What, then, were the contradictory realities which this 'double taxonomy' attempted to articulate together? What did it secure?

If the legislation was neither wholly 'progressive' nor 'socially controlling' in effect, was it therefore negligible? Again, this is too all-or-nothing an alternative. A field of social conduct was restructured, rearranged, reorganised; it was subject to a new disposition, to new strategies; new modalities of regulation were elaborated. This was not a fortuitous development, and it was not without significant effects, both for the field of 'moral economy' itself and for other regions of the social formation. It represented a restructuring of a very distinctive kind. Moreover, it was initiated in what we have now come to recognise as a crucial field – the domain of social reproduction. But this is the site where some of the key social relations of the social formation are reproduced and secured. How, then, can we understand the relation between this internal reorganisation of moral regulation and other structures and relations in the social formation?

Clearly, any presupposition of a fixed, universal or 'necessary correspondence' between them will not suffice.[30] There may, of course, be no relation of any kind – such a position has, indeed, recently been argued. But this alternative would amount to segregating the region of moral conduct as a wholly separate and autonomous kingdom, free of all connections and determinations. This is not an acceptable alternative. Another possibility would be to isolate certain parallels or homologies between the spheres of production and social reproduction, giving to the former a final determinacy. If so, what was it in the new modes of capitalist production and organisation which 'required' such a corresponding movement in the area of social reproduction? Another possibility, then, is to look neither for an absence of any relation between them, nor for a given and fixed correspondence, but rather for the mechanisms which secured an articulation between the different structures. This would situate the question more at the level of what Gramsci called the 'educative and formative role of the state . . . adapting the civilization and morality of the broadest popular masses to the necessities of the continuous development of the economic apparatus of production', a role capable of obtaining 'objective results in the form of an evolution of customs, ways of thinking and acting, morality, etc.' This perspective does not look to the economic structure as the direct source and origin of moral and legal practices, and it recognises the 'relative autonomy' of the state and juridical complex. It poses the relation between structures in terms of over-determination – operating on the terrain of hegemony. This returns us, by a different route, to the political and ideological character of reformism in the conjuncture under consideration.[31]

These connections are pursued more fully in the following pages. Nevertheless, we must not lose sight of what was specific to the domain of moral practices and ideologies. The field of moral conduct was not dismantled or overthrown, but it was dislocated, rearranged; it received a new inflection. The pivot of this re-articulation was the public/private distinction. Around this couple, new modalities of regulation were made effective; a new balance was fixed between them. On the one hand lies the modality of 'public morality', which 'keeps society clean': a discourse whose key interpellation is the 'man on the Clapham omnibus' (Lord Devlin's 'right-thinking man'), whose practical morality is founded 'in the mass of continuous experience half-consciously or unconsciously accumulated and embodied in the morality of common sense' (Devlin, 1965, p. 15). Respectable man is petty-bourgeois man, whatever his actual socio-economic position. On the other hand lies the modality of 'private morality', whose key interpellative structure is 'economic man', whose practical foundations rest on the exchange in private between equivalences. This modality is more individual – possessively individualist – and more 'modern'. It is modern bourgeois man, market man – *homme moyen sensuel*, in his Benthamite or Millian disguise. The reappearance of this ideological figure at this precise conjuncture does not require a simple judgement 'for' or 'against'. It requires, rather, an adequate historical explanation.

Moral reformism was also a signifying strategy. It declared and represented what its practice was aimed at accomplishing. We might treat it, heuristically, as 'signifying' in a more direct sense: saying something, giving a message. What was the message about? What did it say, to whom was it addressed?

Of this there can be little doubt. The message was about the proper way of regulating moral conduct – that is, inevitably, it was about sexual practice. All but two of the legislative measures relate, directly or indirectly, to the regulation of sexuality. The two exceptions are capital punishment and the new laws on 'Sunday Observance'. They did not specifically deal with sexuality, but the preservation of the 'separate' character of the 'Lord's Day' has, throughout its history, been funded by a Puritanical taboo on pleasure which is certainly not unconnected with sexuality. For the rest, the connection is obvious: prostitution, homosexuality, contraception, abortion, divorce, obscenity and pornography, the sex-specific aspects of social reproduction in its social, not exclusively its biological, sense.

To whom was this 'message' addressed? Again, there can be little doubt. Homosexual law reform specifically related to male sexual relations. So did the Obscene Publications Acts, given the male-specific nature of the distribution and consumption of pornography. Theatre audiences released from the Lord Chamberlain's grip included both sexes. But it can hardly be doubted that *women* were the key interpellated subject of the new legislation. Apart from the activities of ponces, Wolfenden and the Street Offences Act were agnostic about male clients. If men dominated the pornographic trade, it was pornographic representations of women or advertisements for female prostitutes which they 'consumed'. Divorce affected both marital partners, but since traditionally the man's freedom of sexual manoeuvre was greater than the woman's, it was women whom the reforms principally released from the bondage of a marriage that had completed its course. Contraception may have incidentally favoured the sexual pleasure of men, but its increased availability after the 1967 Act made the most radical difference for women. Abortion directly affected women with unwanted pregnancies. Even homosexual reforms, though legislating for male sexuality, contained a latent message for women: their position, including the stability of marriage, the family and sexual monogamy would not collapse if the law averted its eye from consenting homosexuality. Overwhelmingly, it was the position of women in the field of sexual practice which provided the legislation with its principal object/subject. What it proposed, in sum, was a measure of relaxation in the social and legal control of selected aspects of female sexual practice. It meant, in effect, a new modality of 'control' over these aspects – a more privatised and 'person-focused' regulation, tacit rather than explicit, invisible rather than visible. Negatively, it seemed to suggest that society would not immediately fall apart as a result. Positively, perhaps society itself had come to recognise, and even to 'require', such a revision.

The reconstruction of femininity

This attempt to reshape the field of female sexual conduct must be set in the context of other practices and discourses concerning women in the period, and against the material conditions affecting their position. These have recently attracted increasing attention, especially in feminist research.[32]

The fifties seem to be marked by an intensified ideological 'campaign' to return women to their 'natural place' in the home, family and marriage. The structuring of popular ideological discourses, especially, around this reconstituted domestic 'subject' is not difficult to explain. It was no doubt aimed at that wider return to 'traditional' social patterns, following the extraordinary upheavals of the war – part of the post-war 'settlement'. But there may be other, more compelling reasons for the extent of the 'religion' of domesticity and motherhood in the popular imagery and ideologies of the period, less part of a smooth process of readjustment and more an attempt to master and secure, ideologically, tendencies pointing in a contrary direction. There is certainly a connection with the concern over the size of the labour force. The birth rate was still falling, and many had been lost in the war. Beveridge certainly believed that 'In the next 30 years housewives as mothers have vital work to do in ensuring the adequate continuance of the British race and of British ideals in the world' (*Beveridge Report*, p. 53).[33]

Yet, in retrospect, the concern appears to have been more practically effective in 'cultivating' the *quality* of labour power than in its quantitative aspect. There was no effective policy of population growth in the period; the trends embodied in the phase of 'affluence' were set against it. The British family, confronting its heroic mission, settled down to its 2.5 children, which rapidly became a nuclear norm. Secondly, the continuing shortage of labour was supplemented from two main sources: black immigration, and female part-time work – the latter, a significant, if uneven and gender-structured, move by women into the labour market, which has proved to be a long-term, not a temporary secular, trend (see Beechey, 1977; and Sivanandan, 1976). Thirdly, this must be related to the very special and augmented role for women in the rapidly expanding surge of domestic consumption which underpinned the productive growth of the mid-fifties – a phase and *type* of selective economic expansion specifically aimed in their direction, at the 'consuming housewife'. The confinement of the British 'boom' to the sphere of private domestic consumption is striking, compared either to previous types of economic expansion or indeed to the character of economic expansion elsewhere at this time in the capitalist world.

> The truth was that a mass-consumption society is dominated by its biggest market, which, in Britain, was that of the working class . . . Henceforth, it was *their* demand which dominated commercially, even their taste and style, which pressed upward into the culture of the non-working classes . . . Business therefore took over the task of filling the proletarian world . . . All workers except the most destitute or isolated were rapidly adopting a style of life based on mass production, i.e. on production geared to their own desires; but that production reflected only certain aspects – and those which least distinguished workers as a class – of their aspirations: notably the desire for a higher material standard of life and more material possessions for individuals and families (Hobsbawm, 1968, pp. 242–3 and 246).

Economically and ideologically, women were the clue, the door, to this selective penetration of the family and privatised consumption by the 'new' capitalism.

This factor, however, contained its own contradiction. For consumption to be stimulated, while being at the same time confined to the private and familial sphere, women had to be located at the heart and centre of the principal unit of consumption, the family. Here capitalism itself profited from what, in the framework of Marx's discussion of reproduction, must be conceived as one of those historical shifts in the 'cultural' element in the determination of the value of labour power (i.e. the 'costs' of its reproduction): that is, an augmentation or expansion in the value of the 'historical and moral element' (Marx, 1967, p. 171).[34] But, to sustain this form of consumption at an ever increasing rate, the wage of the 'breadwinner', traditionally the man, had to be supplemented by the additional earnings of women. There was also the area which concerned the qualitative reproduction of labour power, some aspects of which seemed to call for an intensification in the attention to child-care and mothering, while other aspects, no longer adequately taken care of within the family, decisively became, in this period, the province and responsibility of an increasing state intervention.[35] Women, in short, were being called upon to be both wives-and-mothers – spending home-makers – *and* (part-time) working women.

It was difficult to reconcile all these roles within the dominant representational forms and discourses of a fully fledged ideology of domesticity and motherhood. Hence the proliferation of ideological discourses around 'women's roles' in the period, and the struggle to privilege certain of their interpellative structures against others. The psychological and welfare ideologies stressed motherhood. The economic and consumerist ideologies privileged the woman in the home, the 'little domestic kingdom'. Woman-at-work was, largely, a structured absence in these discourses: working was something women sometimes 'did', it did not define what they, essentially, 'were'. Its economic rewards were defined as 'a little something on the side' – 'a bit of pin money'. Its true role in supporting the mass consumption boom, and in giving capitalist expansion its appropriate form and definition, was displaced from view. The way 'women', including their sexuality, came to be constructed in this period was the outcome of the over-determination of these different practices of ideological representation on one another, and the work of privileging and displacement, which is the effect of their articulation, with one another and with other practices. Without ascribing a single source or origin, the 'privatisation' of some aspects of 'deviant' female sexuality (prostitution) in this period – its 'return' to the regulation of the private economic contract, its parcelling out to the impulse and regime of personalised 'need' – should not come as wholly a surprise.

In the sixties, the period to which the 'consenting legislation' properly belongs, we see a further reconstruction of the ideological discourses which represent women's roles, and a proliferation of one sub-set of those over others: the discourses concerned with 'femininity' and 'sexuality'. Here we see registered a *partial break* with the fully elaborated domestic and maternal ideal. Women remain, in these representations, principally confined to the private and the personal sphere. They retain, 'of course', alongside their secondary social position, their 'unique femininity'. But, far from being permitted to flourish only alongside its marital and maternal elements, 'femininity has been permitted a certain disarticulation from its traditional moorings. Here are "women" reaching out for other things, different images, new interests . . .' Those sometimes include extra- and pre-marital affairs, they include the recognition of the demand for feminine sexual pleasure, and they flatter and cultivate the feminine attributes, the eroticised feminine body. Here is signified a contained and ambiguous 'liberation', whose limits are not to be doubted for a moment: it is the difference, as Janice Winship (1978) has argued, between 'femininity' and 'feminism'.[36]

What reaction these representations bear to the material conditions of most women is difficult to assess. Work, the family and social reproduction – the structures historically determining the 'place' of women – remain the sites of their secondariness and their oppression. But two factors provide us with a clue as to one element of change: the growing struggle, among women, for better provision of and a wider latitude of access to contraception and abortion. Greenwood and Young have noted the parallels in the two struggles, historically, in Britain (Greenwood and Young, 1976, p. 125). Contraception was least available to unmarried women, since it encouraged pre- and extra-marital sex; abortion was most easily available to them, since the strongest grounds were unplanned pregnancies outside the support of marriage and the family. The pre-reform legislation was aimed at maintaining the link between female sexuality and reproduction. The contraceptive pill provided the material basis for breaking this tie. Something was certain to give, once this structural link was dissolved.

We get an inkling of this in the explosion of ideological discourses, from the early sixties onwards, aimed at the reconstruction of female sexuality. The active, modern housewife, well-equipped for her tasks, gives way to more personalised and 'feminised' interpellations. There is a greater stress on the feminine, on the care, cultivation and grooming of the body, on the accentuation of its attractive and seductive power, and its 'availability'. Ambiguous images of feminine 'independence' and of a self-directed pleasure detach themselves from the more outward bound and serviceable images of the fifties. These are not representations of women entering unambiguously into a public world – far from it. But they are women partially detached and disconnected from their 'natural' domestic role, entering a more personalised world of private, 'natural' pleasure. The *sexual valorisation* of popular ideological discourses, above all in mass advertising, is a powerful and distinctly new ideological force. The link is indisputably forged between the pleasurable and pleasured feminine 'subject' (object) and the drives of a sexually valorised and eroticised consumption.[37] Exactly how to understand the articulation here, between a historically specific construction of female sexual representations and the libidinisation of consumption, we can only speculate about. But the shifting homologies between the two, in the era of capitalism, cannot be doubted. For centuries Puritanism provided the dominant interpellative structure of the formal and official ideologies of capitalism, whatever the actual practices of the different classes were. And this, it has been assumed, had to do not only with the ethic of hard work and disciplined effort, of 'suffering in this world for a prize in the next', but with the impulse to save, to accumulate. The partial dislocation of capitalist ideologies from this integrating thread, and its re-articulation around the erotic compulsions to 'spend', represent a significant shift.

Its consequences can be seen elsewhere, in an area not directly related to women. The religious opposition to gambling is, as Peter Fuller has pointed out, essentially a post-Reformation affair (Introduction to Halliday and Fuller, 1977). Despite the Puritan assault, gambling flourished in the 18th century, both amongst the aristocratic classes and the urban poor, in keeping with that century's 'prodigious enthusiasm for all kinds of financial speculation'. The Georges frequently resorted to lotteries to raise quick sums of hot money. It was in the 19th century that the moralistic bourgeois opposition to reckless spending and speculation really came into its own as an aspect of 'moral education', with 'the casinos closed, the lotteries abandoned and the laws regulating betting introduced' (Halliday and Fuller, 1977, p. 41). Though both private gambling among the upper classes and an illicit gambling sub-culture among the poor continued to flourish (and, of course, the turf), the legal framework of bourgeois Puritan morality was preserved until after the Second World War. The Royal Commission on gambling published its report in 1951. Harold Macmillan introduced the Premium Bonds scheme in the late fifties. Off-the-course betting shops were opened in 1960, the casinos in 1963. Lord Wigg assumed the chairmanship of the Betting Levy Board under the Wilson administration. Gradually, through the intervention of the state, the small-time bookies were absorbed into the concentrated ownership of the five largest companies (Halliday and Fuller, 1977). If the corner betting shop was Mr Butler's contribution to the lifting of the Puritan cloak from the shoulders of working-class men, the bingo hall was his gift to respectable working-class married women who wanted a 'little quiet flutter' – and why not? The rationale, he has suggested (its parallels with Wolfenden cannot be overlooked), was justified in that it 'drove betting off the streets, where it was illegal and strained the police', into the arms of the betting chains, presumably, where the market provided a sufficiently strict regulator (Butler 1971, p. 203).

The character of reformism

In their important chapter 'The Control of Morality' in their *Abortion in Demand* (1976) Greenwood and Young quote an interesting observation from the historians of the abortion law reform movement, Hindell and Simms: 'The preponderance of Labour members among the reformers highlights an interesting paradox. The party which believes most in controlling economic behaviour and appetites is the same party which believes most in freeing the private sexual behaviour. Conservatives on the other hand believe that the State should provide moral constraints but economic freedom' (Hindell and Simms, 1971, p. 202). Greenwood and Young go on to argue that, if one looks at underlying 'world views', Labour's attitude to economic and moral reforms is not contradictory at all, since both are predicated 'on the idea that the social order can be adjusted piecemeal, that social progress can be achieved without fundamentally changing the social order'

(Greenwood and Young, 1976, p. 117). While agreeing with the general point, it seems to me that more could be made of the apparent contradiction identified by Hindell and Simms, in pinpointing the precise nature of 'reformism' and in giving its operation in this field a necessary historical specificity.

Both sets of authors seem to assume that there is some homogeneous outlook, attitude or policy which, in this period, can be broadly attributed to each of the two major political parties. Both seem also to assume that Labour emerges as clearly the 'party of moral reform' and that the character of this reformism can be assimilated to the general, moderate, social-democratic, 'Labourist' outlook of the Labour Party in the post-war period. These premises seem to me to be untenable, once they are pressed towards any real historical specificity. On the contrary, we would argue that there are distinct, opposing ideological formations within each of the two major parties in this period. These are as pertinent for an analysis of the emergence of 'moral reformism' as the elements which tie these political fractions and forces back into their respective Parliamentary or party wings. For the formation of a political bloc in support of the moral reformism whose dominant tendency we have been examining, the convergences between the 'Right Progressive' wing of the Conservative Party and the 'Revisionist' wing of the Labour Party are more significant than those things which the Conservative Party shared with its traditionalist fraction, or those which the Labour Party shared with Labour traditionalists. Moreover, we would also argue that the moral revisionism which the 'consenting legislation' set in motion differed significantly from what we might call traditional 'Labourism' or orthodox social-democratic reformism. What follows is a brief attempt to elaborate on these theses, in an effort to identify what was peculiar and specific to the moral reformism of the sixties as a political–ideological formation.

The starting point here must take us back to the nature of the post-war political settlement. Both major political parties made a deep and profound adaptation within the terms of the post-war settlement. Essentially, this required, on the Labour side, the clarification of its commitment to settle for a species of Labourist gradualist reformism within the frame of reference of the 'mixed' capitalist economy, and, of course, the Cold War. (For a fuller analysis of the terms of this compromise, cf. Hall *et al.* 1978; also, *inter alia*, Miliband, 1961, Coates, 1975; and Howell, 1976.) On the Conservative side the settlement required the acceptance of the 'welfare' modification to the structure of pre-war capitalism, and the taking on board of a commitment to increased state intervention in the economic management of the economy. The depths of these adaptations did not, however, fully emerge at once. Indeed, it was only under the peculiar conditions of the economic boom of the mid-fifties that the profound political and ideological adaptations which had been set in train were forced into the open. The thorough overhaul of the internal structure of the Conservative Party in the wake of its massive defeat at the polls in 1945 had helped in the creation of a distinct 'reformist' wing, bringing forward in the leadership ranks the 'new' post-war Conservatives. One notes, for example, the eagerness with which Butler records how he moved, under the archaic shadow of Churchill in the very depths of the war, to the initiation of a 'One Nation' strategy for education. What has been called, elsewhere, the 'social-democratic consensus' in education, which spanned this whole period, owes an enormous amount of its relatively early formation and hegemony to the precocious appearance of a species of Tory educational 'reformism' (see Grant, Finn and Johnson, 1977). Still, the Conservative Government which assumed power in 1951, like its successor in 1959, remained an unholy mixed alliance between 'new' and 'old' forces within the party. It was the deep structures of economic 'affluence', coupled with the immediate and unexpected leadership crisis precipitated by Suez, which cleared the decks, giving the temporary advantage to the reformist wing – what Gamble (1974)[38] correctly defines as the 'Right Progressives' – though this was never an unequivocal hegemony, and it was admittedly, exercised under the generalship of a figure, Harold Macmillan, in whom the 'new' appeared permanently displaced through a studied caricature of the 'old'.

On the fundamentals of economic policy, and on the broad strategy of the politics of support, these two elements in the Tory Party were broadly united. While accepting the basic terms of the post-war settlement, everyone agreed that the whole implicit tendency towards collectivism and statism, latent in the 1945 reforms, had to be disarticulated from their Labourist origins, and given a radically different, Conservative inflection. The return to a modified free market ideology ('Conservative Freedom Works'), to a 'popular capitalism' which would give each individual a personal stake in the system ('the Property Owning Democracy'), to the traditional market themes of competition, 'freedom', and possessive individualism, were theses from which few dissented. Butler's period as

Chancellor is an eloquent testimony to this: the shibboleths of Conservative individualism can hardly have been so openly, opportunistically and damagingly pandered to as in the infamous budget Mr Butler introduced before the 1955 election (see Pinto-Duchinsky, 1970; Oppenheimer, 1970; and Brittan, 1969). Yet the contradictions remained.

In part this was a question as to how to construct and secure a new 'historical bloc', so as to ensure a permanent Conservative hegemony; it was a problem of exploiting to Conservative advantage the new class relations, the more fluid class formations, of the 'affluent society'. Gamble, once again, has put the matter with force and clarity. The 'core of the Conservative Nation . . . was still the middle classes' – the 'unorganized "little men" in the community, the backbone of the "British way of life", society's NCO's, "the bulwarks of local communities" '. These were 'the source of enterprise and invention in the economic field, and at times the guardians of customary life' – the independent middle and lower-middle classes, sturdily independent, who 'ask only to do a fair day's work for a fair day's pay, and to accumulate steadily sufficient property and savings to enable them to be independent' (Gamble, 1974). The central ideal, the key interpellated subject, of these traditional Tory discourses, was the small businessman or shopkeeper. Readers will have little difficulty in also placing this figure as Lord Devlin's 'right-thinking man' – the man 'on the top of the Clapham omnibus'. The problem was that these traditional, independent middle and petty-bourgeois classes were a fast disappearing species (their temporary demise was eloquently hymned by Angus Maude in an influential study, *The English Middle Classes*, in the mid-fifties). Their position was undermined by inflation; and their economic status was threatened, on one side by the rising managerial and new middle classes, on the other side by the rising 'affluent proletarian' threat. Their social position was weakened by these new social formations, and by the emergent 'middle strata' identified with the great concentrations of capital, the growing bureaucracies of the state, by the rising managerialists and the new white-collar strata, and what Hobsbawm (1968) has called 'clean-handed' labour.[39] Their moral world was threatened – affronted is perhaps a more appropriate word, with Wolfenden in mind – by the materialism, the hedonism, the moral agnosticism and cultural fluidity of mass-consumption capitalist society. What the 'Right Progressives' gradually came to understand was the secular erosion of the party's traditional class basis, and the necessity, if Conservatism was to stake out for itself a permanent foothold in a modern capitalist society, to enlarge its social base to include – through the formation of a new historical bloc – the new, emergent social forces of a socially mobile society. Could they be 'won' for Conservatism? What social programme would facilitate its construction?

The older 'new Conservatives' adopted a more flexible and pragmatic approach to this problem, mixing and combining their appeals according to the dictates of the hour. But around and behind them there emerged a more organised and articulate 'progressive force' – that force which found a voice in the radicalism of *Crossbow* – theoretically rather than pragmatically committed, not simply to the politics of electoral support but to the strategy of Conservative modernisation. It is here that we discover a specifically 'revisionist' Conservative wing, one which gradually adopted, and forcefully pressed, an analysis of the emergent sociological trends in modern capitalism, different only in emphasis and inflection from the theoretical revisionism of the 'new' Labour Right.[40] Here the new doctrine was articulated: the dawning of the 'post-capitalist' era, the reformed structure of modern capitalist enterprises, managerialism, the dissolution of class society, the 'end of ideology', the dawning of the politics of incremental reform, the tocsins of 'modernisation' and 'growth'. For this 'progressive party' the seizing of a tactical electoral advantage was not enough. 'Modernisation' for its members constituted an altogether new and heroic Tory programme – Tory, they stressed, not *conservative* – which required the structural overhaul and reform of social and cultural life side by side with economic reform.

If a specific political bloc can be identified within the Conservative political formation which strengthened Butler's hand at the Home Office, and stayed around to lend its support to Roy Jenkins' reformism a decade later, it is here, if anywhere, that its core fraction must be located. *This* was the fraction which understood that economic individualism alone was not a motive force powerful enough to construct a hegemonic bloc. The moment had arrived to begin the construction of a 'revised' capitalist civilisation. For this social force, in substance, 'economic freedom' required an erosion of the traditional Tory commitment to legal moralism.

Though echoes of this 'programme' are to be found, a decade after, in some of the themes of Mr Heath's 'modernisation' strategy, the rise of the 'progressive party' was cut short in the early sixties. It could not survive the economic squeeze (the tapering off of the post-war boom, the revolt of the middle classes against wage inflation) or the ideological squeeze (the return of the party to its old stamping ground: hanging, crime and punishment, social delinquency and violence, immigration, law and order). Traditionalism revived – some, looking forward to Mr Powell, Mrs Thatcher and Sir Keith Joseph, would say 'with a vengeance'. The progressive party went into a slow decline, even though it required the debacle of the Heath interlude of 1970–74 to accomplish its trial interment. Yet the torch, laid low here, had passed to safer and more redoubtable hands, for the same period is marked by the emergence in the Labour Party, on the back of its 'sociological defeats' at the polls in the mid-fifties, and under the leadership of Hugh Gaitskell, a variant of the same political strain – Labour revisionism.[41]

Labour revisionism was, from the outset, more 'theoretical' than the Conservatives'. It, too, took its bearings from a theoretical revised doctrine concerning the new, 'post-capitalist' society: the society in which ownership had become increasingly irrelevant (and thus the theories of Marx and the residual class sentiments, appropriate to an earlier form of capitalism, increasingly obsolescent); where the movements of the economy could be managed by Keynesian intervention and regulation without the need for further bouts of nationalisation; where social mobility was fast eroding that traditional basis of the class structure, creating a more open and upwardly striving society; where the dynamic of capitalist growth was capable of wiping away the older structures of poverty and want; and where (here the doctrine made a descent into the politics of electoral support: *could* Labour win?) a party which could not construct a new historical bloc from amongst the new managerial elites, the technical strata of labour, the 'middle' intelligentsia and the 'affluent worker' – the new bourgeoisie and the newly embourgeoisified – was destined for the historical scrapheap. The defeat of 1959 made the theoretical lesson more vivid.

This political formation was distinctive in at least three respects which are directly germane to our concerns. First, it differed from the traditional left *and* right of its own party. It was clearly demarcated from the traditional economic recipes of the Labour left – nationalization, creeping collectivism, a militantly gradualist economism. But it was also sharply distinguished from the traditional right, committed as it was to the dismal Puritanism of an obsolescent Fabianism. 'The trouble is that some of its [the Labour Party's] leaders', Crosland wrote, 'are radical but not contemporary – they are discontented, but with a society which no longer exists; while others are contemporary but not radical – they realise that society has changed, but quite enjoy the present one' (Crosland, 1962, p. 131).

Secondly, it was significantly distinct from its 'Progressive' counterparts in the Conservative Party, with whom, in some respects, it shared the struggle to command the great, undefined 'floating' political centre. It was far more thoroughly 'radical' in its revisionist programme than the 'Right Progressives' ever had stomach for. Crosland, its most articulate and sophisticated spokesman, was a committed Keynesian interventionist. A fundamentalist in his commitment to 'managerialism', he made no play with the bankrupt doctrines of Tory 'economic freedoms'. He was wedded to capitalist enterprise – to the economies and ideologies of corporate growth, not to the possessive individualism of the rentier or shopkeeper classes. He was a 'radical egalitarianist', if by that we mean pushing 'equality of opportunity' to its extreme limits; indeed, his most influential book, *The Future of Socialism*, contains some spirited pages on 'Why Equality of Opportunity is not Enough'. This was no plea for the structural transformation of capitalism. But it represented an incisive critique of the *traditional* structures of British class inequalities and class sentiment, whose residue, he believed, was still virulently alive in the new, post-class society. Hence his unswerving radicalism on the question of the public schools and the necessity for comprehensive education. Capitalism had rendered the class struggle obsolete. But 'Class, in the sense both of class-consciousness and the existence of clearly-defined classes, is an exceptionally marked phenomenon in British life', he wrote (Crosland, 1963, p. 118). However, he regarded these presistent traces of class consciousness and class resentment as increasingly irrelevant features of a society which had been irrevocably refashioned. For him these obsolescent features of British class society remained – in contradistinction to his 'Progressive' opposite numbers – the object of his revisionist strategy. It was said at the time that Mr Crosland looked forward with relish to the 'steady Americanisation' of British social and economic life. But the truth is that Mr Crosland's 'future' was not that of a rampant economic individualism (he admired, of course, its mobility and fluidity) but of a thoroughly modern and modernised welfare capitalism. Perry Anderson, in the two early essays he wrote for *New Left Review* on Scandinavia, was correct to identify Sweden as 'Mr

Crosland's Dreamland'. Not the least of its attractions was the moderation, the un-Puritanical, tolerant and 'civilised' quality of its social life.

This is the third distinctive feature of Labourist revisionism. The basic, structural economic problems, it argued, had been solved. The object of modern reformism had been transposed from an economic to an ethical impulse. The purpose of reformism was to construct a 'civilised form of social life' appropriate to a civilised and modernised capitalism:

> . . . it is significant that our society is now different in kind from classical capitalism, not only in the socio-economic respects . . . but in almost every other respect one can think of – family relationships, population trends, sexual morality, personal religion, the position of women, literary and artistic standards, and so on. It would be curious if these profound changes in every part of what Marx called the 'superstructure' reflected no fundamental change in the underlying social and economic forces (Crosland, 1963, p. 34).

There, one finds, in embryo, the political charter for the 'legislation of consent'. This programme of moral reformism was no side issue, no icing on the economic cake. Its aim was nothing short of bringing into line and formalising social, moral and ethical trends already set in motion by the reformation of classical capitalism. And the motive and mechanism of this reformism was to 'de-regulate' moral conduct, to 'liberate' it from the compulsions of legal and state regulation, from the cramped Puritanism of the Fabians and the non-conformist respectability of the traditional working class. In moral and economic matters alike, revisionism argued, we had come to the limit of state intervention. It was time to 'let up on the brake', to break the hold of external compulsion and to move certain critical areas of life back into the self-regulation of civil society and the market.

> Society's decisions impinge heavily on people's private lives as well as on their social and economic welfare; and they now impinge, in my view, in too restrictive and puritanical a manner. I should like to see action taken both to widen opportunities for enjoyment and relaxation and to diminish existing restrictions on personal freedom. The first of these requires, it is true, a change in cultural

attitudes rather than government legislation. If this were to come about, much could be done to make Britain a more colourful and civilized country to live in. We need not only higher exports and old-age pensions, but more open-air cafés, brighter and gayer streets at night, later closing-hours for public houses, more local repertory theatres, better and more hospitable hoteliers and restaurateurs, more pleasure-gardens on the Battersea model, more murals and pictures in public places, better designs for furniture and pottery and women's clothes, statues in the centres of new housing estates, better-designed street lamps and telephone kiosks, and so on ad infinitum. The enemy in all this will often be in unexpected guise; it is not only dark Satanic things and people that now bar the road to the new Jerusalem, but also, if not mainly, hygienic, respectable, virtuous things and people, lacking only in grace and gaiety. This becomes manifest when we turn to the more serious question of socially-imposed restrictions on the individual's private life and liberty. There come to mind at once the divorce laws, licensing laws, prehistoric (and flagrantly unfair) abortion laws, obsolete penalties for sexual abnormalcy, the illiterate censorship of books and plays and remaining restrictions on the equal rights of women. Most of these are intolerable, and should be highly offensive to socialists, in whose blood there should always run a trace of the anarchist and the libertarian, and not too much of the prig and the prude (Crosland, 1963, p. 355).

This may not strike most readers as a prefiguring of the Socialist millennium; but it can hardly be doubted that it was, for the reformists, a quite precise sketch for the revisionist Utopia. It is remarkable, both for the valorisation of pleasure (in confrontation with the typically dour social-democratic rhetoric) and for the revelation it makes of the depth and degree to which individualism and privatisation remain at the core of revisionist doctrine. Its alignment with the principle for the regulation of a revised 'moral economy' defined earlier is strikingly exact and precise. Paradoxically, it was the only part of the revisionist programme destined – line for line, and, of course, within its structural limit – to be legislatively enacted. Here the social-democratic variant of 'economic individualism' received, at last, its appropriate hegemonic elaboration.

The fate of progressive reformism

In its pure form this doctrine was not destined to command the centre of political life either. Gaitskell suffered formal defeats, from the 'old' left over Clause 4, from the 'new' over unilateralism; but both turned out to be, in substance, victories. Yet 'Revisionism', like its 'Right Progressive' correlate, never dominated its party's thinking or policy; it had to compromise, and underwent subtle transformations, in the sea-changes which accompanied the early stages of the economic crisis and the political reformulations of the early sixties. It was Wilsonian not revisionist modernisation which secured the political centre, and gained the slender electoral majority in 1964; that was a sterner, more nonconformist variant of the social-democratic gospel, less theoretical, more pragmatic, pivoted more on a state-sponsored 'scientific and technical revolution' than on the revolution in private corporate capital and 'uninterrupted expansion' on which the theses of *The Future of Socialism* had been predicated.[42] If the cultural and 'ethical' impulse remained, it was a junior partner in the Wilsonian alliance, more isolated, largely limited to the 'Home Office' reforms – its most distinctive, 'posthumous', political expression.

We have described this programme as a late return of 'economic individualism' within one wing of social democracy. This catches the element of 'diminishing restrictions on personal freedom', the language which Crosland had adopted. Roy Jenkins, in *The Labour Case*, employed much the same terminology, in the section on 'Liberalising the Home Office': 'First, there is the need for the state to do less to restrict personal freedom. Secondly, there is the need for the state to do more to encourage the arts . . . Thirdly, there is the need, independently of the state, to create a climate of opinion which is favourable to gaiety, tolerance and beauty . . .' Mr Jenkins was also keenly aware of the disposition of support: 'There is undoubtedly a libertarian fringe to the Conservative Party . . . Equally there are in the Labour Party a few members whose views on these libertarian issues are as obscurantist as are to be found anywhere in the country' (Jenkins, 1959, pp. 137–8). Labour, nevertheless, was the only viable political instrument of reform.

But the strategy can be characterised in a different, more accurate, way. It can be seen as one attempt to articulate a culture, a 'civilisation', a moral economy for an emergent state capitalism. In this respect the 'utilitarian' residue is a confusing element. In Britain, when social democracy is required to elaborate a moral–ideological argument, it appears typically to draw on a debased version of the utilitarian repertoire. No full-blooded return to 'laissez-faire' was, in fact, envisaged. The revisionists accepted the interventionist role of the state: they were committed to the modifications which 'welfare' had imposed on the more irrational forces and movements of capital. The crucial move in the game was to fix the limits to state intervention, to circumscribe the sphere of operation of the state: to define the state as junior partner in the state–capital alliance, and to shift the dynamic of economic and social life back, not to the sturdy independence of the *rentier* or small businessman but to the reformed impulses of big, managerialist, corporate capital. This required setting free the impulse – the instinct – of the big private sector of capital accumulation and corporate enterprise, and its managers. It was *this* variant of 'state capitalism' – the Crosland Dreamland – which was slowly eroded and undermined through the deepening economic and political crisis of the sixties. What came to dominate this latter phase was a different variant of state capitalism – the 'Wilsonian' model. It had the the same elements, resting on the same base and alliance of forces, but in a different 'mix', and articulated through a different ideological repertoire. The period of 'moral reformism' was the last flicker of a distintegrating social and economic strategy. Instead of building and expanding this 'modernist' moral/social hegemony, the decade produced, instead, its steady polarisation into its 'progressive' and 'traditionalist' camps.

This break-up of the consensus on which the programmes of both the 'Right Progressives' and the 'Revisionists' depended, can be traced, in terms of the shifting class alliances of the period.[43] During the fifties, and especially under Mr Macmillan, the economic bonanza was large and expansive enough to carry, behind the restoration of 'economic freedom', a broad class alliance – temporarily welding together the old social base of the 'Conservative Nation' and the emergent social strata of the 'affluent' society. Its dynamic was, principally, economic. The success with which the expanded welfare state was absorbed and contained, and the economic boom funnelled into privatised consumption, was sufficient to gloss over the internal contradictions within this composite formation.[44] If the sturdy, independent middle and lower-middle classes were scandalised by the culture which flourished in this economic free-for-all – 'a vulgar world whose inhabitants have more money than is good for them, barbarism with an electric light . . . a cockney tellytopia, a low grade nirvana of subsidised, supervised houses, hire purchase extravagance, undisciplined children, gaudy domestic squalour, and chips with everything' (Curran, 1962, quoted in Gamble, 1974) – Mr Macmillan did not flinch from exploiting its greediest aspects to electoral advantage. After all, 'we have never had it so good'. But once the economic tide began to turn at the beginning of the sixties, and the seamier side of Macmillan's affluence began to show through – the Profumo affair, for instance – the Tory social alliance began to come apart. Mr Butler rightly regarded his virtuoso performance at the Tory Conference of 1961 as a temporary triumph over the 'traditionalist' lobby; but he knew he was riding an untamed tiger. Though the 'Colonel Blimps of both sexes – and the female of the species was more deadly, politically, than the male' were in temporary retreat, 'many members of the party continued to hold this ("soft" on crime and punishment) stand against me' (Butler, 1971, p. 200). 'We are desperately anxious to stop this nation from becoming so morally corrupt . . .' one delegate warned him. And, by the following conference, the signs of the backlash were already beginning to be manifest: 'This is not a liberal revival, this is a middle-class revolt by the civil servants, by the nurses, by the shopkeepers, by the young professional men and women who feel themselves, rightly or wrongly, squeezed between the expense account directors on the one hand . . . and the strength and the power of the trade unions on the other . . .' (Gamble, 1974, p. 80).[45] A familiar note . . .

The whole aim of the Wilson propaganda, leading up to the 1964 election, was to put together an alternative, and more stable, historical bloc, behind the slogans of modernisation and controlled and orderly 'growth'. The principal fractions in this alliance were progressive industrial capital, the scientific managers, key sections of the new technical working class and the 'new petty-bourgeoisie', all submerged by Wilsonian sleight-of-hand into 'workers by hand and brain'. Coupled to this was the great representative engine of the trade unions, through which the aims and aspirations of the older working class and the constituencies of the socially disadvantaged, emerging behind the 'rediscovery of poverty', would be represented – but with the latter decidedly in a subaltern role. This carefully constructed edifice, too, crumbled quickly in the debacle of the 1964–6 period, leaving the Labour Government, presiding over the deepening capitalist crisis, resting principally on the great corporate institutions – industrial capital, the unions and the state machine.

The revisionists doubtless hoped that this new bloc would recognise itself and something of its social aspirations in the programme of moral reform, in the drive to 'make this country a more civilized place in which to live' (Jenkins, 1959, p. 135). But there was really only one fraction to which the programme made a direct and immediate appeal: the 'progressive middle classes'. There were many and varied cultural trends and tendencies in the Britain of the mid-sixties, but *socially* this was the period in which the 'progressive middle classes' came closest to establishing a social hegemony. It was this fraction which learned to 'swing with the trends' in the wake of the 'cultural revolution' of the early sixties, who deserted the second- and third-rate public schools and colonised the new comprehensives and the progressive primary school class-rooms and playgroups, who used their social know-how and confidence to 'manage' the health services and the welfare state to their advantage. The programme of moral reform may have benefited many other social sectors, but it was designed in the image of the progressive middle classes.

The disintegration of this 'progressive' bloc, the formation and disintegration of the Wilsonian variant, and the gradual turn towards a more orthodox, authoritarian moral regime – which, by the seventies, was explicitly defined as a campaign to liquidate the sixties 'permissiveness' and all that – belongs to another part of the story.[46] But the contrasts are vivid. If, figuratively, the emergent state capitalism of the 'boom' period seemed to find a sort of expression in a more fluid and 'liberalised' personal and moral regime, this same capitalism, under conditions of world recession, seemed to require a return to moral and ideological orthodoxy and authority. If, in the first period, the law retreated a little from its intrusive position in certain domains of personal conduct, in the second it became precisely the engine specifically employed to turn the ideological tide. But here we can find no fixed functions or correspondences; here everything depends on the conjuncture, on the shifting balance between contending forces, especially in the ideological field. In this respect, if we are looking for a symbolic turning point, it can be found in the departure of Roy Jenkins from the Home Office, and the assumption of that office by Mr Callaghan. The 'kissing' had stopped. It was Jenkins who had called the Wootton Committee together to examine and advise on the legalisation governing drug use and dependency (HMSO, 1968). It was the *Wootton Report* which recommended a reduction in the maximum penalty for possession and sale of cannabis, the declassification of marijuana from the list which included heroin and the opiate drugs, and a re-examination of police powers to search and arrest on suspicion of carrying dangerous drugs. It was the new Home Secretary who said, in the debate on the *Wootton Report* that the

> . . . House should recognize that the lobby [in favour of legalizing cannabis] existed and from his reading of the Report he thought the Committee had been overinfluenced by the existence of this lobby. The existence of the lobby was something the House and public opinion should take into account and be ready to combat, as he was. It was another aspect of the permissive society and he was glad that his decision had enabled the House to call a halt to the advancing tide of permissiveness.[47]

As the incipient crisis developed, through the sixties, it received its most powerful articulation through a split between the 'new' and the 'old' middle classes, the 'new' and the 'old' petty-bourgeoisie, between its 'progressive' and 'traditionalist' fractions – a division into two, distinct and opposing moral – ideological formations. Each theme in the ideological struggle came to be enunciated through these two constellations – education, crime and penal policy, welfare, law and order, social values, sexual *mores*. This is Gramsci's 'crisis of authority', which is also a 'general crisis of the state' (Gramsci, 1971, p. 211). The earlier manifestations of reformism were one of its principal victims. No transitive causal logic or conspiracy can be ascribed here. Wolfenden did not grasp, at one translucent blow, the 'functionality' for the new capitalism of a modified moral economy. Rather, as a step in a concrete historical process, the *Wolfenden Report* was 'driven' by a diverse set of forces and circumstances to its 'conclusions – the sketch for a modification of the moral economy. Similarly, no ruse of history, no late call for Minerva's Owl, 'selected' Mrs Whitehouse, Mr Muggeridge, Lord Longford or the 'Festival of Light' as conscious agents for the dismantling of moral reformism and the restoration of moral 'legalism'. If we make a tentative historical judgement about the logic of these events, it is only by way of a retrospective decipherment which is not reducible to the ascription of conscious intention and motivation. This theoretical gap between historical 'logic' and historical 'process' remains to threaten the security of the most careful and tentative historical reconstruction, whose provisional nature we again acknowledge.

The problem – closing the gap between 'logic' and 'process' – is clarified but not resolved by the identification of either an organised political force or a social bloc. In neither case can these be ascribed as the 'authors' of moral reformism in a literal sense. The 'legislation of consent' was not an expression of these forces. Nor, as we have tried to show, was it the product of some univocal historical necessity. It was submitted to and shaped by the forces, institutions and apparatuses, the philosophies and ideologies specific to this domain. These were often in opposition to, or cross-cut and limited by, other tendencies and forces. The precise balance or 'settlement' struck in this domain, as well as its subsequent disintegration and reformulation, forecloses on any attempt to disinter, retrospectively, a determinist narrative to the story. Nevertheless, reformism as a complex historical formation does have its own peculiar history in this period, its own distinctive character. It arises from and generates its own distinctive kinds of contradiction. It connects with programmes which give complex tendencies and contradictions a certain formulation, and which aim at a certain effective and plausible resolution to those contradictions, even when such 'settlements' do not hold, or have outcomes which cannot be fully predicted or fail ultimately to secure those relations which they seek to articulate. Specifically, the contradictions identified here amount to something like a 'crisis' in the sphere of social reproduction. Though no one particular class fraction grasped the full dimensions of this crisis in a lucid, circumscribing glance, it had a particular resonance for that fraction. They came to recognise themselves, for a time, as the interpellated 'subjects' of its revised doctrine of moral conduct. While it lasted, it staked out terrain on which they could effectively operate.

The classification and framing of moral conduct

In an important, unjustly neglected, essay on 'visible and invisible pedagogies', Basil Bernstein has developed an argument, put here in terms of the regulation of sexual conduct, about educational pedagogy. Bernstein argues that there are different ways of classifying and framing educational knowledge, and these represent modalities in the regulation and transmission of 'cultural capital' in the education system. These yield distinct educational pedagogies, and each is, in its own way, a distinctive mode of pedagogic control. By classification Bernstein means the relationship established between the contents of a curriculum: in pedagogies with 'strong' classifications, contents are 'well insulated from each other by strong boundaries'; in weak classification systems, contents are less strongly insulated. His other term – framing – refers to the context in which educational knowledge is transmitted, i.e. the relationship of control between teacher and taught. Different pedagogies establish different relationships between elements of regulation and choice: 'Strong framing entails reduced options: weak framing entails a range of options'.[48] Weakly framed pedagogies are, in our terms, more 'permissive'. In a subsequent development of this argument Bernstein identifies the emergence of a new mode of pedagogic regulation, especially in the educational reformism which modified pre-school and infant school pedagogy in the post-war period.[49] And he identifies this development with the emergence of the new, 'progressive' middle classes, which (until Mr Rhodes Boyson and the authors of the Black Papers turned the tide) established a kind of pedagogic hegemony in certain educational sectors in precisely the periods also identified with the emergence of 'moral reformism'.

> If the ideologies of the old middle classes were institutionalized in the public schools and through them into grammar schools, so the ideology of the new middle classes were first institutionalized in private pre-schools and then private/public secondary schools, and finally into the state system at the level of the infant school. Thus the conflict between visible and invisible pedagogies . . . between strong and weak classification and frames, is an ideological conflict within the middle class. The ideologies of education are still ideologies of class. The old middle class were domesticated through the strong classifications and frames of the family and public schools. The second form of organic solidarity celebrates the apparent release, not of individual, but of the person and new forms of social control (Bernstein, 1975, pp. 124–5).

This last point is an important one, since the terms 'permissive' or weakly bounded educational systems have sometimes, erroneously, been equated with an absence of control. Bernstein clearly argues that what he has identified are two distinct modalities of regulation: 'The form of transmission of an invisible pedagogy encourages more of the child to be made public and so more of the child is available for direct and indirect surveillance and control' (Bernstein, 1975, p. 135). In this mode of regulation, however, control is 'vested in the process of interpersonal communication' rather than in imposed hierarchies and externally systematised authority. The penetration of the invisible pedagogy was, in Bernstein's view, uneven; effectively installed in the early years of schooling, it tended to yield to a more 'visible' pedagogy as the child progressed towards those levels of schooling where certification and assessment became more significant.[50]

For Bernstein each pedagogy represents a mode of social reproduction. The shift of emphasis, at certain levels of schooling, from 'visible' to 'invisible' pedagogies marked therefore a transition between two different modalities of cultural reproduction. Each was also more characteristically identified with different social class fractions: the old middle classes with strong framed and bounded systems, which 'convey, tacitly, critical and condensed messages'; the new progressive middle classes with weakly classified and framed systems which 'promote . . . far greater ambiguity' – a person-centred pedagogy, resting upon 'implicit hierarchies which do not require legitimation by explicit and unambiguous values'. Bernstein tentatively remarked the appearance of similar shifts in the symbolic codes and codings in the areas of sex and aesthetics.

We do not wish to push the parallels too far, but they are certainly worth noting, and prove to be highly suggestive. In the sphere of moral and sexual conduct an established mode of public regulation is transformed by the temporary interruption of a more 'invisible' and 'personalised' modality of regulation, resulting in a code of regulation which is, in Bernstein's terms, more 'weakly' framed and classified. This shift is closely associated with the imprint of the progressive elements of the new middle classes. In both instances the shift is accomplished by an internal rearrangement of the field or domain – a reclassification of the elements into a new relation. Theoretically, the important point is that the forces, contradictions and tendencies operative on this field of social reproduction register within the domain of legal regulation in the form of a redisposition of the existing elements into a new configuration. As Marx once observed about the so-called 'correspondence' between economic and legal relations: 'But the really difficult point is how relations of production develop *unevenly* as legal relations' (Marx, 1857). More and more we are coming to understand the unevenness of such relationships as requiring a necessary detour through what at first may appear to be 'simply' a matter of formal rearrangement. The analysis offered in this paper is only a tentative step in the direction of deciphering 'general and necessary tendencies' from within 'their forms of manifestation.' (Marx, 1961, p. 316).

2
The Conservatism of the Cannabis Debate

Its place in the reproduction of the 'drug problem'

Nick Dorn

LEGALISE POT, SAYS MP . . .
Cannabis should be openly sold, but heavily taxed, like cigarettes . . . According to the best scientific evidence there is no case that cannabis promotes law breaking or leads to rape, robbery or other crimes (*Evening Standard*, 30 March 1977).

GLUE-SNIFFING PENALTY CALL
Glue-sniffing should be made a criminal offence. And a shock report is to go to MP's and the Government (*Liverpool Echo*, 30 March 1977).

This paper is largely speculative and has two short-term objectives. First, it attempts to initiate a critical discussion of cannabis law reform and to set that issue within the context of broader drug and non-drug issues. Second, it also serves the function of a first step in the development of a theoretical framework for a research project on alcohol and health education. The statements that follow are therefore provisional and require some further development.

There is a very considerable literature on cannabis. Much of this literature is concerned with the questions of what cannabis is, who is taking it, why, and with what medical effects. More recently sociologists and others influenced by labelling theory have broadened the debate to include consideration of the impact of the illegality of cannabis upon the ways in which cannabis may be used, and upon social consequences of threatened or actual apprehension by agents of the legal system. In the light of the possibility that the overall costs of legal prohibition outweigh benefits to cannabis users or to 'society at large', there have been calls for cannabis law reform.

Such reforms appeal to several groups of people. Cannabis users themselves, for example, once savoured the illegality of cannabis as an aspect of the potential, attributed to it, to subvert the conventional rule-bound world and to transform it into a better place. But today's users, more often tending towards the view that cannabis is simply a recreational pursuit and a matter of personal preference and consumption style, are less happy about prohibition. For liberals of all political parties, Mill's philosophy that one should be free to harm oneself (as long as this does not harm other people's interests) leads to support for cannabis law reform. Sociologists of 'victimless crime', sometimes themselves past or current cannabis users, point to the ineffectiveness of the law in preventing deviant behaviour such as cannabis use, and emphasise the unproductive consequences of prohibition for those who are caught. Law-and-order stalwarts, concerned that the illegality of cannabis may, in the face of its widespread use, undermine respect for the law, need not necessarily oppose reform. Neither are the police very happy about laws which they cannot enforce and which sometimes seem to detract from the war against the 'real criminals'. Governments furrow their brows over the financial costs of enforcement, sigh at the thought of an untaxed commodity, and then cock an ear to those concerned about 'social costs' of cannabis prohibition. The food and drugs industry dusts off its sixties' files on product development.

In comparison with the attention paid to the questions of whether or not there should be reforms, the attention paid to the questions of the practicalities of reform and to its effects has been negligible. A very few studies have focused upon historical or contemporary examples of changes in law relating to cannabis in various countries or federal states (Drug Abuse Council, 1975). However, these studies have been concerned only with the effects of cannabis law reform *in relation to cannabis.* One purpose of this paper is to draw attention to the possibility that reform of cannabis law may have drastic and negative implications for the ways in which individuals and institutions react to use of *other* illegal drugs. The argument developed is that *the tactics employed by those whose short-term goal is to 'liberate' cannabis use may damage the possibilities of achieving the longer-term goal of the abolition of the drug problem.*

In order to discuss this question of the relation of cannabis law reform to the broader drug problem, it is necessary to understand both the historical source of the categories of deviance with which we are concerned ('drugs', 'drugtakers') and also the ways in which these categories are currently being deployed. The following section of this paper discusses the emergence of these concepts as a by-product of the clash between conservative farming/trading and liberal industrial classes in the 19th century. Subsequently, within the framework of a model of analysis of social problems that recognises the interactions between social groups, control agencies and structural circumstances, the deployment of the 'drug' concepts in the sixties and seventies is discussed, with special reference to the relation between the 'drug problem' and reproduction of the labour force. 'Drug problems' in the teenage working class were, in the sixties, a matter for concern because they appeared to threaten the transition from school to work. But now, in a period of increased unemployment, the drug problem offers one non-structural explanation for failure to make that transition. The drug problem, having been fitted into the scenario of 'children in trouble', offers a rationale for the efforts of control agencies to 'cope with' working-class youth 'failing' to make the transition to non-existent work, in ways that are within the ideological and practical capabilities of the agencies involved.

The public meaning of the drug problem, it is suggested, is changing. It is coming to be simultaneously stretched (in relation to chemical substances) and restricted (in relation to the social class of youth involved). Whilst it used to refer to any youthful use of illegal drugs, it is coming to mean use by working-class youth of any intoxicant, legal or illegal (e.g. amphetamines, alcohol, glue). The continued illegality of cannabis presents, because of its particularly middle-class connotations, a contradictory element in the proletarianisation of the drug problem.

It is within this context that alternative tactics and goals of cannabis law reform are discussed. Tendencies towards a clear separation between cannabis and 'drugs' (such as would obtain if cannabis were commercialised) are described as consolidating the concept of 'drugs' and lending tacit support to the 'drug problem' in its emerging role in the pathologisation of working-class youth. Decriminalisation of cannabis (no commercial trade) might be preferable to commercialisation in so far as the former does not draw such a clear line between 'drugs' and 'non-drugs', but it would not remove the more general tendencies towards some kind of individualisation of structural problems.[1] And, by removing an 'anomaly' from the present control system, decriminalisation would enhance the apparent rationality of drug control and hence the objectivity of the 'drug problem'. It is suggested, in conclusion, that an effective practice for abolition of the drug problem may depend not upon limited delabelling exercises but upon an investigation of the conditions of teenagers' rejections of the 'teenage dependencies.'

Historical genesis of the social categories of 'drug' and 'drugtaker'

Calls for cannabis law reform can only be understood by reference to the existing legislation covering illegal drugs in general, and that legislation can in turn be understood only by reference to the historical circumstances from which it emerged. Drug legislation in the UK and in other countries derives from international conventions concerned primarily with opiates. The history of domestic legislation in the UK is essentially the history of international agreements: Britain has consistently legislated to domesticate new international agreements as they have emerged. The so-called 'British System' of heroin maintenance for addicts is hardly an exception to this rule, since it remains the case that experimentation with unprescribed heroin remains a crime in the same way that experimentation with cannabis, amphetamines, LSD, etc. is a crime. Heroin maintenance, sometimes said to characterise the British System of drug control, in fact involves an infinitesimally small proportion of experimenters with illegal drugs, and is more a matter of the spheres of influence of the various professions in this country than a normalisation or de-stigmatisation of drug use. Since Britain has so closely followed the international agreements, it would seem that an understanding of her current domestic legislation relating to cannabis and other drugs must be sought in the origins of international agreements.

This is not the place to attempt any synthesis of the burgeoning literature on the emergence of international drug controls;[2] only one or two points are important for our present purposes. Whilst controls on alcohol and cigarettes have developed over several centuries, controls over drugs now illegal date from the early 20th century and are the result of economic, political and moral issues that date from the 19th century. Parties to the debate included Britain, China, and the United States. The background to the debate was the state of economic relations between Britain and China. Britain had an unfavourable balance of trade with China, since Britain wanted Chinese silks, spices and tea, but China's economy was relatively self-sufficient and she did not require British products, causing Britain to pay her in silver. By tendering Indian opium and other goods in place of silver, Britain attempted to make China adopt a trading pattern more to Britain's advantage; the trade also made a substantial contribution towards meeting the costs of the Indian administration. During the 19th century Britain was foremost amongst western nations in seeking out foreign markets.

Within Britain the farming gentry and trading interests benefited from and supported the trade, and the Liberal Party, representing the growing industrial middle class, opposed it. The Liberal attack on the opium trade, far from originating in any concern about 'drugs', emerged from its more general attack upon its political opponents, and is remarkably similar to its earlier position on slavery and other issues. The Liberals' stance on such issues was underpinned by their philosophical, economic and religious value system, which stressed freedom of the individual, freedom to enter into contracts without coercion, individualism, self-help, self-restraint, and independence. Thus their attack on the policies of the trading and farming interests, such as the opium trade, was informed by these values: the opium trade was attacked as an affront to individual freedom, as undermining self-help and self-restraint, and as promoting dependence.

In outline, this is how the terms of the debate were formed. The debate continued for some decades, its outcome being determined at the beginning of this century by a number of factors. Among these were internal changes within China, changes in the Indian economy, the aggressive trading and foreign policy of the United States, developments within the United States and in the Philippines, and the coming to power of the Liberals in Britain. The important point for our puposes is not why and how the opponents of the opium trade won, but the fact that, as they won, so their views about opium also prevailed. The concept of 'drugs' and 'drug abuse', first applied to opium, was subsequently applied to other substances as these were included within the international conventions and the domestic legislation. One way and another (it was not a matter of great concern to the more powerful countries when it occurred), cannabis was included in these international agreements and thus became characterised as a dangerous 'drug'.

Framework for analysis of social problems

Greenwood and Young point out in the article included in this volume that various authors have claimed that there are contemporary tendencies towards greater coercion, towards decriminalisation of deviance, and towards positivistic control methods (e.g. labelling deviants as 'sick'); they ask how these apparently conflicting tendencies can coexist. The drug field does indeed seem to offer some evidence of simultaneous yet apparently diverging tendencies in control. Since the mid-sixties there have been tendencies towards decriminalisation of simple possession of cannabis, in so far as fines have been reduced (both in the maximum penalties provided by the Misuse of Drugs Act 1971 and in penalties actually handed down by the courts) and in so far as the police may more often overlook cannabis possession nowadays: in the face of several million users, such a strategy makes 'practical sense'. Simultaneously, the maximum sentence for supply has been increased, and so a good case could be made out for the existence of an increase in coercion against suppliers. There have, in fact, been suggestions that this has resulted in the amateur supplier being driven out and in professionalisation and centralisation of the trade. Together with these tendencies towards decriminalisation and coercion, there has been a continuation of positivistic treatment policies. In general, then, we can say that over the last 10 years treatment approaches have at least been holding their own, coercive approaches being focused against 'the real criminals' (e.g. pushers), and de facto decriminalisation of possession, especially by the otherwise 'law-abiding' middle-class, has made some headway. But if we take the last 2 years, these tendencies in relation to illegal drugs have been overshadowed by tendencies for 'social concern' about *legal* drugs, especially alcohol, to increase. This concern is especially marked in relation to teenagers. More recent, and even more marked, is the publicity about solvent-sniffing.

Now it is not possible to explain these recent changes in 'the drug problem' as following simply from changes in teenage behaviour; even if teenage behaviour has changed slightly (and it would not be surprising if teenagers were drinking more today than a decade ago), there remains the question of why and how agencies have recently apprehended this new problem. One might attempt to explain these agency changes in terms of moral entrepreneurship of key individuals, in terms of the status politics of social groups, or in terms of the practical and material interests of the various control agencies (cf. Dickson's account of the US marijuana controls, 1968). But the world is full of moral entrepreneurs, status politicking, and bureaucratic interests, and it is important to ask why and how particular definitions of social problems win, at particular times, in the face of other contending definitions. This question requires us to inquire into how wider structural circumstances provide a frame for interaction of social groups and social control agencies.

Figure 2.1 presents one way of looking at the relationships between structural circumstances, control agencies and social groups.[3] The top half of the diagram may be regarded as acknowledging the rational problem-solving carried out by social groups in response to objective problems caused by their structural position and by the actions of control agencies, resulting in particular social 'solutions' and styles. The bottom half of the diagram refers to the fact that these social solutions may result in problems for the control agencies, given the categories for recognising deviancy that they work with. In what follows we shall be mostly concerned with control problems and solutions, and shall assume that structural circumstances must be afforded a central place in explaining them. Agencies can only carry out their tasks within the limits of their abilities, including the limits imposed by their operational ideologies and categories of deviancy. The existence of the categories of deviancy, in our case the categories of 'drugs' and 'drugtaking' and their connotations (as described in the previous section), is a necessary mediating link between objective conditions and control policy. These categories may, however, have differing meanings and policy implications, depending upon the wider control ideology in which they are articulated (the classical/coercive, neo-classical/positivist, and delabelling/decriminalisation traditions). The way in which the

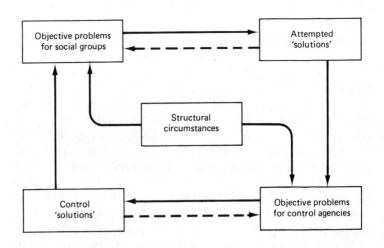

FIGURE 2.1　*Framework for analysis of social problems*

categories of deviancy and the control ideologies are put together will depend partly upon problems the agencies come to face through continued applications of a policy that causes client groups to adopt new practices and/or that directly causes administrative or ideological difficulties internally or in relation to other agencies. But it will also depend upon agency staff's understanding of structural needs. This is assumed true in two senses: first, in the relatively short-term agencies must carry out their tasks in ways that, at the very least, do not appear to sabotage the smooth running of the economy and of social life; secondly, in the longer-term, agencies must secure the reproduction of the central economic structures upon which they rest, and this task includes the proper socialisation of tomorrow's labourers, consumers and managers. In the last resort it will be the reproduction of the economic system that will occupy agencies, even to the detriment of their short-term problems.

Drug control in the sixties

Since the Second World War a central economic concern has been the ever-present possibility of overproduction and slump. This problem is exacerbated by the fact that the rational course of action for each individual economic unit – the expansion of production to attain economies of scale and great (export) sales – is exactly the course of action that creates overproduction and slump in the system as a whole. There are several types of economic solution that may be offered to the problem of overproduction, but for a number of reasons some solutions, e.g. high tariff walls against imports, have not been taken. Rather, there has been an attempt to stimulate consumption by means of market segmentation, fashion trends, planned obsolescence, etc. Now the socially necessary corollary of such economic strategies is an encouragement of diversity, though diversity within fairly clearly defined limits (of consumption). Clearly, criminalisation of emergent social styles that encourage conspicuous consumption is economically dysfunctional in this context. During the sixties there definitely were some tendencies to decriminalisation of illegal social diversity. These trends, however, were not very marked in the drugs area, and in the following paragraphs I shall attempt to say why.

It is clear that circumstances might exist in which control agencies are placed in a conflict position. *Actions and ideology that might be appropriate for the servicing of some short-term needs might endanger the longer-term necessities of reproducing the preconditions of the economic system as a whole.* (Thus, decriminalisation of social diversity as a means to market segmentation and expansion might be curbed by control culture anxieties about the maintenance or the reproduction of a productive labour force.) In retrospect, it seems clear that the trends to decriminalisation of drug use in the sixties were indeed contained in favour of coercive and positivistic control solutions: the threat to production was identified as the central meaning of drug use in the UK in the sixties. But, in order to clarify the argument, it is important to differentiate between the two senses in which drugs might be seen as threatening production – the short-term threat to work-discipline, and the longer-term threat to reproduction of the labour force. Let us take the threat to work-discipline first.

> It must not be thought . . . that contemporary man's work and leisure form watertight compartments . . . They must produce in order to consume. The interrelationship between formal and subterranean values is therefore seen in a new light: hedonism, for instance, is closely tied to what I will term the ethos of pro-ductivity. This states that a man is justified in expressing sub-terranean values if, and only if, he has earned the right to do so by working hard and being productive (Young, 1974, p. 235).

From the Defence of the Realm Regulations of 1916 (designed to preserve the fighting morale of the troops) up until the early or middle sixties, drug use was not regarded as a youth problem. Objectively, there was the evidence of the Home Office statistics, which showed that most registered heroin addicts were over 50 years of age up until the early sixties; not until the mid-sixties did those under 20 years of age make up more than a tenth of those registered (Bean, 1974, p. 104). And in terms of imagery, cannabis was associated with coloured immigrants rather than with teenagers. In this context, drugs, to the extent that they were perceived as a threat, were first perceived to threaten the *adult* order rather than children. Given the historical connotation of drugs (i.e. sloth, loss of freedom of contract, of independence, and of economic rationality), it is not difficult to see how drugs came to be equated with social dependency. But such a dependency role does not, in itself, stand as a challenge to the social order: there is a difference between an individual's loss of his ability to regulate his life and to go to work in order to earn (a loss which leads only to his own loss of consumption), on the one hand, and scandalously unearned pleasure, on the other. It was perhaps through the perceived connection between drugs and immigrants that the connection with unearned pleasure was made: racist resentment of immigrants included the idea that they were getting away with too much pleasure, and not working enough. In any event, it was in relation to adults, to the existing work force, that the moral calculus of the balance between production and consumption was first dislocated by drugs. To the extent that drugs seemed to threaten the ideology of work-discipline, they did so primarily in relation to an existing, adult work force.

As the sixties progressed, however, the drug problem not· only expanded but took on the appearance of a *youth problem*: not only involving youth, but specifically involving youth. It might, of course, be quite reasonably argued that teenage drug use was regarded as a greater affront than adult drug use because teenagers had yet to make any work contribution to society, and that they should continue in a limbo of anticipated pleasure until they had taken their place at the lathe (and at the altar, etc.). This argument could be turned upon its head, however, since, if teenagers are not yet expected to work, such pleasure as they do get is never earned pleasure, which makes it equally or more scandalous. Alternatively, one might argue, if one wished, that social reaction against teenage drug use was a displaced reaction against the conspicuous creation of a teenage consumer market. None of these arguments, however, seem to account for the depth and specificity of social reaction which marked the latest and most extreme manifestation of an ongoing 'youth problem'. What is it about the structural position of adolescents that focuses such concern? Posed in this way, the question indicates its own answer – for adolescence is a historically recent creation, during which children denied a productive role within the nuclear family are *re*socialised into the ethos and practice of extra-familial, adult, labour. A process of *re*socialisation is more vulnerable than is the maintenance of existing socialisation.

To understand how the 'drug problem' came to be defined, first and foremost, as a youth problem, and to understand how it elicited not only moral indignation but also panic, we therefore need a shift of analytic focus, from the relation of the drug problem to the existing adult work force, to its relation to tomorrow's work force. John Clarke has emphasised the importance of the transition of teenagers from school to work, positing that the recurrence of moral

panic about youth stems from anxieties in the control culture about
the continued success of this vital transition. In so far as drug use in
the sixties was seen as a youth problem rather more than a problem
likely to infect older workers, it seems most likely that the threat to
production was indeed perceived to point primarily at the reproduction of tomorrow's labour, rather than at the maintenance of
work-discipline in the existing labour force (in which shop stewards,
rather than drugs, were of primary concern).

'Drugs' threatened the reproduction of the labour force in two
respects. First, it threatened the reproduction of a managerial elite in
the middle class: if the most favoured of the grammar and public
schoolboys were to spend their time stringing beads and denigrating
conventional ideas about careers and rewards, then who was going to
look after the mill? But however anxiety-producing this may have
been for the parents concerned, it was not a big problem from the
perspective of the control agencies, who could see a large pool of
potential applicants for managerial jobs. Control agency concern
centred around middle-class hippies not so much out of concern for
them as out of concern for the example which they were setting for
the working-class youth. 'Setting a bad example' is a fault for which a
rap over the knuckles, rather than indulgence or social work, is an
appropriate response. Thus coercion, in the form of expulsion from
public school, or prosecution and stiff fines, was the favoured way of
dealing with youthful middle-class drug use.

But it was upon working-class teenage drug use (or the possibility
of widespread working-class drug use or interest), and upon the
possible consequences for the reproduction of the non-managerial
work force, that control anxieties focused. The transition of the
working class from school to work is of central concern to the
agencies, dwarfing, quantitatively and qualitatively, the problem of
the socialisation of the middle class. This concern is entirely realistic,
since the transition from school to work is shorter, sharper and
altogether less seductive for working-class teenagers. Not having
such a long educational/transitional stage within which to practise
Utopian social styles as had middle-class teenagers, nor being able to
evade the reality of the power job-market as it faced them, working-
class kids' drug use was of a kind that fitted into their own attempted
'solutions' (or accommodations, or resistance rituals) to the broader
problems they faced: on the one hand, the same example, thrust upon
them by the media, of the good life; on the other hand, the clear fact
that they were not going to get it (as a group); and in the middle the

strengths and weaknesses of their parent culture and of the local community. Working-class youth culture in the sixties represented a variety of solutions to an insoluble problem, and this was reflected in its drug use. The solutions adopted were often recognised by control agencies as 'delinquency', meaning the failure of smooth transition from school to work. What power might drugs have to exacerbate this tendency to delinquency, to disrupt the reproduction of labour, to produce a teenage working class unwilling to accept the privations tolerated by their parents? This anxiety led to an interest in empirical studies of the interaction between delinquency and drugtaking in the working-class (Cockett, 1971).

As the sixties progressed, the drug problem in relation to working-class teenagers came to be more and more absorbed into the more general control tendency to deal with delinquency within treatment and social-work paradigms (e.g. Children and Young Persons Act 1969). The general trend to redeployment of some deviancy categories out of a classical/coercive ideological framework and into a positivist one had several causes, only some of which can be mentioned here. First, there was the overwhelming need to guarantee the reproduction of labour. Second, there was the need to do this in a manner that seemed legitimate and did not cause short-term social conflicts, did not cause the parent working-class culture to line up behind and defend the resistance strategies of their children. Third, coercive control solutions (e.g. Borstals) were becoming increasingly impractical and expensive as a way of handling the mass of working-class teenage deviancy; anyway, some control agencies (e.g. the police) were becoming increasingly aware of the need to reserve coercive control measures for those who most deserved them – 'real criminals' such as train robbers and violent political groups, for example. The redefinition of delinquency into maladjustment had practical and ideological advantages (though perhaps it would be impossible to draw a firm line between these two): drugtaking by working class teenagers was symbolically stripped of any power it might have had to be a tool of resistance to the labour market, and converted into a sign that teenagers needed help to overcome their immaturity and take their place in society.

Thus, I suggest, working-class drug use came to be differentiated from middle-class drug use, not just on the basis of the drugs supposedly used, but on the basis of the type and severity of threat that drugs seemed to offer in the hands of each class and on the basis of the methods of social control seen as appropriate counters. In the *why?*

eyes of the agencies, never given to explicit statements about social class, the working class/middle class differentiation came to be seen. as a differentiation between cannabis (= middle-class) and other illegal drugs (= working class). Middle-class drug use, identified with cannabis, was seen as fairly harmless but naughty: working-class drug use was seen as more harmful to proper development.

By the late sixties any residual fears that drugs would suddenly topple civilisation had been empirically disproved by the passage of time. To the disappointment of some people outside the control agencies, drugs had clearly not infiltrated the mainstream culture to any significant extent and, in any event, it was becoming clear that it took a little more than a pill or a joint to turn a worker into a hippy. To the extent that control agencies may have feared a breakdown, brought about by drugs, in the discipline of the existing work force, these fears were laid to rest.

The passage of time also resulted in convincing demonstrations that supposedly middle-class styles of drug use were by no means incompatible with consumption of other goods and services. As Richard Neville was to say: 'If in the end it means only that Time becomes Time Out, Heath turns into Heffner, Wimpey goes organic, cheque books are multicoloured, Peter Stuyvesant gets stoned, the OZ musical replaces Fiddler on the Roof and God Save the Queen is set to rock and roll, it was still fun on the way' (Neville, 1972, p. 5).

If excitement, understanding, authenticity, sociability, real self, can be got with the aid of illegal consumer goods, they can be got also from legal consumer goods. And whilst it might have been thought that the 'values' of what has been called the 'post-bourgeois' generation would have prevented such a transition, such a thought mistakes an elitist and up-market consumer mentality for rejection of 'materialism'. The young middle class of the late sixties, or at least a portion of it, rejected the arduous patterns of accumulation of consumer durables characteristic of its parents, and substituted for it a policy of immediate access to desired personal and social states. The commercialisation of the new market in 'authenticity' had made clear the potential for increases in consumption and the maintenance of demand. Styles of consumption laid down in the young middle class during secondary and tertiary education were not only compatible with consumption to the limits of their resources during their student years, but were also compatible with subsequent patterns of repeated and conspicuous consumption that exceeded those of their parents.

So, owing to the reassurance offered by the existence of a large pool of potential applicants for managerial jobs, and also to the compatibility of middle-class styles of drug use with consumption of other goods and services, anxieties about the impact of middle-class teenage drug use upon the social order declined toward the end of the sixties. A non-interventionist approach to middle-class drug experimentation, generally equated with cannabis use, thus came to appear more justifiable. But control agency concerns over the reproduction of the working-class labour force remained high, maintaining an official hypersensitivity to possible signs and symptoms of failure in the transition of working-class teenagers from dependency to independency. The possibility of widespread drug dependency in the teenage working class, then, became no less worrying as time went on, and agencies maintained a clear and strong stance against 'drugs'.

The anti-drug stance was bolstered by the concept of the 'pusher'. By directing public feeling against the pusher, a clear public statement against drugs was made, but a statement that facilitated the portrayal of controls as a form of social protection rather than coercion. The focus upon the pusher gave drug controls a humanistic, and hence almost 'natural', appearance.

Young has written convincingly about the media image of the pusher as corrupter, suggesting that 'collectively chosen deviant solutions to problems caused by common problems are thus portrayed as impossible. The corrupter image of deviance is the reverse side of the individualist theory of history' (Young, 1974, p. 249). Social groups do not deviate on purpose, the imagery says, but are tricked into deviancy by corrupt individuals who stand to gain conventional rewards. The pusher imagery is of central importance in the field of drug controls.

Another side to the pusher imagery is also of importance – as an example of how liberal opinion may sometimes supply the ideological tools for its own defeat. In his *Diaries* Richard Crossman described how, when discussing the Misuse of Drugs Bill (which was to become the Misuse of Drugs Act 1971) the Labour Cabinet split 'for the first time into a sociological vote, that is to say, every member of the cabinet who had been at University voted one way and everybody else voted the other' (reprinted in the *Sunday Times*, 13 September 1977). The university-educated and more 'liberal' was for maintaining a distinction between pushers and users, increasing the penalty for pushing and decreasing the penalty for possession. But the distinction between pushers and users rebounded in the faces of its liberal supporters because, in confirming the corrupter and corrupted roles, it confirmed the moral seriousness of drug abuse and the need for firm handling of the whole issue. By its reliance on the pusher concept, liberal opinion helped to structure the debate in such a way as to contribute to its own defeat, because of the moral leverage it offered conservatives for the infliction of symbolic defeats on 'permissiveness' and on liberal opinion in general. The 'soft' liberal explanation of social deviancy – as the result of the corruption of innocents – logically paves the way for and justifies a 'hard' response both to corrupters and to those who might become corrupted: 'As Mr. Callaghan said . . . he was glad if his rejection of the Wootton Report's recommendations had "enabled the House to call a halt to the advancing tide of so-called permissiveness"' (Lanuette, 1972, p. 285).

The *Wootton Report*, which had concluded that cannabis was probably not very dangerous, and had recommended that penalties could be substantially reduced, was thrown out by Mr Callaghan amid great applause and suggestions that the Committee had been 'got at' by the 'pro-pot lobby'. As Mr Callaghan said whilst rejecting the Wootton recommendations: 'I had the impression that those who were in favour of legalising pot were all the time *pushing* [my emphasis] the other members of the committee back . . .' This perception is perfectly rational, given the ideological climate at the time: normal people were being demoralised and misled by the permissive lobby (rather 'soft on drugs'), which was itself infiltrated by the pro-pot lobby (very 'soft on drugs'), and that in turn had been corrupted by pushers:

$$\text{pushers} \longrightarrow \text{pro-pot} \longrightarrow \text{permissive} \longrightarrow \text{misled}$$

Perhaps the characterisation of permissiveness as akin to corruption was a development that had wider and more important results than did the formal implementation of the content of the Misuse of Drugs Act 1971. Looking forward to an issue developed later in this chapter, we can see how the partial fusion of the concepts of the evil pusher and of misguided permissiveness was to prepare the ground for the following logic:

GET YOUNGSTERS OFF THE ROAD TO RUIN

The recent Royal Society of Health's Conference message was

clear and blamed juvenile alcoholics on today's permissive attitudes . . . 'So often I have seen so-called professionals buying the loyalty of young people by allowing them selfish and unhealthy indulgence. Who knows how many youngsters have developed into alcoholics as the result of misguided generosity', said the 43-year-old policewoman. (*Pulse*, 30 October 1976)

But coming back to the 1971 Act, we find that its specific content is quite notable. The Dangerous Drugs Act 1967 had already provided for the more effective containment of the 'victims' (by means of the clinic system, which made it difficult for users to obtain heroin from several doctors). The 1971 Act reduced maximum penalties for cannabis possession (from 10 to 5 years upon indictment), introduced and affixed severe penalties to a new offence, that of possession of drugs with intent to supply, and increased penalties for the existing offence of supply. It was not claimed that this would 'solve' the problem, but it did sort things out somewhat from the administrative point of view (more clearly delineating between deviance categories and more clearly allocating tasks to agencies than hitherto) and also from the ideological point of view. The 1967 and 1971 Acts, then, can be seen as a rational 'solution' to the various problems faced by control agencies during the second half of the sixties. It simultaneously embraces a classical/coercive perspective (punishment for pushers), a positivist perspective (treatment for those who fail to make the transition to work – being in work is often used as a criterion of treatment success, whether or not the person is drug-free), and a move towards decriminalisation (lessening of penalties for possession). The mix of perspectives and practices is an integrated rather than conflicting one.

Seventies' structural unemployment and its reduction to working-class 'pathology'

From the structural point of view, the last few years have been marked by an 'economic crisis' of simultaneous inflation and recession. Unemployment has risen markedly. Whatever the causes of these developments, they have had obvious repercussions upon social groups. In particular, there has been a rise in the pool of unemployed working-class school-leavers, and a fall in average real incomes of those remaining in work. The sixties ('Those days when what is foolishly called the permissive society was in its first bloom, and its rotten fruit was not yet so thick upon the ground', Ronald Butt in *The Times*, 17 March 1977), the period of the consumer boom, is looked back upon as a period in which Britain was not paying her way in the world; but today we are going to have to pay. Contemporary deprivations are the inevitable result of over-indulgence and lack of work; this wisdom bears down upon us as one nation, and particularly upon those social groups and individuals who are suffering most deprivation.

Current economic policies in the UK are orientated to an increase in productivity and exports, at the expense of employment and home consumption. These policies have an impact on the 'drug problem' in two ways. Let us take unemployment first.

In a period of high unemployment the transition from school to work becomes more problematic not only for teenagers but also for those agencies supposed to manage that transition. In a situation of planned unemployment, where the agencies can do little or nothing to create jobs on a permanent basis, they may cope with the failure of the school-to-work transition in two ways. First, they can participate in schemes which give working-class youth 'a taste of work', so that some work socialisation may take place and so that the pool of never-employed is reduced. Secondly, in view of the limited capacity of such job-creation schemes, they must evolve some way of coping with the large number of people who remain without experience of, or with very limited experience of, employment. How might agencies, already committed to an ideology in which drug use is seen as a threat to the school–work transition, rationally respond to this situation? I would suggest that their existing deviancy categories and ideologies predispose them to a simple expansion of their existing practices. Whilst agency staff may know that unemployment is structural, *they cannot respond to it in those terms*; they therefore seek some rationalisation for the fact that they are best equipped to respond to unemployed youth as messed-up *individuals*. Working-class drug use is a symptom to which agencies can so respond.

Lest this should appear entirely speculative, there is some evidence that the agencies have recently begun to respond co-operatively to unemployed youth in a way that identifies drug use as a reason for its 'instability'. A 1975 UK Government report said:

Considerable progress has been made towards the setting up of an experimental short stay residential unit in London for unstable young multi-drug users . . . It is hoped that the project may tell us whether such a service can assess and help to stabilise the young people who will become its clients. Although the unit will be run by a voluntary organisation, the hospital service, the local authority and the DHSS have been involved in the planning of the project and will be jointly responsible for its funding (UK Government, 1975).

In fact, this unit had been under discussion for 5 years. Funding was finally agreed in 1977, as continuing high levels of unemployment reinforced the funding agencies' tendency to respond to 'instability' as 'drug misuse'. The Unit is the first of its kind in the UK and the timing of its multi-agency funding is significant.

Clearly, though, this form of response can help agencies to cope with only a small proportion of unemployed youth, since it is evident that few teenagers are taking illegal drugs; rather more working-class teenagers do, however, take legal drugs, such as alcohol and glue, and over the last few years this country has apparently developed youth alcohol and glue problems. Whether or not youth unemployment has 'caused' a change in youth behaviour, it has provided the conditions for changes in social reaction.

Although it is nowhere said explicitly, newspaper cuttings and TV programmes about these problems make clear that it is working-class kids who constitute the problem population – see, for instance, the *This Week* TV presentation, 'On the Glue', reviewed by the Institute for the Study of Drug Dependence (ISDD, 1976); or local and national press cuttings in the ISDD press cuttings library. Such a perception of the situation could, however, only be developed alongside changes in definition of alcohol and glue. Hitherto neither of these commodities had been seen as drugs open to the same sort of abuses as heroin. Yet it is clear that only these commodities were available to the mass of ordinary teenagers. The means whereby the transformation of alcohol and glue into full-blown 'drugs' was undertaken is quite striking. The *This Week* programme (noted above) 'On the Glue' introduced such hitherto unknown terms as 'glue addict' and 'glue den', and spoke of the problem of 'relapse' after treatment for the 'addiction'. The internal structure of the programme and the signs used (e.g. a 'glue addict' interviewed with his face in shadow), together with the special use of language, clearly indicated that glue use was akin to heroin use. The label 'drugs' and all it symbolises has been extended to a new activity, which is invested with all the horrors attributed to LSD-type and heroin-type 'drugs' plus a few new ones. An information resource in a British police station was recently found to list twenty-three 'well-authenticated complications of glue sniffing' including:

– a feeling of omnipotence such that the glue sniffer may jump off a high building feeling that he can fly or he may assume a fighting stance before an on-coming train;

– damage to the nerves;

– rupture of the lungs due to the lung sticking together and tearing;

– engaging in anti-social behaviour such as damaging property, theft, larceny, shoplifting, rape, homicide.

A person armed with such Angslingeresque knowledge is unlikely to turn his back on a person suspected of having sniffed glue, or to treat him as in any way a normal person. Yet this is the kind of knowledge that can credibly be put about by the simple strategy of calling a common substance, in this case glue, a 'drug'.

Cannabis reformers are quite often even more strongly committed to the maintenance and expansion of the concept of 'drugs' than is the general population or the allegedly conservative control agencies. Consider, for instance, the following extract from an article on glue in *High Times*, the leading cannabis paraphernalia merchandising magazine in North America and the UK:

Indeed, chronic huffers tend to be anti-social individuals from broken homes and backward environs . . . Apathy is the disorder of the day, and the more gone gunk geeks sport self-styled ostentations of their antisociality: crude, homemade india-ink and razor-blade tattoos like 'Born to Lose' . . . Tru glue ready gunk geeks squeeze the last bits of morality from their souls as deliberately as they roll down and squeeze out the last remaining drops [of glue] . . . (Schenkman, 1976, p. 109).

Transformations in the meaning of youthful alcohol use were less abrupt. For some years 'alcoholism' in adults has been seen primarily in disease terms (Linsky, 1970), and loss of control and loss of responsibility for one's economic well-being have been an integral part of this image. It remained only to fit this image on to the drinking patterns of youth. This was done in a manner that emphasised the new and alarming extent of drinking by young people – language terms used included 'The Teeny Drinkers' (Panorama, BBC TV, 1976) and *The New Drinkers* (Smart, 1976).

As noted above, the transition of the working class from school to work has, since the Industrial Revolution, been of acute concern to control agencies. Alcohol and glue, potentially available to the bulk of working-class teenagers, offered an explanation of the failure of many to make this transition that fitted better into the categories and capabilities of these control agencies than did the alternative explanation that work was short. This is not to say that the personnel of these agencies are stupid, or conspiratorial, or blind to unemployment: rather, *they must respond to the problem in a way within their capabilities of response, and these capabilities determine the types of deviance categories and rationales that become dominant.* (Needless to say, this raises specific problems for teenagers to which they will evolve their own 'solutions'.)

But (as indicated by the dotted lines in Figure 2.1, above) control solutions can directly cause certain problems for the agencies concerned. Today the concept of drug dependency has been 'stretched' to cover the use of a wide range of substances, some of which are illegal and some not. It is becoming increasingly clear that the concept is now being deployed to describe any use of any intoxicant by working-class teenagers, and seen as an indicator of failure in normal development as a marker of the need for some kind of treatment. In other words, the concept is shifting its focus of application from the substance taken, to the type of persons supposed to be taking it. As this shift takes place, it becomes increasingly improper, from the points of view of the agencies that facilitate it, for the appellation 'drugs' to apply to a substance which is perceived to be taken primarily by the middle class.

So far we have considered one way in which agencies' methods of managing sustained youth unemployment (especially severe at the 'bottom end' of the teenage labour market) may be related to tendencies to 'un-label' cannabis. But as noted above, current UK economic policies involve not only unemployment, but also a holding-down of home consumption as an encouragement to exporting. In so far as cannabis today 'stands for' social diversity and for styles of conspicuous consumption, any tendency to reflation of the economy and to encouragement of home consumption may also facilitate cannabis law reform. But this factor may 'not be so important as that associated with youth unemployment, given the threat to reproduction of the social order which the latter implies.

We are, then, entering a period of time in which cannabis law reform, hitherto an issue exciting few people outside the small, single-issue groups set up to promote it (e.g. the Cannabis Action Reform Organisation), may be taken more seriously by official agencies of the state, and by the media. Reform may even become a more explicitly political issue, as support is sought from left and liberal groups. In these circumstances the question of what is a progressing stance in relation to cannabis law reform becomes important.

Cannabis law reform: a step towards or away from the abolition of the drug problem?

At the present time[4] cannabis occupies a somewhat ambiguous status – a 'drug', yet not quite a 'drug' (see Figure 2.2). As a marginal member of the set of things we call drugs, it has tended to straddle the boundary between drug and non-drug, to blur that boundary, and hence to weaken the concept of drugs. It is this ambiguity that the cannabis law reformers wish to resolve.

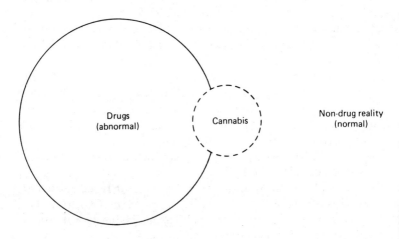

FIGURE 2.2   *The ambiguous position of cannabis as a drug*

In straddling the boundary between 'drugs' and 'normality' cannabis calls into question the separation of these domains, and provides a link between them. One can have shades of drugtaking.

Take away this ambiguous case, and one is left with an in-or-out situation; *either* one is normal *or* one is a drugtaker and damned.

Now the unfortunate aspect of the tactics of most would-be cannabis law reformers is their forgetfulness of the situation of the users of drugs other than cannabis. Cannabis law reform is being advanced by means of the argument that cannabis ought not really to be considered a 'drug' in the same sense as other drugs. Let us examine the form of this argument: cannabis, is not dependency-producing, not really very harmful to health, not psychologically or morally harmful, not abnormal, not a drug. The hidden corollary of this is that some other things really are drugs. Cannabis law reform appeals to its audience by agreeing, yes, *you're perfectly right about drugs*, they embody many evils: *it's just that cannabis isn't a drug.* Thus cannabis law reform often proceeds by confirming and strengthening the concept of 'drugs' (see, for instance, the celebration of the image of the working-class drug/glue user in the *High Times* article quoted on p. 62).

If these tactics are successful, if the marginal status of cannabis is resolved by contrasting cannabis with the defiled conceptual domain of 'drugs', and by extracting cannabis from that domain, then God help the people who remain defined as 'drugtakers'! Drugtakers, like everybody else, construct their identities and biographies from the themes publically available. Were the tactics of cannabis law reform to be successful, a number of persons would find themselves trapped within an even more 'druggy' identity than is currently available. Having taken a 'drug' would be an even more significant and damning event than it is today.

In developing tactics for reform in this area of social policy, as in any others (see, for instance, Mathieson's work on prisons, 1974) we have to concern ourselves with the relation of tactics for achieving relatively short-term goals (e.g. cannabis law reform) to the chances of achieving longer-term goals. If our longer-term goal is to abolish the drug problem, then tactics that get in the way of this goal should not be adopted. But this raises the question of what we mean by abolition of the drug problem. Such a goal may seem facile: a goal more to be endorsed in theory than in practice.

By talking of abolition of the drug problem I do not mean that it is realistic to anticipate a situation in which no person comes to harm through the use of chemicals. Rather, I mean to draw a distinction between the necessary effects of chemicals upon the body, on the one hand, and, on the other hand, the additional physical, psychological and social consequences of particular modes of use, expectations, role-modelling and social reactions that stem not from the chemical itself but from the way we conceptualise its meaning. ('If that was LSD I took, then I must be about to lose control of myself.' 'If this is heroin you've been taking, then you must be disturbed', etc.)

Minimising the harm people do themselves and each other would require the dissolution of the conception of drugs rather than its confirmation and application to a wider and wider set of behaviours. This is what abolition of the drug problem means – the abolition of unnecessary, socially caused harm. Essentially it means the eventual dissolution of the very concept of 'drugs'.

It is from this perspective that I now consider two distinct possibilities for cannabis law reform – decriminalisation of small-scale cultivation of the plant and of possession of small quantities, and full legalisation of a commercial cannabis market. Two government bodies, the American Shafer Committee and the Canadian Le Dain Commission, have proposed versions of decriminalisation. Roughly the proposal is that small-scale cultivation, private use of cannabis, small-scale supply-not-for-profit, and possession (but not use) of small amounts in public, be permitted by law, or punished only by light 'parking-ticket' fines; but commercial supply not be allowed. Cannabis grows well enough in North America (indeed in the UK) in window boxes or outside, for an occasional or moderate user to supply himself and to offer hospitality from a few plants. Versions of decriminalisation have now been enacted in several states in the USA and the Carter administration is in favour of an extension of the principle, partly on pragmatic grounds of the unworkability and expense of prohibition. For some commentators, however, decriminalisation does not go far enough:

> 'I am living, walking proof of the evils of marijuana', said author/journalist Hunter S. Thompson to the laughter and applause of participants at the fifth annual conference of the National Organisation for the Reform of the Marijuana Laws . . . After being introduced as the 'spokesman for the drug culture', Thompson's entertaining speech opened the conference, and raised an issue that was debated throughout the three-day gathering: decriminalisation vs. legislation (NCCDE, 1977).

Many commentators, such as Thompson, are primarily concerned with winning a symbolic crusade, and do not concern themselves with the merits of decriminalisation except as a stepping-stone in this crusade. The crusade that concerns them is that issuing from the remains of the sixties' middle-class hippie youth culture, and the final acknowledgement and incorporation of that culture. Decriminalisation of cannabis denotes too grudging an acknowledgement of that culture to be very attractive. Furthermore, the question of social reaction towards working-class use of other substances does not penetrate the constituency of the middle-class cannabis user; social reactions to users of other drugs is something that can be considered 'later'. It is because many cannabis law reform enthusiasts are concerned primarily with cannabis, and with its eventual commercialisation, that they work with the two social categories, 'drugs' and 'non-drugs', contrasting one against the other. But in so doing they, the apparent radicals, confirm the objectivity of 'drugs' and help to legitimise social reaction to 'drugtaking'.

A goal of decriminalisation of cannabis, on the other hand, would require us to forsake altogether the language of psychopathology which reproduces the dichotomy drugs non-drugs. The goal of decriminalisation, because it confronts these established categories with a new category, would demand a different and more difficult strategy: one would not seek to redefine cannabis by denying that it has the properties attributable to 'drugs'. Instead of criticising the efficiency with which existing categories are applied, one would have to make a positive case for classification that cuts across those categories. One possible vocabulary for the making out of such a case might be derived from the discourses of civil liberties, personal choice, and bourgeois rights in general. Decriminalisation arguments could thereby be extended to all 'drugs', not just to cannabis.

But there are at least three problems inherent in any advocacy of decriminalisation. If, as earlier sections of this paper have argued, the 'drug problem' currently functions as a way in which economic and structural problems are reduced to a more 'manageable' individual level, then decriminalisation is unlikely to get any further than cannabis during a period of high unemployment. Secondly, decriminalisation alone would not, in present conditions, remove less formal aspects of social reaction. Indeed, decriminalisation can be seen as part of an ongoing and broader trend towards 'soft' methods of social control (the drug user as sick rather than bad), which may have more insidious effects than illegality, and which legitimises 'hard' treatment of other deviants judged to be 'real criminals'.

Thirdly, decriminalisation of cannabis would, because cannabis is believed to be a middle-class drug of choice, have the effect of facilitating the current tendency to redefine drug dependence less in terms of the substance taken and more in terms of 'non-middle-class' forms of intoxication. So cannabis decriminalisation, falling in the context of this tendency to redefine all working-class teenage intoxications as forms of drug dependence, would facilitate the pathologisation of the teenage working class.

It follows that, if our attention is not totally taken up with cannabis, and if we are to develop reform strategies that are, at the very least, compatible with the abolition of the drug problem and of the social and medical harm it causes, we should not give support to campaigns for the commercialisation of cannabis, or for its decriminalisation, as these are currently conceived.

These remarks underline the inadequacies of a simple de-labelling position, from which one would simply recommend decriminalisation or legislation, firstly of cannabis and then possibly of other drugs. Such a recommendation overlooks the functions of the drug problem, and overlooks the manner in which a de-labelling posture can lead 'progressive' workers to act 'conservatively'.

The question of practice

The conservatism of the cannabis debate lies in the failure of many participants to consider any issue other than cannabis, a failure that has the effect of, quite literally, conserving or reproducing the 'drug problem'. A practical alternative is not, however, easy to grasp.

Possibly the way forward lies in devising ways to facilitate those actions by control agencies that contribute to a solution of wider structural problems, rather than translating them into 'more easily dealt with' individual problems; but this answer was, perhaps, predetermined by the analytic focus of this essay, and makes light of the difficulties. Let us glance quickly at some of the difficulties as they present themselves in one area of practice – that of 'education' about alcohol.

The school system and the agencies delivering drug information and education to the general public form parts of the control culture and share in development and dissemination of the kinds of 'solutions' discussed above, including the broadening of the concept 'drugs' to cover working-class teenagers' use of alcohol and glue. An early drug education booklet for children posed the question, 'criminals, or just sick?' (Wood, 1969). The answer to this question is becoming clearer – the middle-class deviant is possibly criminal but the young teenage working-class deviant is just sick! Health education trends over the last few years have been away from purely informational, 'factual', substance-focused approaches and towards a person-focused approach on social attitudes, values, mental health and personal problems. Such education is increasingly being time-tabled for 'non-academic' schoolchildren. At present, most drug education consists of both these strands, substance-focused and person-focused. In the substance-focused strand the criteria for a 'drug' are learnt (dependency-producing, sick-making, work-preventing, etc.); when the teaching is conducted by more liberal teachers, these criteria are sharpened by discussion of whether or not cannabis satisfies them. In the person-orientated strand children learn concepts and procedures for diagnosing their social problems as failures in their development or mental health. Unfortunately, we know little of the impact of such education upon health, since such evaluation research evidence as is available focuses on impact upon attitudes and deviant behaviour, measures of these outcomes having been substituted for measures of health outcomes. An alternative education approach to purely substance-focused or person-focused approaches is the recently developed 'situational education' approach, which focuses upon choice-situations and how these might be perceived by participants in them (Dorn, 1977). This offers a tangential alternative, rather than a challenge, to the 'it's a symptom of a personal problem' approach. A more radical approach would be one that aims to help teenagers to minimise the health consequences of experimentation with legal or illegal drugs. Such an approach must be based in an appreciation of the framework of broader cultural solutions and styles within which intoxicants are used.

But the success in getting any such pro-health approach implemented would depend upon one's success in appealing to some constituency that would find it preferable to the anti-health approach of individualisation of structural problems. Teachers active in the Labour Movement might form such a constituency, but it is unfortunately precisely amongst young affiliates of the Labour Movement that counter-productive trends, such as support for the couplet of liberation of cannabis and treatment of working-class teenagers, is most fashionable.

Might a more hopeful source of support be the rock press? Whilst it is sometimes quite as given as is the straight press to wallowing in stories of 'slow decline of sudden and tragic death' ('Save our Stars', *Melody Maker*, 13 March 1976), the rock press is at least capable of a sense of humour. In a spoof entitled 'In-depth probe dept. – sniffin' craze gathers impetus', *Sounds* magazine reports: 'Loo paper is a groove, claims reader . . . When you roll yourself a ball of that soft virgin bog paper and insert it up your nostrils the feelings is just far out! With the added advantage that no-one else need know your secret!'

Another 'reader' writes:

> We're all aged between fourteen and sixteen and we not only sniff glue but also the saddles of women's bicycles! I myself pour glue into my ears as it reaches the brain a lot quicker like that. It has also made me partially deaf so that I don't have to hear any music by boring oldies like the Stones . . . Wanna hear some of our lyrics? . . . 'Well, I'm only a kid/But I like a lot of sulphate/I sniff a lot of glue/I shot my cat, I cut/My hair but I'm always in trouble (*Sounds*, 23 October 1976).

The extent to which teenagers are able to follow *Sounds* magazine and to mock the pictures that the straight press offers to them is a question open to investigation. But, in any event, the ability to mock a social performance does not necessarily help one to understand its roots, nor does it prevent one from acting it out (as feminists know, as junkies know, etc.).

This leads one to the question of how working-class youth are today negotiating the 'teenage dependencies', as satirised by *Sounds*, but as offered earnestly by welfare and educational agencies and as further disseminated by the mainstream media. The possibilities range from simple acceptance by teenagers of the possibility that interest in or episodic use of intoxicants represents a form of teenage drug dependency; through creative renegotiations of the meaning of the teenage dependencies to various 'resistance strategies' that might subvert welfare agencies' attempts to deal with structural problems in individualised forms. However teenagers negotiate the teenage dependencies (and this question requires empirical research),[5] their 'solutions' will pose new problems for the agencies concerned (see Figure 2.1). Any understanding of these problems must include the ways in which members of agencies and of 'client groups' make sense of their structural position in particular economic and social conditions.

It is from this perspective that the question of practice must be considered. This requires a movement from discourses employing psychopathological categories, through discourses on civil and individual rights, to a discourse on the consequences of and opportunities offered by failures in the smooth running of the economics that require and guarantee that latter discourse. This means a refusal to accept the parameters of a debate that simply shifts definitions of dependency from cannabis users to the young working-class user of legal and illegal drugs, and an insistence on redirecting public and agency attention back to the real structural problems of reproduction of socio-economic relations of formal independence. It is within that broadened debate that it will be possible to articulate a programme of reforms relating issues such as cannabis to the abolition of 'dependency problems' in general.

This might explain why people take various drugs but not why it is morally right

3
Social Democratic Delinquents and Fabian Families

A background to the 1969 Children and Young Persons Act

John Clarke

> These are not issues on which socialists have had much to say
> (David Donnison, 1958).

> It is a truism that a happy and secure family life is the foundation of
> a healthy society and the best safeguard against deliquency and
> anti-social behaviour (The Longford Study Group, 1966).

The Children and Young Persons Act 1969 is one of the most
discussed pieces of criminal legislation introduced in this country,
and this chapter looks at one part of the background to the Act, or,
rather, offers a reinterpretation of part of its background, since a
variety of accounts of its creation already exist. The chapter focuses
on the development of social-democratic thinking on the juvenile
court and juvenile delinquency between 1958 and 1968 through the
Fabian Society and the Labour Party as one of the central elements
of this process of policy-making. The arguments of the Fabian
pamphlets and Labour Party documents are reviewed in some detail
in order to situate this alternative interpretation – alternative in the
sense that it analyses them not as specifically criminological or
penological questions but as the development of a specific political
strategy for restructuring one particular aspect of the post-war
capitalist state in Britain.[1]

The juvenile court

The contributions from the Labour Party and the Fabian Group to
the disussion of delinquency and the juvenile court are, quite
clearly, not a revolutionary breakthrough in the ways in which those
problems had previously been conceived. As I have argued elsewhere

(Clarke, 1975), the central elements of these social-democratic analyses, the three-sided connection of delinquency, deprivation and the family, are present as organising elements in the 19th-century reform movements which concerned themselves with juvenile delinquency. Similarly, the blurring of the distinction between the 'deprived' and the 'delinquent' is formally visible as early as 1927 in the Report of the Interdepartmental Committee. The establishment of the children's departments following the report of the Curtis Committee in 1944 provides one of the institutional and organisational forms for blurring this distinction further, given their increasing involvement in the operations of the juvenile court.

As well as these institutional expressions of the combination of the family, deprivation and delinquency, we must also note the intellectual framing of the problem of delinquency. I do not propose to offer an exhaustive survey of English work on juvenile delinquency in the period before 1958, but just to note some major strands. Among these are the 'discovery' (and persistent rediscovery) of the 'problem family' by a variety of surveys themselves not specifically concerned with delinquency (child neglect, mental hygiene, health, the consequences of evacuation in war-time and so on), but all of which testify to the presence of delinquency as one of the range of indices on which these families score highly (cf. Blacker, 1952). Equally important is the emergence of psychological and psychiatric approaches to the problem of delinquency in a number of ways: the work of Cyril Burt, and his connection with the establishment of the psychiatric social work training course at LSE, in which child guidance was a main element (cf., *inter alia*, Timms, 1964); the establishment of the Institute for the Study and Treatment of Delinquency under the directorship of Edward Glover; and, subsequently, the work and widespread influence of John Bowlby.

However, it is just as important to note the growth in the mid-fifties of work on delinquency, which, though not predominantly psychological or psychiatric in its theoretical approach, nevertheless had the consequence of focusing attention still further on the family and socialisation in the causation of delinquency. I am thinking of the 'ecological' work of Liverpool University (from Caradog-Jones, through Simey to Mays), and the beginnings of 'community studies', such as the work of Jephcott and Carter. Though more overtly sociological in form, these studies nevertheless identity the family as the central transmitting agency of social values and behaviour, as this quotation may indicate:

In Gladstone Road, however, stealing is stealing and children are taught from as early as possible that stealing is wrong. The standards of Gladstone Road were different, money was saved for the future and children must be taught its value. They keep themselves to themselves in Gladstone Road and frown upon gossiping on the doorsteps; they think ahead and plan for the future. Above all they think of their children as presenting a problem – the problem of bringing up. In Dyke Street, the children just grow (Jephcott and Carter, 1954, p. 55).

Elsewhere, others have noted the influence of similar forms of sociological work on the community, family and socialisation for the development of Labour policy on education in this period (Finn, Grant and Johnson, 1977), and, as we shall see, the social-democratic conceptions of delinquency and the family also relate to this analysis of socialisation.

Finally, in this section, the precise context of the Labour Party's development of policy towards the CYPA 1969 was set by the establishment in 1956 of the Ingleby Committee by the Conservative Party. This forms the precise context in two senses. Firstly, the Committee was asked to report on *both* the operation of the juvenile court and the workings of local authority children's departments, and it was around this double connection that Labour Party policy subsequently developed. Secondly, the Committee formed the forum in which the first formulations of Labour Party policy on these questions became visible, at first in the form of evidence submitted by members of the Fabian Society (Stewart, Donnison, Halpin, Jay, MacColl and Townsend, reported in Donnison and Stewart, 1958), and subsequently in the response to the *Report* by Donnison, Jay and Stewart (1962).

Where, oh where, is that family service?

Both Fabian contributions are concerned less with the juvenile court than with the reorganisation of the personal social services: their main aim is to press for the creation of a unified 'Family Service'. This has two main aspects. First is their assessment of the achievements and failures of the welfare state. The Beveridge-designed safety net is seen to have largely eradicated 'primary poverty', though there remain 'loopholes' through which people still slip, and it is these people who are the object of their attention. This small proportion slips through the net for two reasons. The net is designed to meet specific and specifiable material needs, thus for those whose needs are not easily categorised, or who have multiple needs, there is either no provision or unnecessary duplication; and, secondly, there are those who are too 'ignorant or apathetic to make use of the services offered to them' (Donnison and Stewart, 1958, p. 3). From these observations two major directions are proposed – the rationalisation of the personal social services to provide a family service; and the humanisation of the social services, attuning them more to people and less to defined categories of need:

> Every system of government bears the marks of its rejected predecessors. The early Fabians' determination to build up a technically competent, specialist service to assure nation wide minimum standards of care in a wide variety of fields arose from their rejection of the chaos, cruelty and social wastage of the Poor Law. We still have far to go before we can be satisfied with the standards of our housing, our mental hospitals and schools, but Fabians today should be increasingly concerned about a new problem – the tendency of large scale, specialised (and frequently competing) services, organised to meet arbitrary defined 'needs', to lose touch with the individuals and families that form the complex human reality they are dealing with, and to disregard human needs for which there is no appropriate administrative category (Donnison, Jay and Stewart, 1962, p. 7).

Donnison supports the proposed new direction for the personal social services by a review of current trends in social services in which he notes:

> They appear to be based on a realistic appreciation of the nature of human needs. One study after another has shown that the personal social services devote most of their resources to a small proportion of their clientele, and many of these people need help from several different services. Human needs do not come in self-contained, specialised packages; they are entangled, involving whole families – and sometimes whole neighbourhoods (Donnison, Jay and Stewart, 1962 pp. 2–3).

The new family service is to be less concerned with the straight forward provision of material benefits and assistance than it is with helping families and individuals to cope with them – the humanising direction is as relevant here, for the service's work is seen as focusing around the area of family relationships:

> The service that is needed must set out by concentrating on the few families that get into serious difficulties, but would be available from the beginning to all those who wish to make use of it (it would be a 'family casework service', not a 'problem families service'). It must be manned by workers with a sensitive understanding of family relationships, and special skills in mobilising the will and energy of the bewildered, anxious and aggressive people (thus it would be based primarily on the skilled use of personal re-lationships, rather than the provision of material help and expert advice) (Donnison and Stewart, 1958, p. 7).

What then does the Fabian Society have to say about the problem of delinquency? For its members this is essentially a secondary category, and though the terms delinquent, deprived and malad-justed are used separately to some extent, they tend to become subsumed within the same set of causative relations – those of family disturbance, incapacity and breakdown – and thus are one of the focal points on which the demand for the family service is hinged. This is primarily argued through the evidence of the large numbers of children who are taken into public care (i.e. in spite of the welfare provision available post-Beveridge). Donnison quotes a study in which

> . . . it appears that one third of the children in the care of the local authorities have been committed under 'Fit Person' orders by courts which were convinced that the parents were failing to look after them properly. About another third were received into care because they were deserted by their parents, because their families were homeless (generally through failure to pay rent), because their parents were in prison, because arrangements made for their care by their parents had broken down, or because home conditions were unsatisfactory in other ways. The rest were children whose mothers were unmarried, ill or dead; and there is reason to believe that those children, too, were frequently victims of a breakdown of the supporting human relationships that surround the normal family – they are, after all, a very small proportion of all the children whose mothers are unmarried, ill or

dead. A high proportion of all the children in the care of local authorities thus come from homes which have broken down – not through illness, death or destitution, but through human unhappiness and the failure of parents to cope with the job of bringing up children. There is no reason to believe that children in the care of voluntary societies differ greatly from those in the care of local authorities, and it is now generally agreed that unhappy and broken homes play an important part in producing the delinquents who enter approved schools (Donnison and Stewart, 1958, pp. 5–6).

Thus, delinquents merely form one segment of a much more significant group, those in need of care through the breakdown of family arrangements, not through illness, death and destitution – thanks to Beveridge – but because of the inability of parents to cope with human relationships. It is here that the work of the proposed family service is situated. This conception of delinquency is repeated in Margaret Stewart's contribution to the second Fabian pamphlet:

> Some delinquents are, in a medical sense, abnormal or subnormal, but the great majority come within the normal range and are not in need of psychiatric treatment . . . There is little doubt, nevertheless, that many delinquents suffer from grave social handicaps. The parents of many of them are not equipped to cope sensibly with the pressures and problems of the modern world, many are educationally backward (Donnison, Jay and Stewart, 1962, p. 18).

This focus on the family situation by the Fabians forms one of the planks on which criticisms of residential forms of treatment are mounted:

> . . . parents with little insight, with few of the skills required for the care of children in the modern world and without the self confidence and poise needed to seek advice and follow it. Social workers with heavy case loads have little time to spare for parents once their children have been removed from home. Often when the children return, the material conditions and parental attitudes which contribute towards their delinquency or maladjustment are still present (Donnison, Jay and Stewart, 1962, p. 25).

It is to facilitate intervention in this sort of family context that the reforms put forward in the Fabian pamphlets are aimed; the relevance of the other aspects of remaining material deprivation are only treated here through their appearance in the family situation or where caused by the inadequacies of the family.[2] It is perhaps worth noting that although the Fabians here propose a rationalisation of the social services, it is primarily a rationalisation only of those elements which taken together constitute the personal social services; the questions of material deprivation (financial, housing, education etc., except where connected with the phenomena of personal inadequacy) are left to the pre-existing appropriate branches of the state.

The procedural reforms then return to the question of the civil/criminal procedings. The central proposals are these – the raising of the age range of the juvenile court to 18, and children under 15 only being brought before the court on care or protection proceedings. Alongside these proposals goes the recommendation to add 'case committees' to the existing juvenile procedure. In the case committees children under 15 may be dealt with away from the 'more formal and public jurisdiction of the juvenile court', and these committees would operate on more informal and relaxed principles. However, not all cases would be removed to this new setting; it would be reserved for the children whose parents 'were for the most part *co-operative*' (my emphasis). This would serve a number of functions – keeping many children away from the stigmatising effects of the judicial process, separating what Donnison and Stewart call the 'sheep' and the 'goats', the 'unruly from the well-behaved', and the mature delinquent from the immature deprived and maladjusted. These, however, are in a sense secondary to the distinction drawn about the attitudes of the parents, and the centrality of this co-operative/unco-operative distinction is re-emphasised in a number of ways. First, it is stressed that this will enable the juvenile court to be reserved (with its full legal authority) for those children who will not admit the facts, and for those whose parents 'will not accept the recommendations of the case committee'. Since the whole of the Labour strategy in this period was built on the evidence that it was only a tiny minority of cases in which the facts were in dispute, the attitude of the parents moves to the centre of the proposal. Similarly, if parents were requested to attend a meeting of the committee and failed to do so, it was firmly stressed that this failure 'would be followed by a summons to appear before a juvenile court'. Finally, the pamphlet emphasises that the case committees must be sensitive to the attitude of the parents. The committees are given the power to transfer (without parental agreement) cases to the juvenile court, and 'it is important that they should do so without delay if they believe their clients to be uncooperative'.

Sheep and goats: some interim conclusions on the Fabians

What is significant about the Fabian contributions is the development of a set of distinctions and categories which provide the basis for the proposed strategies of problem solution both via the reformulated court system and the agency of the family service. So we are given the following divisions, constituting the 'complex human reality' with which the various branches of the state will have to cope: (1) the materially deprived (the object of the welfare state proper) and the socially inadequate (the object of the human skills of the family service); and (2) the co-operative parent (the raw material for the case committees) and the unco-operative (subject to legal procedure). The anomaly in this system of categorisation is the distinction between the 'sheep' and the 'goats'. The previous two sets of divisions are generated at the level of the social composition (and social causes) of the groups for whom appropriate administrative forms have to be found. However, in the comments on the social factors associated with delinquency, no distinction is made between the sorts of problem connected with delinquency, deprivation or maladjustments. The divisions between the 'sheep' and 'goats' are not then social divisions in terms of identifiable differences in the pattern of causation. Rather, they are administrative divisions, only appearing as distinctive groupings at the level of how they are to be dealt with, at the level of what administrative procedures are best suited to keeping them separate. They are not even distinguished by whether or not they have committed offences, merely on whether they are unruly or well-behaved or whether they are mature or immature – they are the categories of processing and disposal. The existence of these categories indicated the persistence of an administrative separation between the 'hard core' and the rest which continues to play an important role in Labour policy.

The other aspect of the Fabian Group's contribution to which I want to draw attention here is its political form. By this I mean not that it is broadly social-democratic, but the question of which of the numerous strands that make up the complex ideological ensemble of social democracy it represents. First, then, it is located largely within the revisionist position in the Labour Party of the late fifties – that of accepting the broad terms of the post-war solution of the mixed economy and welfare state, though with reservations about the completeness of the welfare state's accomplishments. Their response is one of *administrative rationalisation*, the further reformation of the state apparatus, a response firmly within the tradition of the Webb's administrative socialism.

However, this is connected with a position which is not part of that element of the social-democratic tradition, that of their emphasis on the *humanisation* of the state's apparatus, their vision of both the 'complex human reality of need' and of the socially inadequate. It is important to be precise about what this humanisation involves for them: theirs is not a vision of state-provided psychiatry and psychotherapeutic services; their conception of the family and in-adequacy is not one which is much influenced by psychiatry and psychology, it is primarily a 'sociological' one, which focuses on the skills necessary for coping with the complexities of modern life and with the task of bringing up children (cf. the Jephcott and Carter comment, p. 78). They are not the advocates of a welfare-state Freudianism, but rather of a welfare-state human relations theory; the skills which they envisage the workers of the family service possessing are not those of psychoanalystic diagnosis (in fact, in 1962, Donnison explicitly rejected the 'medical model') but those of sensitivity to human relations and educative abilities – the social workers are to civilise or resocialise their clientele.

I have made this point at some length because it seems to me that there are two views of Labour policy in this period which would equally serve to divert attention away from this emphasis on human relations. The first would be to collapse the Labour Party espousal of a family social service into the dominant practice of the social workers who came to constitute that service – that of psychother-apeutic 'case workers'. But this collapse would fail to give sufficient weight to important problems about the relation of political policy-making to the operation of other branches of the state apparatus.[3] The second error would be to over-unify the direction of social-democratic revisionism in this period with the 'modernising' and 'scientistic' programme developed by the Wilson regime in prep-aration for the 1964 election. An over-emphasis on this theme of economic modernisation and the role of science omits a second theme of Labour's revisionism, that of humanising and civilising the civil society of reformed capitalism. The Fabian Group's proposals are doubly connected with this 'civilising' vision, first, in that they are attempting to enable those without the skills, intelligence and commitment to develop them to be able to take their part in the benefits of this new world; and second, that this 're-equipping' is to be done precisely through the skills of human relations, in the person of the family service worker.[4]

In a crucial sense the report of the Longford Group forms the bridge between the observations of the Fabian Group and the subsequent policy documents produced by the 1964 Labour Government (the 1965 and 1968 White Papers, and the 1969 Bill), and, as will be seen, connects importantly with significant elements of the Labour Party's intended government programme. The *Report* begins by locating the challenge of crime in a set of arguments already familiar from the Fabian pamphlets.[5]

> Of these evils, the external ones – poverty and squalor – are much less extreme than in the days of Dickens, but the gulf in living standards between the poorest and the best off (or even the average) is hardly more tolerable; while social inadequacy, the failure to fit in, may be, if anything more widespread as the technical apparatus of life becomes more complex (Longford Study Group, 1966, p. 4).

The division is again between material deprivation and social maladjustment, and subsequently (as with the Fabians) this division becomes the basis for a double-edged strategy of reform. But the arguments about these reforms come later in the document, for what the Longford Group first produced was not an analysis of crime or delinquency but a diagnosis of the state of Britain, in which crime appears as by-product and indicator. The first central component of this diagnosis is to connect the material inequalities already mentioned with their spiritual accompaniment – the 'get rich quick ethos', which has led to a 'weakening of moral fibre'. The values which this ethos emphasises are traced to their role in the causation of crimes:

> The values that prevail among those who dominate society may be expected to spread to all its levels. If men and women are brought up from childhood to regard personal advancement and ruthless self interest as the main considerations, material success will certainly not train them in social responsibility, and wordly failure

may lead to social inadequacy and a resentful sense of inferiority. (What is commonly called the inferiority complex is found in a remarkably high proportion of adult criminals and young delinquents (Longford Study Group, 1966, p. 5).

Again what focuses the Group's attention here is less the problem of crime than the social inadequacies resulting from the 'acquisitive society', and against this ethos the group proclaims an alternative 'socialist' vision which would 'substitute the ideal of mutual service and work towards a society in which everyone has a chance to play a full and responsible part'. Though the centre of this socialist conception is essentially a moral one, it does also have its material side. In addition to the criticisms of material inequalities, the *Report* also concerns itself with class inequality in the law: 'There is also an element of class discrimination here. Working class youth who break windows are taken to court; at once there is the stigma of a police record. Oxbridge undergraduates who break windows are "dealt with" by their college authorities: there is no legal or social stigma at all' (Longford Study Group, 1966, p. 6).

The concern with inequality before the law taken together with the concern for the socially inadequate has, as we shall see, profound consequences for the Labour Party's proposed reforms of the juvenile court system. The approach of the Longford Group is summarised in the concluding paragraph of the first section of the *Report*:

Although society may be justified in demanding a measure of retribution to deter the criminal, this is a negative approach. Something more is needed for the true protection of the citizen: the prevention of crime by the care of the inadequate and immature, the healing of the sick, the rehabilitation of the offender, the restoration of his self-respect and his training in respect for the rights of others (Longford Study Group, 1966, p. 6).

We can see the composite of the strategies with which the group proposes to deal with the crime problem reflected in their review of the causes of delinquency:

Chronic or serious delinquency in a child is in the main, we believe, evidence of the lack of care, the guidance and the opportunities to which every child is entitled. There are very few children who do not behave badly at times: but the children of parents with ample means rarely appear before juvenile courts. The machinery of the law is reserved mainly for working class children, who more often than not, are also handicapped by being taught in too big classes in unsatisfactory school buildings with few amenities or opportunities for out of school activities.

Anti-social behaviour in a child may arise from difficulties at home, from unhappiness at school, from physical or mental handicaps or maladjustment, or from a variety of other causes for which the child has no personal responsibility (Longford Study Group, 1966, p. 21).

We must note some of the main themes of this account. First is the range of factors proposed to be connected with delinquency, involving both social and psychological inadequacies, again not focusing specifically on psychological or psychiatric accounts of delinquency. Second is the emphasis placed on education, reflecting the centrality of the alliance between the teaching profession and the Labour Party around conceptions of educational disadvantage and deprivation which was to dominate educational theory and policy in the sixties (see Finn, Grant and Johnson, 1977). Finally, we might also note the conception of the working class implicit in the Group's report: it is essentially one which locates the working class on a hierarchically arranged ranking that measures differences along indices of distribution of material wealth, of housing, of educational opportunity and of social skills – it is fundamentally an inert class defined primarily by what it lacks.

From this point, too, we can also begin to see the workings out of the Study Group's three-part 'solution' to the challenge of crime – the problem of material inequalities, the problem of social inadequacy, and the problem of class discrimination in the law. The first of these is dealt with in the section entitled 'Forestalling Delinquency', which deals with the achievement of the original aims of the welfare state 'held back by financial restrictions' under Conservative Governments. This section deals with the need for more egalitarian and universally available access to health, housing, social amenities, education and vocational guidance, work and industrial training; and pays special attention to the 'Family on National Assistance', the 'Special care of the handicapped' and the 'Unmarried mother and her child'.

The strategies for this first set of general categories bear more than a passing resemblance to Labour's proposed social programme in *Signposts for the Sixties*, but each section is couched with special reference to the effects of disadvantage on the causation of crime or delinquency. For example, in the education section they note: 'Probably a quarter of all children of school age have special needs which are not being properly catered for – and it is just from this group that so many delinquents (as distinct from the merely naughty or mischievous) emerge' (Longford Study Group, 1966, p. 14).

Here, then, the Study Group deals with the genesis of 'full social provision, as of right, for every individual' as the response to the material inequalities, and this in part is seen to require the administrative reorganisation of the social services, of which the central plank is to be the family service. For the Longford Group this is vital, because 'It is a truism that a happy and secure family life is the foundation of a healthy society and the best safe guard against delinquency and anti-social behaviour. Many pay lip-service to this belief: all too little has been done seriously to attempt its realisation' (Longford Study Group, 1966, p. 16).

The family service is especially related by the Group to the categories of 'special' need mentioned above, and would act in co-operation with other local and central state services in the meeting of family needs. What is significant here, as in the Fabian proposals, is the administrative 'separation of powers' proposed, which is based on the double definition of need – the main services of the welfare state are seen as meeting specifically material needs, while the family service acts in part as a guide and supplement to these but is centrally focused around social and personal inadequacy (the lack of emotional and social skills).

The family service is also destined to play the central role in the proposal for the reform of juvenile justice – it is the proposed strategy not only for coping with delinquency but also for resolving the problem of class discrimination in the law. The report proposes to resolve the problem of class discrimination by removing most of the cases presently dealt with by the juvenile court from the operation of the law altogether; instead they would be dealt with by the family service acting in agreement with the parents. There is a complex logic at work here, which is summarised by the report writers as follows:

No understanding parent can contemplate without repugnance the branding of a child in early adolescence as a criminal, whatever offence he may have committed. If it is a trivial one, such a procedure is indefensible, if a more serious charge is involved this is, in itself, evidence of the child's need for skilled help and guidance. The parent who can get such help for his child on his own initiative can almost invariably keep the child from court. It is only the children of those not so fortunate who appear in the criminal statistics (Longford Study Group, 1966, p. 24).

We can break this logic down into a series of propositions:

1. minor offences are unproblematic and are signs of what the report earlier calls 'naughtiness', a part of the normal process of growing up;
2. more serious offences are an indicator of some more deep-rooted defect or inadequacy, in view of which the child is in need of treatment;
3. priviliged parents can arrange this sort of treatment for their children privately;
4. therefore, what is needed is not a systematic legal mechanism to deal with those 'not so fortunate' but a state-provided equivalent to the care or treatment which the privileged can provide privately.

So what begins as the unequal administration of the law becomes redefined as the unequal distribution of facilities of care or treatment through the redefinition of delinquency from criminal offence to symptom of neglect, defect or inadequacy. The machinery of the law is only to be reserved for those instances where the service and the parents cannot reach agreement – here, too, the problem of the class inequality of the law is to be resolved, since the law is not to be employed on the grounds of the type of child (class background) but on the technical and administrative criteria of parental refusal to co-operate. The juvenile court as such is to be abolished and be replaced by a family court dealing with referrals from the family service for all children of school age; this family court would, in addition, take over the various functions of magistrates' courts which presently dealt with family matters.

Finally it is important to note that the report also recommends that the family service should also have the responsibility for the provision of the range of residential facilities for young offenders, and a central proposal among these is the following: 'High priority should be given to the special units for the small number of violent and disturbed adolescents who require treatment in a setting of closer security and the care of people with special skills and experience' (Longford Study Group, 1966, p. 22). What is significant here is that within the logic of the 'permissive' approach of the *Report* is its 'hard core', in which the supposedly alternative logics of the 'soft' treatment model and the 'hard' punitive model intermingle quite comfortably – these adolescents are (fortunately) violent *and* disturbed and in need of security and special care.

After Longford: directions and misdirections

Here I can only deal briefly with the subsequent Labour Party policy and strategy which led up to the Children and Young Persons Act 1969, and largely in terms of its relation with what has already been discussed. The analysis and recommendations of the *Longford Report* provided the foundation and most of the content of the Labour Party's 1965 White Paper *The Child, the Family and the Young Offender*, which proposed the establishment of family councils and family courts for those up to 16 (on the grounds that this would shortly become the school leaving age). Along with arguments derived from Longford about the preferability of the family council system, the White Paper adds a central criticism about the present juvenile court system: 'Although when children appear in the juvenile courts their parents attend whenever possible, the present arrangements do not provide the best means of getting parents to assume more personal responsibility for their children's behaviour' (HMSO, 1965a, p. 15).

Here, quite forcefully expressed, is one of the central themes of the Labour strategy for juvenile delinquency. In the midst of the debate about care, inadequacy and treatment, lies the commitment to the informal and 'permissive' methods of the family council or family service as being a central mechanism through which to implicate the parents more fully in the control of their children; in effect, to get the parents to *internalise* the controls previously handled externally through the more formal mechanisms of the law.

The White Paper was withdrawn by the Labour Government in the face of extensive criticism from a variety of directions, and was subsequently replaced by the 1968 White Paper *Children in Trouble*, from which the most contentious formulation of the 1965 version, the family councils, was withdrawn. Juvenile courts were to be retained as the formal mechanism through which delinquents were to pass. But this procedure was to be modified in the direction of the Longford and 1965 White Paper distinction between 'normal' delinquency and that which appeared as symptomatic of other problems:

> It is probably a minority of children who grow up without ever misbehaving in ways which may be contrary to the law. Frequently such behaviour is no more than an incident in the pattern of a child's normal development, but sometimes it is a response to unsatisfactory family or social circumstances, a result of boredom in or out of school, an indication of maladjustment or immaturity or a symptom of a deviant, damaged or abnormal personality (HMSO, 1968a).

Consequently the White Paper proposed a double set of conditions which had to be met before a child (up to 13) could be brought before the court. It was not sufficient that the child should have committed an offence; he or she had also to fall within a number of categories which indicated the need for 'care, protection or control', a decision to be made through enquiries made by local authority social services departments.

Social-democratic delinquency

In this section I want to draw together the conception of delinquency as found in the Fabian and Labour Party documents of the period and to connect with the trajectory of the party itself in that time. This will be very schematic, and should not be seen as an exhaustive analysis.

First, then, the conceptions of delinquency are all situated within a fundamental acceptance of the accomplishments of the post-war reconstruction, the nature of the mixed economy and the construction of the welfare state. The major arguments about delinquency are raised within this structure, and indeed are pre-eminently about the inadequacies of the state (rather than the society) in meeting the needs of its members.

The first area of criticism lies in the failure of the welfare state itself to have resolved the problems of material inequalities: both the Fabians and the Longford group stress that the level of state provision remains inadequate to deal with the problems which confront it (especially housing, education and industrial training). The Longford Group especially traces delinquency indirectly to the effect of these factors, and proposes a further programme of state intervention and reform, and we have already noted the close connection between these proposals and the Labour Party's social programme as established in *Signposts for the Sixties*. However, what is crucial is not the presence of these factors in connection with delinquency (as part of a relatively unauthorised set of causative factors) but the administrative separation involved through their distinction between material inequalities and social inadequacy (the family situation).

This distinction means that, practically, the proposed reforms for the system of juvenile justice have an overwhelming weight attached to those factors connected with the matrix of the family/social inadequacy/the family service, rather than with the questions of reforming material inequality. What organises Labour Party thinking on juvenile delinquency is not the theoretical conceptions of delinquency causation (which run through a whole range from material disadvantage, boredom, psychological maladjustment or maldevelopment, to parental inadequacies in coping with the skills of bringing up children in the modern world) but the proposals for reform, which are wholly centred around the proposal for a family service. Even the proposed abolition or reorganisation of the juvenile court is secondary to this central theme, and is seen as being dependent upon the establishment of this service.

If the attention to the questions of material inequality, as I have argued, falls within the same structures as do the Labour Party proposals for their 'social programme', then the argument for the family service connects with another, more submerged, strand of social-democratic thought in the period – that of humanism in the new world created by the post-war settlement.

These values are seen to run counter to both some older values in the socialist tradition and to some of the prevailing values of the new reformed capitalism. We can trace both these strands in the social-democratic arguments about delinquency and the family service. For example, Donnison, though accepting the achievements of the welfare state, locates the demand for the family service against the 'technical' orientation of the Fabian tradition deriving from the Webbs. The new family service for Donnison is to be the bearer of 'human' rather than administrative values, to help with the human side of reformation (the social skills of parental coping) rather with material deprivation. It carries with it a sense of the difficulty of human relationships, and attempts to involve the state in educative work to allow those without the necessary skills to be able to receive the benefits of the improvements in the material standards of life.

Though clearly aligned with this direction, the Longford Group adds another aspect to this argument through its criticism of the values prevailing in the new Britain – those of acquisitiveness and material success – and proposes to draw instead on an older social-democratic tradition (the Group names Tawney) which stresses the values of co-operation, mutual service, and self-respect allied with respect for others. More overtly than the Fabians, the Longford Group is proposing a remoralisation of sectors of the society; its members are concerned with the promotion of *proper* values (and against the 'weakening of moral fibre') and guarding against 'vulnerability to temptation'. Again, it must be stressed that here we are not dealing with a psychiatric or psychotherapeutic version of crime causation (except for a minority of deviant cases) but one which is centred around values, socialisation and the family as an educative institution. Like the Fabians, the Longford Group proposes that all children should have equal access to a stable and caring – in a word, 'normal' – family, and where this does not exist, the state must intervene to promote it. The family service is therefore central to their proposals, since none of the state welfare agencies is, as presently constituted, capable of performing this task by having the family as its central focus.

In terms of criminological and penological analysis these documents provide little in the way of overt criminological theorising about the causes of delinquency. They do not pretend to be unified 'theoretical' texts, and are not amenable to analysis in such terms. Rather they form part of a political programme which takes delinquency as one of the critical axes of the relationship between social life, the family and the state. Similarly, their proposals are inadequately grasped if they are merely seen within the framework of questions about the reorganisation of the juvenile court between a legal and a welfare model of its practice. What this omits is the political centre of the proposed reorganisation – the rearrangement of the relation between the state and the family through changes in one particular state apparatus. This question has to be situated in a very different theoretical terrain.

The state and the family

To understand the central role attributed to the family in social-democratic thinking in this period, it is necessary to consider the wider context of the relation between the family and capitalism. The family performs a number of vital (though largely 'invisible') functions for capitalism, which may be drawn together in the term *social reproduction of labour power*. In capitalist societies this function of reproduction is necessarily performed (for the most part) privately, that is, outside of the world of capitalist production, and the dominant form in which the reproduction is accomplished is the family. Here, through the performance of domestic labour, the individual labourer is produced and reproduced in the appropriate forms in order to be able to sell his/her labour on the market. The reproduction of labour power involves more than just the simple provision of labourers who are physically able to sell their labour, since it is necessary at each stage of the development of capitalism that the pool of labour available be organised and divided with the appropriate levels of skill, and 'correct' ideological orientations to work, and social and political life.[6]

However, this process of reproduction is too significant to the possibilities of continuing capital accumulation to be left to 'private' processes, and it is here that the forms of connection between the state and the family are of central importance, since the state is the agency through which it is possible for interventions to control and regulate this process of reproduction to be made. Gramsci has described one major role of the state as that of 'conforming' civil society (the sphere of private institutions) to the demands of the sphere of production, and state intervention to regulate the family is one mechanism through which this control of civil society has been accomplished.

In this process of reproduction the securing of the stable provision of future generations of labour power is one of the most critical areas, and one of the areas in which the British state has intervened on a major scale. From this standpoint delinquency appears not as a crime problem but as an indicator of breaks in the supposedly normal patterns of reproduction – or where the mechanisms to ensure continuity have failed. The close interconnection between the problem of delinquency and the family in English criminological and political thought is from this standpoint no accidental and ideological irrationality; rather, it reflects a focus on specific problems of the stable reproduction of future generations of labour power under capitalism.

From this standpoint the central character of social-democratic thinking on delinquency is not the lack of systematic analysis of the causes of delinquency but the force with which the family is constantly located as the central problem to be faced.[7] What is attempted in the development of these policies is a means of changing, through the reorganisation of areas of the state apparatus, the relationship between the state and the family (or, more particularly, certain types of family.)

Here lies the importance of the Longford and subsequent distinctions between delinquency which is merely normal naughtiness and that which indicates severe problems – problems of the home. It is only the latter which is to be taken seriously, and under the proposals of the 1969 Act, it is the family itself (not the act of delinquency) which is to be the decisive factor in this distinction. This concern with the family is also manifested in the proposed procedural reforms discussed earlier, which largely hinge on the following triple relation between the state and the family. First, where possible, agreement should be arrived at between the family service (or its particular variant) so that the family itself (rather than the external power of the state) becomes the carrier of the values, discipline and controls necessary to stabilise the process of social reproduction (see Wilson, 1977). Each of the documents we have considered stresses the importance of getting the family to accept what are defined as its 'own responsibilities'. Second, where it is the problem, the policy is to promote the agreement of the family to having *itself* 'treated' – to create a non-repressive means of entry to the family for social workers. This attempts to circumvent the problems of (1) the 'apathetic' family, which would not actively seek social work assistance, and (2) entry to the family being enforced by a visible legal power (and therefore perhaps being no more than tolerated). Third, the repressive legal apparatus (i.e. some form of properly constituted court) is retained to deal with the occasions on which these consensual approaches fail – in the cases of 'unco-operative' families (not children).

It is important not to be misled into neglecting this final aspect through a concentration on the substitution of a 'welfarist' model of delinquency control for a 'legalist' one. What is at issue here is not a simple shift from a formal and repressive legal process to an informal and non-coercive one – not a matter of the magistrate versus the social worker. The aim is a more complex reorganisation of the balance between consensual and repressive processes – a new strategic balance which provides methods of operation more suitable to dealing with the problems of reproduction which are *registered* in delinquency. It is a commitment to a policy which suggests that intervention in the social and psychological processes which are held to underlie serious delinquency is best constructed without the oppressive weight and formality of legal process – that is, to create an internalised set of controls rather than externally imposed ones.

Finally, it is important to register that, though the family service is intended to be a 'universal' one (the 'door on which to knock'), its function in this context is a more strictly selective one – most importantly, selective in relation to the working class. This is not a reorganisation of the state aimed at the class as a whole, but at particular sectors of it – those who cannot cope with or adjust to what the Longford Group calls 'the technical apparatus of life'. The new forms of organisation of social, economic and political life in the reorganisation of post-war British capitalism were in no sense uniformly distributed across the British working class, and have produced forms of dislocation in social, economic and political aspects of class relations and class cultures (the full extent of which we have not yet fully registered, but among which changes in the structuring of age relations within the working class were certainly one significant part). The Longford Group benignly testifies to this sort of selectivity when it observes: 'On the whole, however, criminals do not come from stable and closely knit working class families, however poor their circumstances' (Longford Study Group, 1966, p. 5).

The overall perspective of social democracy in this period on the relative success of the post-war reorganisation is also reflected here. Welfare capitalism is understood to have largely accomplished the 'incorporation' of the mass of the working class into some form of stable involvement in English society. What is called for in the family service is only possible on top of the base level of that accomplishment. The family service is the agency through which the new working class 'residuum' – those who have not adjusted to this new stability – can be helped to an adjustment, and taught to catch up with the 'fortunate majority': 'a family service with the aim of helping every family to provide for its children the careful nurture and attention to individual and social needs that the fortunate majority already enjoy' (Longford Study Group, 1966, p. 1).

Conclusion: rehearsing state policy

What is important about this process of creating a state re-organisation is not some form of conflict between two abstract models of juvenile justice, but the rehearsal and working through of alternative state strategies for dealing with sets of problems thrown up by one particular historical moment. The development towards the 1969 Act through the various policy documents of the Fabian Society and the Labour Party must be seen as the defining and testing out of a social policy with two distinct aspects – that of redefining the problem as the 'social residuum' (the unskilled and incompetent families) and of defining the ways in which state apparatuses must be reorganised to deal with this problem. This working out of state policies involves a number of processes. First it is important to note that the policies are constructed through relationships between the party itself (the political representatives) and the party's intellectuals (Donnison, for example), with the role played by these intellectuals being a significant one in both the formulation of these policies, and in formulating the ideological rationale within which they are situated. This is most visible in the relation between the Fabian definition of the problem, which situates the inadequates as falling outside the accomplishments of the welfare state, and the dominant political composition of the party in the same period, which envisages the party's task as being that of completing the achievements of 'welfare capitalism' by clearing away the residual 'dead wood' (in both its economic and its social programmes) – a programme of completing the rationalisation of post-war Britain.

Second, the construction of the policy involves a variety of dialogues with the existing state experts and professionals, especially in the work of the Longford Group. These experts and professionals include those already in charge of particular state apparatuses (the Magistrates' Association, child care officers, the probation service and so on) and the 'disinterested' experts (primarily of course academics working in these fields). Part of these dialogues is the tentative construction of possible alliances with these groups within the state, which also form one of the crucial 'audiences' for these proposals. As well as the construction of alliances (for example, with the emergent social work groups), there is also the work of concession, for example, to the probation service and the police, who form a crucial part of it the Longford proposals.

Finally, there is the critical, but hidden relation between the political development of the policy and the internal administrative work of the state, in this case the role played by the civil servants at the Home Office. Though difficult to penetrate, the intellectual and political composition of this group does, as Tony Bottoms (1975) indicates, appear to have played an important part in the transition between the 1965 and 1968 White Papers.

These points direct us to a significant political consideration. In analysing the role of the capitalist state it is tempting to see it as a homogeneous bloc acting on behalf of capital against the working class. In fact what is revealed in the development of the 1969 Act is the complexity of its internal composition. As the debates both before and after the Act indicate, there are competing ideological and political positions within the dominant class and its political representatives (both strictly political and other groups of state agents) about social policy.

However, the political nature of this debate is complexified and hidden because it is carried on in other ideological forms at the level of administrative argument, at the level of definitions of delinquency and at the level of questions of the law, legal ideology and legal processes. Unlike the 19th century, where social policy is often ex-plicitly defined in terms of the problem of the working class, we are dealing here with debates and arguments which must situate themselves in the pre-existing technical, legal and intellectual ideologies which have evolved with the creation of previous state apparatuses. Engels describes this complexity as follows:

> But once the State has become an independent power vis-à-vis society, it produces forthwith a further ideology. It is indeed among professional politicians, theorists of public law and jurists of private law that the connection with economic facts gets lost for fair. Since in each particular case the economic facts must assume the form of juristic motives in order to receive legal sanction, and since, in doing so, consideration has to be given to the whole legal system in operation, the juristic form is, in consequence, made everything, and the economic content nothing (Engels, 1968, p. 617).

And, indeed, it is precisely in the form of 'juristic motives' that the debate about the 1969 Act is carried on. The argument over different strategies of state intervention in the problem of reproduction indexed by delinquency does appear in the juristic forms of 'the legal rights of children' and 'inequality in the law', as well as in other equally opaque sets of categories. However, this should not be taken to mean that these languages are simply masks which make it difficult to discern the essential content – they do represent real branches of the state, with their own specific 'relative autonomy' from what Engels calls the economic facts. This relative autonomy, the material reality of these apparatuses and their accompanying ideologies and representatives, are perfectly testified to in the creation of the 1969 Act, in which 'legalism', not in the form of its abstract philosophy but in the concrete political manifestation of an alliance between the Conservative Party and the representatives of the legal apparatus (notably the magistracy, but also the probation service), made severe inroads into the original Labour strategy.

But in general is it a good or bad thing?

4
Where Have All the Naughty Children Gone?

Steven Box

Let us thank the medical and allied professions for our daily medicine. On our behalf, they have been, and still are, constantly searching for new diseases from which to save us, with treatments and cures they have also discovered. It is indeed comforting to know that, even at this very minute, there are, in some Viennese laboratory, doctors, psychiatrists, technicians, and other medical moral entrepreneurs, busily hatching a new disease and an effective treatment, so that we might eventually be safer in our beds and they might move closer to professional immortality, and the filthy lucre of the Nobel Peace Prize.

The mention of peace in this context is not a Freudian slip, a sign of dysgraphia, or an indication that my brain is damaged; indeed, it is my belief that this reference to peace is not a symptom of any medical disease. Rather, it is a deliberate intention on my part to draw your attention to an activity which the medical and allied professions are increasingly getting involved in, namely *the production of civil tranquillity and social harmony*. They are getting into this by proposing definitional shifts of moral, ethical and political problems into medical conditions, so that the conflicts, disputes and disagreements implicit in the former can be avoided by systematically labelling some of the antagonists, usually the least powerful, as diseased. In this way structural or cultural changes which might otherwise become the focal point for solving social problems are replaced with a terse medical injunction: get them and cure them, and do not be too sentimental about the means.

An illustrative case of this 'medicalisation of social problems' was provided by Mark, Sweet and Ervin (1967). They argued that those individuals, mainly blacks, who participated in the urban riots in America in the sixties were suffering from (an unspecified) mental illness, and that the government ought to implement immediately a national medico-psychiatric screening programme so as to be able to identify potential urban rioters. These diseased individuals could then be isolated in hospitals and perhaps cured of their illness. According to these doctors, urban riots had nothing to do with political, ethical or moral problems, nothing to do with economic conditions or racism; they were instead merely signs or symptoms that a large section of the urban population was mentally sick and needed treatment.

Can you imagine! Can you imagine these doctors taking themselves seriously! Can you imagine anyone taking them seriously! No? Well, read on.

Many of our schoolchildren are 'diseased'

Hyperactivity is a disease; it is a disease that afflicts schoolchildren. If you do not instantly recognise this diagnostic label, you might be familiar with one of its various synonyms, such as minimal brain dysfunction or damage, learning disorder, hyperkinesis, over-activity, or maladjustment.

There is, as with most major scientific and medical discoveries, some dispute as to priority; some writers consider that it was discovered over 100 years ago, but the strongest contestant is Dr Maurice Laufer, a Providence psychiatrist, who claims to have discovered the disease as recently as 1957. Whatever disagreement remains, it is apparently quite clear that since 1957 hyperactivity has become a disease of extreme national and international importance for two reasons. First, like diphtheria nearly 70 years ago, it is a disease which has now reached epidemic proportions; second, if untreated, its prognosis is disastrous for the individual and a major catastrophe for the rest of us.

What is apparently alarming about this schoolchild disorder is that, since the mid-sixties and particularly during the seventies, it has rapidly spread throughout the population, thus making it a problem demanding the most urgent attention. Thus Ross and Ross write:

One reason for the urgency is the sheer number of children involved and who are presumed to be in need of some kind of intervention. In the United States, conservative estimates indicate that this cluster of symptoms is present in from 4 to 10 percent, or 1.4 to 3.5 million children whereas educators believe that 15 to 20 percent represents a more realistic estimate . . . [Furthermore] the age range and number of children so labelled, can be expected to increase sharply in the next few years (Ross and Ross, 1976, pp. 288 and 295).

As if developing this latter point, Witter reports: 'Already specialists . . . state that at least 30 percent of ghetto children are candidates [for being treated as hyperactive] and this figure could run as high as four to six million of the general school population' (Witter, 1971, p. 31). Finally Cole argues:

> Contrary to the view of many, hyperactive children *constitute a social and educational problem of major proportion.* It has been estimated by the U.S. Federal Office of Child Development that three percent of elementary school children demonstrate enough traits (mild and severe) to be classified as 'hyperactive'. Such a percentage implies that, in a group of 30 to 35 pupils, one might expect to find one such child (Cole, 1975, p. 29).

He continues, almost hysterically, and, as will be obvious later, misleadingly, 'no country, geographical area or social class seem to have immunity' (Cole, 1975, p. 29).

These are all estimates for the future, and as such they may be wildly mistaken. However, with a little more certainty, we can say that at the present there are in America anywhere between a half and 1 million schoolchildren diagnosed as hyperactive. This makes it 'one of the major childhood behaviour disorders of our time. It is the single most common behaviour disorder seen by child psychiatrists, a problem frequently presented to paediatricians and a major problem in the elementary school system' (Ross and Ross, 1976, p. ix).

In the UK hyperactivity and synonymous or overlapping disorders are less well documented, relatively unanalysed and under-discussed; furthermore, differences in disorder classification and diagnostic procedures make strict comparisons difficult and open to numerous criticisms. Nonetheless, it is clear that an epidemic of schoolchild psychiatric disorders is taking place, on a pattern similar to the American although as yet on a much smaller scale.

The diagnostic category 'maladjusted' provides a graphic illustration of this pattern. Although hyperactivity (or hyperkinesis) is officially recognised in the UK, in practice the diagnostic criteria are much stricter than those in operation in the USA. However, the criteria relevant for the category maladjusted include most of those currently employed by American clinicians to label a child hyper-active, so that maladjusted becomes a comparable English category despite the fact that it is not strictly identical. What is interesting about the concept maladjusted is its increasing use to identify and treat the misbehaviour of British schoolchildren. Thus there were in 1950 only 587 so classified full-time pupils in special schools. In the next 20 years this figure rose to over 5000, and only 5 years later had leapt again to nearly 14,000. This increase of nearly 2500 per cent is far, far in excess of the 50 per cent increase in the total school population. In addition, there has also been a doubling, during the last 10 years, in the number of so-called maladjusted children who are not in special schools, but who are either awaiting a place in one or are being treated within 'normal' school in units for 'problematic' children. When we combine maladjusted schoolchildren within a special or ordinary school we find there were just over 8000 in 1966, but by 1976 this population size had risen to over 20,000.

This is not the only diagnostic label which has been increasingly applied to an expanded population of 'handicapped' schoolchildren; within that group there are also many more 'medium educationally sub-normal' (particularly teenagers), 'autistic' and 'epilectic'. Further evidence of schoolchildren being 'medicalised' can be gleaned from the Department of Health and Social Security's triannual in-patient surveys. During the period 1967–73 admissions to mental hospitals for the general population over 15 years of age remained virtually constant or slightly increased, yet for children beneath this age there was a 33 per cent increase controlled for population changes.

A second cause of alarm is that experts now believe hyperactivity to be an indicator of worse things to come. Rather than viewing it as an isolated child disorder, they now increasingly recognise it as being intimately linked with and a precursor of serious adult psychotic disorders. Thus Cantwell (1977) argues that if left untreated, the prognosis for hyperactivity is poor. In his estimation both re-trospective and prospective studies indicate that anti-social be-haviour, educational retardation and depression, and psychosis are prevalent in 'grown-up' hyperactive children. In support of this he cites from, *inter alia*, the work of Menkes *et al.* (1967). In this study fourteen hyperactive children were followed up 25 years later. Although only three were still hyperactive, four were in mental asylums for psychotic conditions and two more for mental retardation. Of the eight who were still self-supporting, one had a prison record and two had been institutionalised as juveniles.

A similar grim and warning prognosis is made by Ross and Ross (1976). Summarising progress in the study of this disorder, they write: 'one important advance pertains to the increased awareness of *the duration of effect of hyperactivity*' (their italics). Originally viewed as a problem of middle childhood and early adolescence, it is now clear that 'hyperactivity may span the major developmental stages, often being apparent in the last trimester of pregnancy and continuing well into adulthood'. Thus, hyperactivity is not 'conceptualised as the tip of the iceberg, a catalytic agent which, *in the absence of effective intervention* [my italics] can trigger off a chain reaction of secondary problems . . . such that we have a chronic disorder of potentially major importance throughout much of the life span (Ross and Ross, 1976, pp. 289–90).

Finally, and once again dramatically highlighting the importance of preventing and/or diagnosing and treating hyperactivity early, is a letter by Drs Carmen and Tucker published in a British medical journal. They firmly believe that study of the neurochemical determinants of hyperactivity may open up avenues of insight into sociopathy, alcoholism and hysteria, since all four are 'characterised by cognitive or attentional defects and aggressive impulsivity of varying severity' (Carmen and Tucker, 1973, p. 1338). If they, Cantwell and Ross and Ross are correct, in the very nub of victory over hyperactivity lies the potential for conquering many of our most serious forms of disruptive and injurious mental illness, especially psychopathy. Indeed, for every hyperactive schoolchild cured we shall be spared the murderous villainy of a later grown-up psychopath.

So let us give thanks to the medical and allied professions: another disease attacking the very brains of our young has been identified, the alarm has been sounded, and we can, with the help and guidance of the medical and allied professions, look forward to victory; diphtheria yesterday, poliomyelitis today, hyperactivity tomorrow. But before we drop off into a state of reverential stupidity, let us take a closer, more critical, look at this disease that is debilitating so many schoolchildren and causing so much alarm. What are the social characteristics of children diagnosed as hyperactive? What causes hyperactivity? How is it recognised? How is it cured?

The 'disease': who, why, how and so what

Unfortunately there have been few epidemiological studies of hyperactivity. Nonetheless, from the available data, one observation important for understanding the 'real' nature of hyperactivity is this: it is a respecter of sex differences. In America boys diagnosed as hyperactive outnumber girls by a ratio of never less than four to one, and occasionally researchers have reported a ratio of nine to one. In this country maladjustment is similarly sex-linked, and again by a ratio of about four to one. Beyond the well established over-representation of boys amongst the hyperactive, very little else is well documented. What there is, however, does not correspond to Cole's (1975) assertion that 'no country, geographical area or social class seem to have immunity'; for example, the disorder is virtually non-existent in primitive Pacific cultures (Prescott, 1968, 1970), in rural areas of England (Bax, 1972) or amongst Chinese–American children in New York (Sollenberger, 1968). On the other hand, some sections of the community seem to be less immune than others. For example, in a prevalence study in twenty-five schools in New Jersey in 1973, Lewis found that black and Spanish-surnamed pupils were much more likely to be labelled hyperactive than were white children, and especially so in suburban areas, among children who had formerly resided in an urban ghetto (Lewis, 1973, p. 60). Another study, this time in Baltimore county during the 2-year period 1971–3, reported that there was an increasing incidence of hyperactivity amongst state-run schools compared with private schools, and that within the state-run schools the highest rate of increase was amongst those children whose parents' income was less than average (Krager and Safer, 1974, p. 1119). Thus the prediction, reported by Witter (1971), that at least 30 per cent of ghetto children are candidates for being diagnosed as hyperactive is both consistent with the New Jersey and Baltimore prevalence studies and does not suggest a random distribution.

These data, which admittedly are not conclusive, can be partially supplemented by the knowledge that IQ, measured in whatever way, is both class-linked and a diagnostic feature of hyperactive children, and, secondly, hyperactivity has been arguably linked with lead poisoning (Wiener, 1970; David *et al.*, 1972) and food additives (Moyer, 1975; Baldwin *et al.*, 1968), which are frequently more of a problem among children from low-income parents living in dilapidated urban areas. Clearly more studies on a total nation-wide population, with a total age-range of children, concentrating on numerous demographic factors are required before the issue of incidence and prevalence can be settled (Omenn, 1973). However, at the moment the best evidence available indicates that hyperactivity afflicts (or is ascribed to) the socially and economically under-privileged male schoolchild living in or having recently moved from an urban area.

In order to legitimate a diagnostic label as being a 'real' disease, medical 'experts' invariably attempt to locate its cause in a histo-pathological lesion or pathophysiological processes (Szasz, 1977). Hyperactivity is no exception. Hundreds of research workers have attempted to 'prove' that it is caused by some organic impairment, flaw or malfunction. Thus it has been claimed to be a direct result of or dysfunction within the brain or within the central nervous system, which itself was probably caused prenatally by encephalitis in infancy or early childhood; others assert it is due to under-arousal of the central nervous system, genetic variation, 'constitutional de-terminants', chromosome abnormalities, and so on. But, not surpris-ingly, no conclusive proof has yet been produced. In a recent sum-mary of this body of research, Baxley and LeBlanc suggest that 'there appear to be many questions that remain to be answered about the etiology of the problem. There are several extant theories about the cause of hyperactivity, but none of them is completely satisfactory . . . so that . . . at the present time . . . the etiology of hyperactivity remains an open question' (Baxley and LeBlanc, 1975, pp. 13–14).

A growing awareness that this search may be as futile as the quest for the Holy Grail has led some commentators to take refuge in a plea for more multi-disciplinary research (Ross and Ross, 1976, pp. 92–4) or the argument that we do not need to know the cause of a disease before we can diagnose and treat it (Werry, 1968). We can borrow the imagery of Oscar Wilde's view of people who marry for the second time and suggest that the plea for multi-disciplinary research represents the triumph of hope over experience and should be left to those with enough faith and their *own funds* to carry on the quest. The latter argument leads us to examine just how some children are recognised to be hyperactive and what happens to them as a result.

Since the medical 'cause' of hyperactivity is unknown, maybe a better understanding of it can be gleaned from consideration of how it is diagnosed. The first, and most important, point is that it is not made on the basis of located impaired physiological and/or neurological factors; neither is it determined by procedures based on psychological factors, such as any of the various intelligence tests – Rorschack Inkblot Tests, Children's Apperception Tests, or the Goodenough Harris Draw-a-Person Test. For all practical purposes, and this is the vital clue, the diagnosis is based solely on the children's behaviour. This immediately raises the crucial question – are there objective culture-free procedures for measuring this behaviour?

In an attempt to prove that there are, and thereby firmly establishing hyperactivity as a descriptive category, researchers have concentrated on the excessive quantity of physical movement. Hoping to demonstrate that hyperactive children do move about more than normal children, experimenters fitted their 'subjects' up with self-winding wristwatches (Bell, 1968; Schulman and Reisman, 1959), photoelectric counters (Ellis and Pryer, 1959), ballistographic or stabilimetric chairs (Sprague and Toppe, 1966; Werry and Sprague, 1970), ultrasonic devices (McFarland *et al.*, 1966), and telemetric devices (Werry and Sprague, 1970). Summing up this research, Cantwell writes that the 'results have been inconclusive and there is serious question whether hyperactive children actually have a clearly *greater amount* of daily motor activity or a different type of motor activity than non-hyperactive children' (Cantwell, 1977, p. 525).

Because of this lack of success, the favoured practical procedure for diagnosing hyperactivity has been to obtain teachers' 'measurements' of children's behaviour by means of the Conners' Teaching Rating Scale. A critical examination of this instrument provides a massive clue to the non-medical understanding of hyperactivity. It includes such items as *classroom behaviour* (fidgeting, hums or makes other odd noises, easily frustrated, restless, excitable, inattentive, overly sensitive, serious or sad, daydreams, sulks, cries easily, disturbs other children, quarrels, acts 'smart', is destructive, steals, lies or loses temper), *group participation* (is isolated from others or unacceptable to them, is easily led and lacks leadership, does not get along with same or opposite sex, teases others and has no sense of fair play), and *attitude towards authority* (defiant, impudent, stubborn, unco-operative, truant). Even if this particular instrument is not used on every diagnosis, it is the case that the typical symptom pattern for diagnosing hyperactivity includes these teacher-reported and teacher-interpreted 'behaviours': extreme excess of motor activity (the child is restless and fidgety); very short attention span (the child flits from one activity to another, wild oscillation in mood, the child is fine one day and a terror the next); clumsiness due to excess activity; aggressive-like behaviour; impulsivity in school (he cannot comply with rules, and has a low frustration level). There is a similar set of behavioural 'symptoms' in the Department of Education and Science's classification for recognising maladjustment. These include 'unmanageable, defiant, disobedient, aggression, stealing, begging, lying, truancy, romancing, sex difficulties', as well as 'nervous disorders' such as 'phobias, withdrawal, depression, excitable, apathetic, obsessive and hysterical'. Furthermore, informal communications with members of the Kent School Psychological Service reveal that 'over-activity', without any known brain damage, is often an important 'symptom' in classifying children as maladjusted.

It does not take a very sharp student of deviance to realise that all these behaviours said to be symptomatic of hyperactivity and synonymous disorders could, with equal, if not more conviction and justification, be called deviant. These behaviours violate important school norms about paying attention to teacher, obeying teacher, and being responsive to teacher's wishes, instructions, or commands; about not interfering with other children; about not answering teacher back, threatening teacher, or actually assaulting teacher; about not mistreating or damaging school property; about comporting oneself in an orderly and disciplined fashion.

In other words, when teachers employ the Conners' Teaching Rating Scale, or make their own assessment, they are interpreting and labelling behaviour of which they disapprove because it violates situational schoolroom norms or authority relations. Hyperactive children are judged by the social inappropriateness of their behaviour rather than by any generalised quantitative excess. Thus, 'the best definition of hyperactivity remains a social judgement of the frequency and intensity of specified behaviours displayed at "inappropriate times"' (Zentall, 1975, p. 549).

Not only could these behaviours be regarded by students of deviance as 'deviance', they were seen as just that before the 'manufacture' of hyperactivity. Children who behaved in these ways were called disruptive, disobedient, rebellious, anti-social, a bloody nuisance, naughty, and received a clip round the ear, or a cane on the hand, or a slipper on the backside. In extreme cases they were expelled, and a few may have been transferred to institutions for mental retardation or mental illness, or treated as being 'emotionally disturbed'. But since most of them were simply violating school norms, they were regarded as naughty little sods and punished for it.

Apparently there has been much medical progress since those uncivilised times. Children are no longer naughty, they are medical cases, and, with this reconceptualisation of the problem, American schools, particularly in poor negro ghettos, and English schools in urban slum areas, are being transformed from places where children attend educational courses to places where children receive courses in medical treatment.

And what type of medical therapy is advocated and practised? At the extreme, a few hyperactive children have undergone brain surgery (Breggin, 1972; Andy, 1970); these may have been isolated cases and this form of intervention, at least, does not appear to be given much prominence or recommendation in the relevant research reports. Nonetheless, innovatory methods of brain surgery, such as transorbital lobotomy, cingulectomy, topectomy, gyrectomy and bimedial leucotomy (Schevitz, 1976) have revitalised this type of medical intervention (Breggin, 1972), and there is no reason to believe that schoolchildren with psychiatric or behavioural problems will remain exempt as these techniques become more widespread.

Another slightly more popular treatment is individual psychotherapy, although, as Cantwell (1977) points out, evidence for its efficacy is lacking and in any case hyperactive children often lack the linguistic or social skills necessary for this form of intervention. Behavioural therapy and altering environmental contingencies is also advocated, probably more so in England with maladjusted children than in America (Kolvin, 1976).

But by far the most favoured and widely practised treatment is drug therapy (Sandoval *et al.*, 1976). Following Bradley's discovery in 1937 that a stimulant administered to children had paradoxical effects in that it made them less active, less excited, less overstimulated, it did not take much imagination to realise that the new psychiatric disease, hyperactivity, might be controlled by stimulant drug therapy. Soon after Laufer's discovery of the disorder, a number of pharmaceutical companies, particularly CIBA and Abbott Laboratories, began experimenting and then producing drugs for hyperactivity. Legitimated mainly by the research of two notable medical moral entrepreneurs, L. Eisenberg and K. Conners, both of whom received much of their funds from pharmaceutical companies, it was not long before hundreds of thousands of hyperactive schoolchildren were being legally drugged. At the moment the main drugs being administered to hyperactive schoolchildren are stimulants, such as methylphenidate (Ritalin), dexamphetamine (Dexedrine) and magnesium pemoline (Cylert), although in a minority of cases non-stimulants such as thioridazine (Mellaril), chlorpromazine (Chorizine), hydroxyzine (Atarax), diphenhydramine (Benadryl), tricyclic impramine (Tofranil) and lithium carbonate, and antidepressant anticonvulsants, such as Dilantin, are also administered. Of all these, and other psychoactive substances, methylphenidate (Ritalin) is the most favoured treatment because it is alleged to be the most effective and essential. This belief was well documented by Sandoval *et al.* (1976) when they reported that more doctors than not agreed with the statement 'depriving a hyperactive child of Ritalin is similar to depriving a diabetic of insulin'.

As yet, the author has no official data on drug therapy being administered to misbehaving schoolchildren. However, evidence for its existence is available both directly and indirectly. Following the publication of an article in *New Society* (Box, 1977), the author received a number of letters from parents and teachers confirming that drugs were being prescribed for children by medical practitioners. Thus a headmaster in the West Country, wrote: 'At a previous school in the Midlands I had a great deal of experience of what might be termed "excessive drugging" of severely sub-normal or deeply maladjusted children. Many of the latter were of West Indian origin.' An ex-teacher from Yeadon wrote complaining that instead of attempting to comprehend the causes of a child's misbehaviour, the local Educational Psychological Service 'to my great disgust . . . prescribed barbiturates'. A father from Rye, East Sussex, complained to me that his daughter had been placed on a course of Valium even though the child disagreed with this decision, which was taken by the mother and the house mistress. From Bristol a teacher wrote: 'We have a small special class of disturbed children (about eight in all) at my primary school. When I heard that one of them was being given drugs to keep him docile I expressed horror only to be told by the teacher that she had personally been involved in the decision and that he was "much better".'

In addition to this direct evidence, of which only a small fragment has been reproduced above, it would seem reasonable to infer the use of drug therapy from the following. First, two leading articles appeared in the *British Medical Journal* (1973, 1975) and a survey report appeared in the *Drugs and Therapeutics Bulletin* (March, 1977), and in all three the condition of hyperactivity was legitimated and qualified approval of drug therapy was given. Secondly, articles and letters have appeared in leading medical journals reporting on various experiments with drugs on overactive children (Spencer, 1971; Triantafillow, 1972; Montagu and Swarbrick, 1975). Thirdly, a professional teacher's journal carried an article (Simon, 1974) entitled 'A Teachers' Guide to "Drugs"' in which sedatives and tranquillisers (including most of the drugs mentioned above) were some of the products indicated for childhood behaviour disorders, and increasing advertisements are appearing in medical journals. It would be naive, given these processes of legitimation, experimentation, publicisation and commercial advertising, not to conclude that the use of drug therapy on children who have been given one of a number of diagnostic labels was not increasing.

From naughty to hyperactive children: private problems

A disease does not just have to be invented for it to become widely diagnosed and socially acceptable. Following the advice of Mills (1959), we should consider both the personal troubles and public issues which are related to and at least partially resolved by a disease such as hyperactivity assuming epidemic proportions. We should look, in other words, both at how hyperactivity and synonymous diagnoses are interpreted as, or transformed into solutions for, individual problems, and how these individual problems are themselves reflections and refractions of wider social issues.

It is often the case that parents, teachers, and ordinary physicians become convinced that a so-called new disease exists only after they have been saturated with artful persuasion and concealed propaganda. Hyperactivity does not appear to be immune to this social process of certification. In this persuasion and propaganda US pharmaceutical companies – sometimes referred to by cynics as the real drug pushers in industrial society – assisted by medical entrepreneurs, played a major, if not the dominant, part. Viewing with much anticipation the vast profitable market of childhood diseases, leading pharmaceutical companies began a two-pronged attack. Through a massive programme of advertising they sought to persuade doctors and teachers (and through these, parents) that many, if not all children thought to be naughty were really suffering from hyperactivity, a disease largely physiological and neurological in its etiology. Secondly, they sought to persuade the lay public, and the teaching and medical professions, that they had benevolently and altruistically developed a treatment at great cost to themselves. Here is an example of such an advertisement, which appeared in 1971:

> MBD [a synonym for hyperactivity] . . . MEDICAL MYTH OR DIAGNOSABLE DISEASE ENTITY. What medical practitioner has not, at one time or another, been called upon to examine an impulsive, excitable hyperactive child? A child with difficulty in concentrating. Easily frustrated. Unusually aggressive. A classroom rebel. In the absence of any organic pathology, the conduct of such children was, until a few short years ago, usually dismissed as . . . spunkiness, or evidence of youthful vitality. But it is now evident that in many of these children the hyperactive syndrome exists as a distinct medical entity. This syndrome is readily diagnosed through patient histories, neurologic signs, and psychometric testing [although of course it never is:] – and has been classified by an expert panel convened by the United States Department of Health, Education and Welfare as Minimal Brain Dysfunction, MBD (Conrad, 1975).

This is followed by the advertiser announcing that the company's product Ritalin is the established and effective means of treatment. In the same year, 1971, CIBA, the manufacturer of Ritalin, made $13 million profit on this one drug, an amount which represented as much as 15 per cent of the total gross profits. This compares favourably with the estimated $21 million profit made a couple of years earlier by Cosa Nostra from the importing and wholesaling of narcotics (Cressey, 1969, p. 92).

This advertising campaign would not have been possible had it not been for a number of medical moral entrepreneurs, amongst whom two of the more famous were Leon Eisenberg and Keith Conners. During a decade they acquired research grants, mainly from the National Institute of Mental Health, but also drug companies, to the sum of over $1 million. They became 'not only the leaders in paediatric psychopharmacology research, but also the country's most influential proponents of the use of stimulants for hyperactive children' (Schrag and Divoky, 1975, p. 79). Since most of their research was on poor or black kids attending fifth and sixth grades in two Baltimore ghetto schools, it would not be unreasonable to conclude that in a very real sense they had discovered a relatively safe and profitable way to make the inner-city classrooms more bearable for teachers and at the same time to reduce the anxiety of parents concerned for their child's education.

Of course, it would not have been possible for these companies to have persuaded parents and teachers both of the disease existing and its treatment if those same parents and teachers had not already been receptive to such a shift. Some members of both groups could be, and were, persuaded on liberal humanitarian grounds that the 'moral' persuasion and/or punishment previously practised on naughty schoolchildren was less civilised and less effective than the prescription of drugs. In our culture the medical profession is already held in 'awe' by large sections of the population because of its undoubted victories over diseases which merely one or two generations ago were mass 'killers'. The medical profession's motives have always been portrayed as care, concern and cure; the interest of the patient has always appeared uppermost in the ideology that seeks to legitimate the expansionism of the medical and allied professions. Consequently, when prominent members of that profession discovered and offered a cure for poliomyelitis, parents rushed to have their children orally vaccinated; and when prominent psychiatric researchers discovered and evaluated a treatment for hyperactivity, many parents and teachers sighed with relief, gave their thanks to the medical and allied professions and eagerly sought to have their children drugged.

If parents care about their children in school, they care both about their behaviour and about their academic achievement – although both seem to go together. If the child comes home with reports of his being disruptive, rebellious, anti-social, a poor learner, this must in some sense reflect badly on his parents, for the family is known to be, and most parents seem to believe this, the main agent of socialisation (even if they do not know that concept!). The discovery of hyperactivity provided an opportunity to be released from the pains and anguish of being a bad parent, for although parents might feel guilty that they have not taught their offspring the appropriate way to comport themselves in schools, they cannot feel guilty about their offspring being the victim of a brain disorder – they may feel unhappy about it, they may even be anxious about it, but they will not feel guilty, because no one, no member of the medical profession, is suggesting that parents are *responsible* for their children having hyperactivity. And the unhappiness or anxiety need not be intense or long-lived, because accompanying the disturbing revelation that their child is suffering from hyperactivity is the reassuring claim that he can be cured easily; in fact, he can be cured by a technique with which they are already very familiar for curing many of their own physical and psychological ailments, the mere taking of a few pills each day (Grinspoon and Hedblom, 1975). No wonder many parents, particularly in a generation already feeling considerable guilt about their country's military involvement in South-East Asia, and bothered about the apparent moral disintegration of urban and school systems and the explicit moral and physical threat on which the Nixon/Agnew 'law and order' campaign was successfully based, were relieved to discover that not all their problems were moral but in fact many of them were medical. To some extent out of gratitude and a sense of relief many parents allowed their children to become transformed into objects fit for psychochemical therapy.

Although 'awe' and 'relief' may explain some, or maybe even most, of the receptivity of parents towards hyperactivity and its psychochemical treatment, there remained a third group who were reluctant but pressurised by the threat that their child would be expelled, kept back a grade, transferred to a special class for the 'mentally retarded' or even transferred to another school. Some schools have even been known to threaten parents with legal action for the maltreatment of their children – namely, not permitting the school authorities to administer drug therapy for a disease the medical experts say exists, and if this results in keeping the child away from school, then the threatened court order for truancy. Under this barrage of threats it is no wonder that some parents have felt bludgeoned into allowing their children to become medical cases fit for drugging. It was not until 1976 that a fight-back was staged by reluctant American parents. A crucial court case, which has not yet been heard, is being brought on behalf of eighteen schoolchildren, mainly from poor and working-class backgrounds. Their parents started to notice symptoms like nausea and cramp, and, on inquiry, discovered that their children had been diagnosed by the local school doctor as hyperactive and been placed in a special class for learning disabilities and given Ritalin. They are suing the authorities for unlawfully placing the children in these special classes, for coercing their children into taking Ritalin, and for making their children suffer a stigma. But apart from this handful, the vast majority of parents have willingly, and sometimes zealously, embraced a medical solution to what they were experiencing as a personal trouble, namely, the difficult or disappointing behaviour of their child.

As for the teaching profession, their acceptance of hyperactivity as a real treatable disease is not that difficult to understand. Many of the behaviours said to be diagnostically symptomatic of hyperactivity and synonymous diagnostic labels could be seen, by unkind cynical observers, as symptomatic of a schooling system which many children view as irrelevant to their interests; which does not and never intends to educate them in ways suitable for managing their future lives better; which is authoritarian, oppressive and intent on instilling them with the virtues of conformity, acquiescence and passivity. It does not do much for a teacher's self-image to be seen as an instrument of class oppression, as an authoritarian custodian of a dominant class culture, or as a peddler of mindless mediocrity. Thus many of them would be and have been willing to accept hyperactivity as a 'real' disorder because it resolves some of their personal troubles; it further distorts the already inarticulate protests of schoolchildren, and it castrates what is often a moral protest or a gesture of moral outrage and turns it into a morally neutral sign of disease. Furthermore, hyperactivity makes the recurrence of these unwanted 'communications' from schoolchildren less likely; the prescribed drugs 'work' – they do subdue children, they do make them less troublesome, they do make them more manageable within a social system that demands obedience and conformity within a regime of routinised activities. Teachers, and beyond them the educational system, are thus protected by a medicalisation of children's behaviours which could otherwise be viewed as symptomatic of a pathological educational situation, but which under the benign and benevolent hand of medicine is seen merely as symptomatic of a disease common to many poor children – children who accidently happen to be boys and not girls, negroes more than whites, and poor rather than well-off.

It is not possible to explain adequately the epidemic, the manufactured epidemic of hyperactivity, merely by observing that pharmaceutical companies had a profit motive urging them along, that some doctors had pointed out the similarity in some behaviour manifested by children with brain damage and the behaviour of some 'disruptive' schoolchildren, that some medical moral entrepreneurs had validated the therapeutic effectiveness of psychoactive chemicals on hyperactive children, or that parents and teachers had personal troubles which could be reduced by accepting the medical view that their offspring and pupils were disordered and not disruptive, diseased rather than disagreeable. It is also necessary to consider the way in which the judicial handling of 'delinquent' children was changing during the sixties, since this altered the availability of accepted 'solutions', and how the alleged treatment and intervention programmes based on sociological positivism were discredited during the same period, thus creating a vacuum for non-sociological solutions to fill.

Throughout the sixties the American method of handling juveniles was criticised by lawyers and criminologists, including Matza (1964), Platt (1969) and many labelling theorists in general. In some way the conflict can be viewed as between two systems of social control, one emphasising an adversary, due process and punishment as desert, and the other emphasising a process of expert-diagnosis-and-treatment as a 'need'. Since its inception, juvenile delinquency in America has been viewed as a maladjustment, as a kind of pathology of growing up and not as an act of wickedness, moral indifference, or ideological protest. Consequently, two processes of justice developed: for adults a punitive system of social control was considered appropriate, whilst for juveniles a therapeutic system based on the concept of 'individualised justice' was thought more suitable. Under this therapeutic system it was not important what the child had done, what was important was his or her needs. Indeed, to appear in a juvenile court, the child need not have done anything considered to be illegal; he or she merely had to be perceived as someone whose needs could be satisfied by the court or agencies to which it would direct those requiring treatment. The rampant paternalism of the juvenile justice system stripped away the principle of offence and with it the adversary system and due process. It was the absence of these foundation stones of justice which made many lawyers and criminologists view juvenile courts critically. Indeed, it was the major reason for and the central analysis of Matza's (1964) brilliant critique.

Largely as a response to this massive assault on it by leading authorities in the legal and academic professions, the juvenile justice system underwent a change in the late sixties. Whether this change was radical or retrogressive depends from which position it is judged. What occurred was a move towards reunification of the system of justice – juveniles were given the right to due process, the protection of an adversary confrontation, and the principle of offence was affirmed. Consequently, legal institutions became less available to control or sanction those whose behaviours were considered disorderly but not necessarily illegal. Until the time of these legal changes juvenile courts had formed a kind of much used and overstretched long stop for problematic pupils ejected from schools; now, because of these reforms in the late sixties, that long stop was withdrawn, and it was into this vacant position that the medical profession and its pharmaceutical company allies substituted themselves. They provided a function for schools which the juvenile court had previously carried out; they provided a means of dealing with troublesome youths, and thus resolving personal troubles of teachers and parents. Instead of referring difficult, disorderly and disobedient children to juvenile courts, the school began referring them to psychiatrists, school physicians or the local Mental Health Community Clinic.

It is ironic that at the time America was 'legalising' her juvenile justice system and thus making medicalisation of schoolchildren more likely, the British system was decriminalising juvenile courts, and this had the effect of massively legitimating a medical approach to troublesome youth. Since the end of the Second World War there has been an increasing trend in Britain to separate adolescent from adult offenders and graft them on an amorphous body of non-offending 'children in trouble'. The Children and Young Persons Act 1969 marks the high-water mark of this trend, in principle if not in practice (Giller and Morris, 1976).

The 1969 Act, the debates and the Government reports and Opposition papers which preceded it, all radiated the medical model of delinquency (Balch, 1975). The whole issue was peppered with such words as 'treatment', 'cure', 'prevention', 'symptom', 'diagnosis'. Social workers were pitchforked into a major role in the control of delinquency; their main purpose was to provide for 'early detection of situations which unchecked may *lead* to delinquency, and the application of remedial and educative processes at that stage' (Scottish Office, 1964, para 250). And this pitchforking was no accident: the profession of social workers had been an extremely strong pressure group behind the 'reform' of juvenile justice in Britain, and within the profession the strongest emphasis was on psychiatric social work. In their view, and this was a view ingrained in the 1969 Act, delinquency was to be explained in terms of an individual's maladjustment and not in terms of the law, its administration, societal reactions and individual modes of adaptation to reaction. Most important of all, delinquent behaviour *per se* was not the real problem, rather it was viewed as merely an indicator, a symptom of 'maladjustment or immaturity, or . . . of a deviant, damaged or abnormal personality' (HMSO, 1968a, para 6). This is most important because it is the existence of these conditions, shared by many adolescents other than those who commit illegal acts, that form the ultimate justification for the state, in the form of medically and psychiatrically oriented social work, intervening in families and in schools. Thus 'persistent truancy, staying out late at nights, even refusing to accept the advice of the social worker become indicators of the "need for treatment"'. This is quite clear in the *Kilbrandon Report*: 'What we mean by persistent truancy is often *the first sign of serious maladjustment of psychological disorder*. If unattended to (like all disease prognosis) it may have repercussions in after life more serious than delinquency itself.' Here then, simply and briefly, is the essence of the present position: if unattended to, behaviour which experts say is symptomatic of so-called mental disorder such as hyperactivity or maladjustment, will get worse, so that early intervention and treatment is justifiable. Since the whole concept of mental disorder is so vague, so broad in its possible catchment area, so capable of being stretched to cover almost any behaviour disliked by those in a position of authority, it gives the widest possible scope for medically solving the problem of difficult, disruptive schoolchildren, and it was this view the 1969 Act both expressed and legitimated.

The Act denies any need for an overriding principle of offence, since the proceedings of the court are based upon expert medical opinion that the offence is not the real problem at all; the real problem is what the offence behaviour signifies about the psychiatric condition of the offender. There is no need therefore to protect children brought to the court, for the motives of those referring them are essentially medical – to get them treated and normal again. Consequently, all the formalities of due process can be chiselled away.

Thus, whereas in America it was necessary for the medical and allied professions to enter schools directly because the legal institutions became disinclined to process children with mere *needs* but no *misdeeds*, in Britain the medical and allied professions directly entered the juvenile justice system. The basic reasons for bringing children to court were so vague and ambiguous that it needed expert opinion to clarify them: 'being beyond the control of his parents', 'falling into bad association', 'exposed to moral danger', 'being caused unnecessary suffering', and 'proper development being avoidably prevented' are not objective conditions recognised easily or agreed on by all who might have them before their very eyes. It needs an expert to pronounce, and because of this elevation of the expert, the administration of juvenile justice in this country passed from the magistrates and police to the social workers, with their psychiatric, psychoanalytic and quasi-medical training, and their intense willingness to help schools cope with troublesome children. Ironically, then, two juvenile justice systems, changing in opposite directions, had a similar effect; for different reasons they both helped to extend the medicalisation of schoolchildren's misconduct.

At one level, then, the recent epidemic in schoolchildren's psychiatric disorders, particularly hyperactivity and maladjustment, can be seen as one solution to individuals' personal troubles. Parents were relieved of the guilt and anxiety surrounding their claim to be good parents, teachers' identity *qua* teachers was afforded some protection, the sheer physical and spiritual effort of controlling some children was reduced, quasi-medical professions were further legitimated, and pharmaceutical companies were provided with another rich human seam from which to gouge back huge profits. All their relative contributions to schoolchildren's behaviour are denied, and instead the blame is firmly located in so-called mental disorders. whatever the symbolic nature of the behaviour, whether it is against the law or not, its significance is denied; no protest, moral or political is heard, no cause to rebel against recognised, no alienation from an oppressive educational family system perceived. The real demons are diseases in all their multifarious disguises; so let us thank the medical and allied professions for our daily medicine. They are certainly making life easier for some of us.

From naughty to hyperactive children: public issues

The personal troubles which I have just suggested underlie the steady drift towards medicalising naughty schoolchildren can be viewed as both reflections and refractions of public issues. Furthermore, since medicalising naughty schoolchildren is merely an illustration of a much wider process of medicalising social, moral and legal problems (Box, forthcoming; Kittrie, 1971; Szasz, 1963; Zola, 1972), it is necessary to broaden our understanding of it by introducing some historical and structural analysis. In order to understand why this process has gained rapid momentum during the last decade, it is necessary to bear in mind some of the contradictions in contemporary industrialised societies, the public issues these produce, and the possible modes of solving these within the constraints of contemporary ideology and material interests.

Industrial societies are criminogenic; through their contradictions they produce problematic populations, groups or classes of people who pose potential puzzles or threats to groups or classes of people in positions of power. The unemployed, the unemployable, the economically underprivileged, the ethnically oppressed groups, and the sexually exploited, are some of the problematic populations whose potential for disruption, deviance and rebellion has to be defused. The state and those whose interests it ultimately serves constantly search for ways and means of containing and controlling these groups, but never by way of resolving the contradictions which gave rise to them (Spitzer, 1975).

In a period of rising, often chronic, unemployment, reflecting Marx's notions about 'the organic composition of capital', many schoolchildren, particularly lower-class and ethnically underprivileged boys, become problematic. A lot of the frustration, rejection, humiliation and oppression they experience manifests itself in delinquency, truancy, disobedience and other behaviours to which figures of authority take exception. The state, as a custodian of moral and legal boundaries, searches for ways of containing and controlling these behaviours, and, naturally, it supports those groups or professions who come up with possible solutions. But if they fail to deliver the goods, they are rejected and another group or profession conscripted to replace them. So it was with those advocating solutions based upon sociological positivism. They were given their chance, and in the wake of their failure came those with solutions based on biological positivism.

For example, during the late fifties and early sixties a number of prominent sociologists assembled extremely plausible accounts of delinquency and other forms of youthful misconduct, focusing mainly on social processes of street-gang life. Cohen (1955), Miller (1958), and Cloward and Ohlin (1960) all stressed the importance of gang beliefs and membership as essential precursors of delinquent behaviour. Largely on the basis of these 'theories' Federal and Local Government enthusiastically sponsored delinquency-prevention programmes centred around the idea of neutralising or co-opting gang membership. However, 'street-gang work' hardly proved effective. Indeed, in a recent appraisal of this intervention strategy, Klein writes that it has 'proven only slightly successful, ineffective or even contributory to gang delinquency. They have employed inadequate resources in combating and entrenched foe. Some of their normal and almost necessary practices have acted as boomerangs, effectively increasing gang cohesiveness and delinquency' (Klein, 1971, p. 55). Another venture, based upon sociological positivism, was the Midcity Youth Project. In assessing this, Miller wrote: 'It is now possible to provide a definite answer to the principal evaluative research question – was there a significant measurable inhibition of law-violating or morally disapproving behaviour as a consequence of project efforts? The answer with little necessary qualification is "no".' All major measures of violent behaviour – disapproved actions, illegal actions, during-contact court appearances, before-during-after appearances, and Project Control appearances – provide consistent support for a finding of 'negligible impact' (Miller, 1962; p. 512). Other major examples, such as the Mobilisation for Youth in New York, based upon Cloward and Ohlin's (1960) analysis of gang delinquency and opportunities, and the Chicago Area Project loosely based on Shaw's (1942) urban research findings, were also unable to demonstrate a substantial improvement in the behaviours they were ostensibly designed to reduce.

By the end of the seventies the promise of sociological positivism was either seen as counterfeit because programmes based on it failed to reduce delinquency and youthful misbehaviour (Lerman, 1975; Wilson, 1975), or totally impractical because they required social reform on a scale that the dominant class was quite unprepared to contemplate (Schur, 1973). Thus, whilst lip service was still being paid to these types of programmes, there was already a preparedness to look elsewhere for alternative solutions to the delinquency problem. One of these was already under way and only required more funds and official certification to mushroom: this was a new version of biological determinism – the conception that delinquents and predelinquents were essentially ill, either mentally or, as in the case of hyperactivity, physically and organically, and required treatment, especially drug therapy.

Medicalising difficult populations of schoolchildren can be viewed then as a solution to a number of major public issues which in part reflect the potent contradictions between cultural and institutional features of industrialised society. One such contradiction is between school and work; during education children are supposed to acquire capacities and commitments for an adult life of work, but the growing economic crisis in many industrialised societies makes it increasingly likely that for certain sections of the male population these capacities and commitments will be under-used or not used at all. By individualising and depoliticising this public issue, and the personal troubles that reflect it, the medical solution helps to fragment a potentially disruptive population; it turns what might be a reflection of a flawed social system into a sign of a flawed individual and delivers the job of controlling these poor souls into the hands of a widely acceptable professional group who, unlike the police or courts, are more difficult for the lay public to visualise as part of the state's control apparatus.

Another contradiction is between the ideological value of equality and the institutional value of racism. During the late fifties and sixties, both in America and this country, there were changes in the ethnic composition of schools. In America these were deliberate changes brought about by civil-rights legislation and the decision to integrate schools. According to Broudy, this forced integration created a major problem for educational establishments. He argued:

> Perhaps the proximate cause or occasion of the problem of the use of the drugs in the treatment of hyperkinetic children lies in the turmoil that disrupted so many of the inner-city schools when an effort was made to implement the civil rights and the Great Society legislation of the late fifties and the sixties by integrating the schools. Of all the difficulties that this effort engendered, none was mentioned more often than that of maintaining classroom discipline, and despite the plethora of hypotheses as to the causes of the difficulty, there was general agreement that the conventional middle-class school depended for order and discipline on family and community sanctions that apparently were not functioning for some of the inner-city children . . . The hyperactive child, whatever the cause of hyperactivity, who threatens to disrupt the fragile fabric of conventional classroom order is dreaded by the teacher pretty much as the hurricane is feared by the mariner . . . Inner-city school . . . discipline became a matter of survival for teachers and probably heightened the attention given to hyperkinesis as part of the problem of maintaining order in the classroom.

These difficulties were raised to a dramatic pitch when the public schools were faced with the demand to provide equal education to all segments of the population. In the inner-city schools those pupils who were not nurtured in the white middle-class mores of schooling and those teachers who were unaccustomed to anything else were traumatized. Talk about blackboard jungles, physical attacks on teachers and school property, police in school corridors, focused attention on the child who could not keep still long enough to note what was being asked of him, who could not seem to sort out the stimuli of his school environment, and who could not respond in an organized way to these stimuli – a child whose ineptness combined with high energy earned him the tag of hyperkinetic. Inasmuch as even one such pupil could disrupt a classroom and several could turn it into a nightmare, it is understandable that the teacher would welcome the use of a drug that would quiet the pupil, if it did nothing else. If there were grounds for believing that the drug not only improved the pupil's scholastic achievement, teachers and many parents would be tempted to discount warnings about possible physical and psychological side effects (Broudy, 1975, pp. 45–6).

Discussion

There is little percentage in getting into the issue of whether drug treatments for hyperactivity work or whether associated clinical iatrogenic illnesses, such as insomnia, anorexia, and depressed height growth, can be controlled by refining drugs. I think that it is a fatal trap to fall into; for it is exactly where the medical and allied professions want their critics. There is no doubt that non-iatrogenic drug specific treatments have been and are being produced, and that these modify behaviours which someone, somewhere has defined as objectionable. But 'from a political and social perspective, the most dangerous psychoactive drug is precisely the one that is medically the safest and psychologically the most effective' (Schrag and Divoky, 1975, p. 106). To meet the medical and allied professions on their own ground, then, is to invite defeat. Rather it is the ideology which encourages us to view ourselves as surrounded by diseases, and not moral/political problems, which should be the focus of our critical attention. For unless we do, we may end up with a society whose normative boundaries are not only supported by medicine but have been medically constructed in the first place.

What I suggest this medical ideology leads to is an entirely new and frightening conception of school health care. Under the guidance or dominance of a therapeutic system of social control, the school system has shifted from screening, preventing and treating real diseases – that is, diseases of an organic kind, which refer to cellular pathology, to screening, preventing and treating non-organic behaviour disagreements – in such a way that it deliberately confuses curing diseases with controlling deviants. Ross and Ross write: 'Having always professed concern about *the whole child*, the school system is for the first time now assuming its rightful responsibility in this area', and that this has 'the potential to be the most important of all major advances in the 1970s' (Ross and Ross, 1976, p. 293). But they fail completely to spell out from whose vantage point, and with whose interests in mind it is a major advance. Surely it cannot be to the advantage of those thousands of schoolchildren who are suffering from nothing more than a desire to rebel at school, from boredom, from a sense of failure, born of an achievement-orientated school environment, who are fearful of a future of unemployment and the welfare, and who demand more of school than school can possibly give.

The discovery and treatment of hyperactivity should not be viewed as an accidental incursion of medicine into matters essentially moral; rather, it should be seen as merely another illustration of an ever-increasing process which has a long and continuous history. The medical profession has always been involved in transforming some moral and political issues into medical conditions. Its capacity to perform this definitional shift was enormously expanded when it annexed and acquired a legal monopoly of the mind as well as the body, for this allowed the discovery of diseases without the need to establish any observable or detectable organic impairment or malfunction (Scull, 1975). Removing the demonstrable organic basis for a disease enabled the profession to discover a whole spectrum of so-called mental illnesses, and for these to cover an ever-growing proportion of human behaviour. The wave of medical expansion, including hyperactivity, was given a shot in the arm by the pharmacological revolution over the last three decades, for it could now be seen to have greater technological control over the 'symptoms' of diseases, and therefore the medical profession to be the right one in charge of treating and containing illnesses.

Fortified by this massive 'technological–pharmaceutical' breakthrough, the state and its welfare apparatus have rapidly expanded, as reflected by the swelling army of prison medical officers, joint forensic consultants, social workers, mental health visitors, child care officers, school psychologists, and so on. A cynic might say that this army is deployed in such a way as effectively to occupy impoverished urban areas inhabited by the unemployed and potentially unemployable. This occupation has not merely consisted of 'treating' those already known to be violent, deviant or criminal, although the increasing employment of medical 'torture' in prisons and mental hospitals should not be minimised. It has also included a programme for subduing the population of 'potential' violent, deviant or criminal individuals. Since the medical model contains a justification for early detection and prevention, the discovery of numerous new diseases and disorders and the stretching of old diagnostic categories have provided the ideological justification for the welfare state and its control professions screening large sections of the potentially disruptive and recommending treatment for their conditions. In this way future urban riots might well be minimised. A generation of urban poor, many of them on prescribed drugs since their infancy, are hardly going to transcend their medication and revolt. Instead, they are likely to have internalised the medical view that they are indeed sick cases and merely seek medical or quasi-medical treatment should they even glimpse the possibility that industrial society is unfair, unequal and unjust.

At a structural and historical level, then, the growing medicalisation of social, moral and legal problems has developed as a series of rational and efficient solutions to contradictions thrown up by increasing industrialisation. The previous social control institutions, religion and then law, have been increasingly shown to be neither rational nor efficient, the first because it requires a leap into the arms of God which fewer and fewer people feel like taking, and the second because it provides too many rights and protections to those whom the welfare state views as 'dangerous' or 'potentially dangerous'. Medicalising these social issues justifies actions otherwise not permissible under religious or legal social control. It justifies intervening before any offence has been committed, it takes the issues out of public moral debate and places them into the secretive and impenetrable hands of the medical and allied professions, it avoids issues of civil rights and due process, it depoliticises, and it justifies the continuation of treatment long beyond the desert of any infractious behaviour, for it is no longer concerned with desert but with health. A modern Government can hardly turn such a gift-horse away: it offers so much and requires so little to establish. So let us thank medicine and its allied professions for our daily medicine; they are doing some of us a power of good, whilst the remainder are being stupefied into conformity. Social harmony is only a magic pill away.

But is not a 'welfare' system better than a 'rights' system.

5
The Contradictions of the Sixties Race Relations Legislation

John Lea

The aim of this chapter is to advance a hypothesis concerning the nature and effects of the race-relations legislation enacted during the period 1962–71. A decade later it is clear that the crisis in race relations has achieved dimensions that few, during the mid-sixties, would have conceived possible. It will be my contention that a major contributing factor to the present crisis is to be found in the contradictory nature of the sixties legislation, a contradiction arising from the dual function of the legislation in both promoting racial integration and at the same time securing the availability of a force of low-wage labour for certain sectors of the British economy.[1]

The ideological framework of state intervention in race relations

One of the characteristics of the British economy since the last war has been its low rate of growth. The post-war years of 1950–60 were years of comparatively rapid expansion in which Britain, like the other major European capitalist economies, experienced a severe shortage of labour. This shortage was met by labour immigration from underdeveloped areas, predominantly the ex-colonial territories of the new Commonwealth.

After 1960 growth rates began to decline, slowly at first, and differentially between the European economies. Britain's performance was among the worst. The resultant decline in excess labour demand was greater than that of other European economies, with the result that immigrant workers now constituted a smaller percentage of the work force than in the other major economies. The most recently available figures for immigrant workers as a proportion of the labour forces of the major European economies are as follows:

Britain 7 per cent, France 9 per cent and West Germany 11 per cent (Department of Employment, 1976).

It might be thought that such comparatively small numbers would make for easier assimilation, and this was undoubtedly a widely made assumption during the early years of immigration, when questions of immigrant assimilation were left to voluntary agencies. However, the low rate of economic growth had another consequence which strongly counteracted any such tendency, namely the concentration of immigrant workers in low-wage occupations, and in the areas of urban decay. This has resulted from the expansion of low-wage public service employment in the inner city, from the dependence of industrial modernisation in declining sectors such as textiles on low-wage labour and intensive use of shiftwork,[2] and, above all, from the lack of sufficient demand pull from the expansion of higher paid sectors of the economy. During the period 1961–9 Britain experienced a net population loss through migration of 600,000. Thus, while immigrants were entering to take up low-paid jobs being deserted by native labour, the expansion of higher paid employment seems to have been more than met by internal migration. From 1961 to 1966 there was in fact a decline in the proportion of male immigrants in white-collar occupations while the working population in general increased its representation in this category (Cohen, 1971). If British workers had been emigrating despite a labour shortage in higher paid white-collar occupations, then a gradual increase in the proportion of immigrants in this sector would have been expected.

It is not surprising that at the outset of a period of migration immigrants should be concentrated in low-paid jobs with bad working conditions. This is to be expected, since, initially, shortages in high-wage jobs will tend to be met by internal migration. What caused concern to observers of race relations during the sixties was the lack of any tendency for this concentration to break down. The first systematic survey of race relations in Britain was published in 1969 and confirmed this. Surveying the available data from the two census years of 1961 and 1966 the report sombrely concluded:

Finally, the concentration of coloured immigrants in certain sections of employment and their absence in others coupled with the fact that there has been little or no change between 1961 and 1966 gives most cause for concern. If this pattern continues into the 1970's then the assessment that the situation is still fluid and has not hardened into a class-colour or colour-caste structure may well be over optimistic (Rose *et al.*, 1969, p. 181).

Other indices pointed in the same direction. On the basis of comparisons of the data from 1961 and 1966 for London, Deakin and Ungerson confirmed that:

> . . . the position of blacks in the housing market showed very little improvement between 1961 and 1966, a period in which the housing circumstances of white families living in similar kinds of areas showed a substantial improvement. When allowance is made for a change in definition of a room between Censuses, the position of Indian and Pakistani migrants, taken together, actually deteriorated (Deakin and Ungerson, 1973, p. 228).

In other words, post-war economic expansion had been sufficient to draw immigrant workers into low-wage occupations vacated by native workers moving to higher paid jobs, but insufficient to break down the concentration of immigrants in such occupations (and consequently in certain areas of the city) and cause them to follow native workers in a process of occupational and geographical mobility. The result was that the benefits to capital of a labour supply suitable for the maintenance of low-wage jobs was being counterbalanced by the cost in terms of social tensions arising from the necessary concentration of this labour force in areas of housing shortage and general economic decay. On the other hand, any tendency to alleviate the concentration of immigrant workers in low-wage jobs and in the inner urban areas would threaten to eliminate precisely the supply of cheap labour. Only the intervention of the state could hope to resolve this contradiction.

The strategy of state intervention emerged at the beginning of the sixties, spurred on by the racial disturbances in Notting Hill in 1958, and crystallised around two main components – on the one hand, immigration controls, and, on the other, the erection of a system of law and quasi-state institutions designed to eliminate racial prejudice and discrimination in favour of equal opportunity for immigrants and their descendents with the general population in terms of access to jobs, housing, education, and social resources in general.

The main components of the sixties race-relations legislation are well known and can be briefly summarised. Firstly, immigration control in the form of the Commonwealth Immigration Act 1962 ended unrestricted immigration, that is, immigration governed solely by the state of supply and demand in the labour market, and instituted a voucher system of controls. This was amended and strengthened in various respects in 1965, 1968, 1969 and 1971. The changes included an ending of all unskilled labour immigration except for specific jobs, the ending of the automatic rights of British citizens to enter the country and, finally, the radical change brought about by the Immigration Act 1971, which brought British immigration law into correspondence with that of the EEC, thus ending the legal distinction between Commonwealth citizens and other immigrants.

The conception of immigration control as reciprocally linked to racial integration policies never wavered throughout the sixties and into the seventies. R. A. Butler, speaking for the Conservative government in the debate on the Commonwealth Immigration Bill 1962 claimed that 'the drive for improved conditions will be defeated by the sheer weight of numbers and the immigrants will be among those to benefit most if the powers in fact prove, as we hope, effective' (Hansard 16 November 1961, cols. 687–95). Nearly fifteen years later Roy Jenkins, speaking for the Labour government's Race Relations Bill, repeated these sentiments, which in 1961 his party had bitterly opposed: '. . . the third principle of government policy is that there is a clear limit to the amount of immigration that this country can absorb, and that it is in the interest of the racial minorities themselves to maintain a strict control of immigration' (Hansard, 4 June 1976, col. 1548).

The logic behind this thinking is quite straightforward. Other things being equal, notably the supply of housing and social expenditure, then a regulation of numbers is necessary to avoid racial conflict over the allocation of scarce resources until such time as the process of assimilation has ensured that immigrants and their descendents are no longer regarded as outsiders. The implausibility of this view and an alternative account of the relationship between immigration control and racial integration will be the subject of discussion below. For those immigrants already here and for their descendants integration was to proceed, in the words of Roy Jenkins, 'not as a flattening process of assimilation but as equal opportunity accompanied by cultural diversity in an atmosphere of mutual tolerance' (Rose *et al.*, 1969, p. 25).

The legislation to achieve this aim was mainly concentrated in the Race Relations Acts 1965 and 1968. The 1965 Act declared racial

discrimination illegal only in 'places of public resort'. Soon found to
be irrelevant to the main areas of racial discrimination, the law was
extended under the 1968 Act to cover housing, employment, and
other previously excluded areas. Employers were, however permitted to discriminate in order to retain a 'racial balance' in their
work force. Also established under the 1965 Act was the Race
Relations Board. Intended primarily as a mechanism of conciliation,
the board could only act indirectly, through the Attorney-General, if
conciliation procedures had failed to reach a settlement in a case of
alleged discrimination. The 1968 Act strengthened both the membership and the powers of the board, enabling it to act through the
county courts in cases where discrimination had failed. The board,
however, had no powers of subpoena and could only act in receipt of
a complaint. Finally, the 1965 Act established the National
Committee for Commonwealth Immigrants to co-ordinate the work
of local voluntary committees. It was transformed under the 1968
Act into the Community Relations Committee, a more centralised
structure in closer relation with the state, its functions being widened
to include both the promotion of 'harmonious community relations'
through local committees and educative propaganda, and, in addition, to advise Governments on race relations matters.

The organising concept of the integration programme was, as
defined by Jenkins, 'equal opportunity'. This concept is drawn from
the central tradition of liberal reformism, and like many other
conceptions of such origin it serves to articulate a view of social
equality compatible with the inequalities of income, property, and
conditions of life which are the necessary accompaniments of
industrial capitalism. This compatibility is achieved by the making of
a distinction between the socio-economic structure of capitalist society, with its attendant inequalities, and the individuals who
participate in that structure. Social equality can thus be defined as
attainable not in terms of the elimination of structured inequalities
but in terms of the opportunities for the mobility of individuals
within that structure.

The coherence of this separation between social structure and the
mobility of individuals within it is dependent on the location of the
constraints to individual mobility outside social structure itself. In
the case of immigrants and ethnic minorities two such impediments
to mobility are generally cited. Firstly, racial prejudice. If prejudice is
regarded as the major impediment to social mobility, then, as long as
the source of prejudice is not itself located in the social structure (e.g.

as a manifestation of class interest), the reforms necessary to achieve racial integration can be seen as changes in attitudes and not changes in social structure. Prejudice itself can be seen as stemming from personality dynamics, from the clash of cultures between immigrant and native, and even seen as having once corresponded to class interest but no longer doing so (though remaining as a hangover from the past, perpetuated in the popular consciousness, and out-of-date school history books containing prejudiced stereotypes etc.). The danger now is seen as prejudice, whatever its origins, being perpetuated and reinforced both among the native population in general and in particular those sections of it who may come to see themselves in competition with immigrants for employment or access to social resources. Secondly, came the attributes of the socially immobile themselves. People forced, for whatever reason, into slum housing and low paid, unsteady, employment develop, it is often argued, a 'culture of poverty', combining a resignation to poverty and a set of aspirations and habits which may prevent them from taking advantages of any opportunities for social mobility that do present themselves (Ryan, 1971).

The source of unequal opportunity is located, then, according to this conception, outside the fundamental inequalities functionally necessary to a capitalist society. It is freely admitted, however, that such inequalities of opportunity, once established, tend to perpetuate themselves. The main lines of this process of self-reinforcement – or to use Myrdal's phrase, 'cumulative causation' – are suggested in Figure 5.1.[3]

This conception of the essentially self-reinforcing process of racial prejudice, discrimination and the oppression of minorities leads to a very clear conception of the main tasks and methods of state intervention. Such intervention is seen as aiming to break the lines of reinforcement and indeed to reverse the process of cumulative causation. Thus educative measures aimed at reducing the incidence of racial prejudice will in turn reduce the incidence of discrimination. The latter can be reduced further, even among those who remain prejudiced, through legal action to outlaw discriminatory practices. The reduction of discrimination will result in increased social mobility for immigrants. This will reduce the self-confirming effect of racial stereotypes whereby racial prejudice, through discrimination and the forcing of minorities into the poorest sections of society, provides the very data that 'confirm' the view of immigrants as inferior in the minds of the prejudiced. At the same time increased

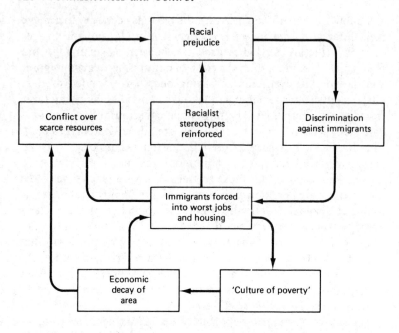

FIGURE 5.1   *The process of self-reinforcing inequality of opportunity*

immigrant social mobility will tend to separate the conflict over scarce resources in the poorer urban areas from the question of race, thereby removing a further cause of the reinforcement of racial prejudice.

This, then, was the internal logic of liberal strategy for racial integration as it was theorised by many of those who supported it and participated in its design. I have not intended to suggest that the British legislation necessarily explored thoroughly all the avenues derivable from these conceptions. Many aspects of British intervention in race relations were mild adaptions of strategies adopted on a grander scale in the United States. But, most important of all, in what follows I shall attempt to show that this conception is in fact a one-sided mystification and gives a false coherence to the sixties racial integration programme, removing from view its essentially contradictory nature. That contradiction, it will be argued, is rooted in the need of the legislation both to promote a programme of increased immigrant social mobility while at the same time preserving the advantages to certain sectors of employment that flowed from the existence of a pool of immigrant labour concentrated at the bottom of the socio-economic ladder, and held there by a combination of racial prejudice and the lack of demand pull from higher wage employment.

The failure of racial integration

Racial integration, as envisaged in the sixties legislation, has not to any significant extent occurred. The tendencies referred to above, which had been noticed by comparisons of the 1961 and 1966 census data, have generally continued into the seventies. The available evidence from the 1971 census on the socio-economic distribution of immigrants can be compared with similar data from the 1966 census. This is set out in Table 5.1. The situation described in the *Colour and Citizenship* report (Rose *et al.*, 1969), based on the comparison of the

TABLE 5.1 *Socio-economic distribution of economically active males born in certain New Commonwealth countries in 1966 and 1971*

Specified socio-economic groups	All persons in GB		West Indians		Pakistanis		Indians	
	1966	1971	1966	1971	1966	1971	1966	1971
Employers, managers and professional workers	14.3	16.5	2.1	2.8	5.6	7.5	16.9	17.2
Intermediate non-manual and personal service workers	18.1	18.5	6.4	8.2	7.8	8.3	20.3	16.8
Skilled manual workers, foremen and supervisors	35.1	33.6	40.0	40.5	19.5	21.5	24.8	27.1
Semi-skilled manual workers	14.9	12.8	25.9	23.6	31.8	32.7	20.3	20.5
Unskilled manual workers	8.3	7.7	21.5	15.8	30.6	22.8	11.5	11.1

SOURCE Department of Employment, *The Role of Immigrants in the Labour Market* (London: HMSO, 1976) table G5.

1961 and 1966 census data, has thus not altered significantly over the period between 1966 and 1971, certainly not sufficiently to enable one to conclude that the sixties legislation has set up a tendency for increased occupational mobility among immigrant groups. Most significant perhaps is the increased concentration of Asian immigrant groups in semi-skilled manual work, where the working population in general has been falling. In those areas of white-collar and professional employment towards which the working population as a whole is shifting immigrant groups are not making gains at a rate likely to overcome their under-representation in these categories. This situation is of course quite compatible with the existence of areas in which large proportions of both the working population in general and immigrant workers are to be found, as in skilled manual work. The developing situation appears to be one of polarisation at either end of the socio-economic scale.

More recent research, notably that carried out by the Political and Economic Planning organisation (PEP) does not give any reason to modify these conclusions. D. J. Smith, in his recent summary of the PEP research, argues:

> If the minorities were upwardly mobile we would expect to find that those who came to Britain recently were at lower job levels and had lower earnings than those who came to Britain longer ago. Unfortunately the interpretation of such analyses is complicated by a number of factors . . . Nevertheless some tentative conclusions can be drawn . . . The job levels of those who came to Britain up to 1962 and afterwards are very similar . . . The analysis is enough to show that the concentration of minorities in poorer jobs is not a temporary phenomenon which will be corrected quickly, for those who came to Britain twelve or more years ago are still doing substantially inferior jobs to whites . . . In short there is little evidence that racial inequalities in the employment field will be quickly corrected by upward mobility of Asians and West Indians (Smith, 1977 pp. 189–90).

As regards geographical concentration, Smith concludes: 'From all the available evidence the answer to the question "is dispersal happening?" seems to be no. In some areas there is an increasing tendency to concentration' (Smith, 1977, p. 297). If immigrants were achieving significant social and occupational mobility, a degree of dispersal would be expected as rising incomes and new job locations stimulated movement out of the initial areas of concentration. Ability to disperse would, of course, irrespective of income, be constrained by racial prejudice in new housing areas. Nevertheless the strong tendency reported by Smith (1977, p. 296) for middle-class Asians to live outside the immigrant concentrations shows that some movement would be possible. But what is lacking is evidence of such movement. The PEP research 'shows that there is no relationship at all, either for Asians or for West Indians, between the length of time they have lived in Britain and the level of concentration of immigrants in the areas where they live' (Smith, 1977, p. 296).

Smith himself is of the opinion that the Race Relations Act 1968 has not been without a measure of success. It is important to study his argument:

The first substantive issue is whether the 1968 Act has proved a failure. Our findings show that there has been a sharp decrease in the extent of discrimination in the field of housing since 1967; all the indications are that there has been a similar decrease in the field of employment too, although the data for 1967 and 1974 are not here strictly comparable. There has certainly been a change in the general climate of opinion, leading to a decrease in open and admitted acts of discrimination: few employers will now admit that they have discriminated on racial grounds, and advertisements specifying 'no coloureds' which were very common in 1967 have almost disappeared. Partly because of the actual decrease in discrimination, and partly because it has become more covert, many fewer Asians and West Indians than in 1967 think they have been victims of a discriminatory act; also those who came to Britain recently are far less likely to believe that discrimination occurs and to claim experience of it than those who came earlier, at a time when there was massive discrimination, some of it quite crude and open. The statement that the 1968 Act has been a complete failure flies in the face of the facts (Smith, 1977, pp. 311–12).

Smith's optimism is hard to square with his carefully documented conclusion as to the absence of upward social mobility for immigrants. It is based in fact on empiricism which cannot be allowed to pass without comment. He places major emphasis on the decline in reported discrimination between the two PEP surveys of 1967 and 1974. Firstly, in other parts of his book he is more cautious as to the conclusions that can be drawn from a decline in reported discrimination. Thus 'the proportions claiming that they personally have experienced discrimination are low . . . This further reinforces the point that the victims of discrimination are not usually aware of it' (Smith, 1977, p. 128). One could only reconcile this with Smith's general conclusion if it could be shown to be the case, for example, that a *constant* proportion of respondents in the two surveys were unaware of the fact that they were being discriminated against. Under such conditions a decline in reported discrimination would indicate some decline in actual discrimination, though how much would depend on what proportion of respondents in the surveys were unaware of the discrimination imposed upon them. Smith does not discuss this question, though he tends to suggest (see below) that the proportion of cases of actual discrimination that could be proved is very small.

Secondly, it is important to recall that the manifest aim of the sixties legislation was 'equal opportunity'. It is quite possible for a decline in reported discrimination to accompany a decline, as well as an increase, in opportunity. Increased immigrant concentration in declining and inner-city areas may result in diminishing contact with and therefore immediate competition with natives for certain types of housing and employment. Smith (1977, p. 182) cites evidence of a tendency on the part of immigrant workers to apply for jobs where there is a known chance of acceptance. Finally, declining experience of discrimination may well represent the opening up of some new areas of employment to immigrants. But this does not necessarily imply social mobility; it may mean simply that the range of low-paid, low-status jobs into which immigrants are accepted for employment is widening. This is no gain in the direction of equal opportunity.

One is aware that Smith has separated the question of discrimination – that is, reported discrimination – from the question of equal opportunity. Thus his conclusion represents in fact a retreat from the aspirations of the sixties legislation. A decline in reported discrimination is quite compatible, I have argued, with the lack of social mobility of immigrants. Low-wage employers not only get used to, but may positively seek, immigrant labour. Landlords in immigrant areas get used to immigrant tenants as native applicants become scarcer. If a buoyant economy were creating labour shortages in areas previously closed to immigrants, then the latter would be encouraged to apply for jobs and houses in new areas. Under such circumstances reported discrimination would remain high or even increase as employers, landlords, and native workers initially reacted to the presence of immigrants. In the long run discrimination would decline as conditions in the labour market made for the acceptance of immigrant workers.

Thus it seems that a decline in reported discrimination indicates more than anything else a stabilisation of race relations. Such a stabilisation may or may not be associated with the achievement of social mobility for immigrants and a state of affairs approaching equal opportunity. Stabilisation short of equal opportunity means the persistence of potential discrimination awaiting any immigrant who should attempt to move into new areas. In other words, a decline in actual experienced discrimination against individuals may be a result of socially entrenched discrimination.

However, there is a far more fundamental problem which arises at this point, and that is the problem of the nature of discrimination. Smith and many other commentators define racial discrimination in terms of refusal of access to employment, certain social rights, and other resources. While this is of course a correct description of the effects of discrimination, it is important to distinguish this effect from the mechanisms which achieve it. The mechanism of discrimination comprises a combination of refusal of access to employment etc. in some areas and an acceptance of immigrants in others. These two aspects are interdependent. Acceptance of immigrants is associated in a large number of cases with their 'willingness' to accept wages and conditions of work that native workers would reject. This 'willingness' is a product of their exclusion from other areas of employment, coupled with the ability of employers to deny immigrants access to effective trade-union rights. The *Colour and Citizenship* report studiously avoided this dual nature of the discrimination process: 'The basic problem should not, however, be seen in those sectors of employment that have over-concentrations of coloured immigrants but in those that have few. It is in the occupations and industries where the coloured immigrant is rare or absent that answers to the concentration, lack of achievement and frustration are to be found' (Rose, *et al.*, 1969, p. 181).

It is important to understand that only such a one-sided conception of the nature of the discrimination process is compatible with the 'equal opportunity' strategy. Such a strategy depends for its coherence, as I have argued, on the analytical separation of the socio-economic structure from the mobility of individuals within it. If the elimination of discrimination is seen as involving simply the widening of access to areas of socio-economic structure, then it would be difficult to see how it could have much effect on the structure itself. However, once it is understood that the process of refusal of access to some areas of the structure is part of a mechanism which guarantees the availability of the immigrant for employment in other areas at the wages desired, then it can be seen that the 'elimination of discrimination' is no simple matter. Specifically, we are presented with the problem of how low-wage sectors of employment previously dependent upon immigrants are to retain their labour force in the absence of racial discrimination against immigrants in higher paid jobs, given that racial discrimination has been a major mechanism serving to guarantee the availability of immigrants as a pool of cheap labour.

Under conditions of economic expansion this problem can be self-solving. The upward social and occupational mobility of existing immigrants and their increasing unwillingness, due to socialisation, to accept low-wage employment can be offset through their replacement in the latter sectors by fresh immigration. This solution is maximally effective for capital if any decline in racial prejudice towards existing immigrants does not apply to new immigrants, as would be the case if new immigrants came from different regions or ethnic groups to the existing immigrant communities.

Under conditions of economic stagnation, however, where there is little new immigration, owing to low levels of labour demand, two problems present themselves from the standpoint of capital. First, if a strategy of equal opportunity is not to disrupt the socio-economic structure by placing in jeopardy the survival of low-wage sectors, then some mechanism must be found to prevent the removal of discrimination (in the sense of refusal of access) from bringing about the collapse of the other aspect of discrimination (use of immigrants as low-wage labour). But, second, under conditions of economic stagnations there is, quite apart from racial prejudice, little occupational and social mobility of the existing immigrant community, and therefore the actual task of removing discrimination falls to the state. However, the elimination of racial discrimination by law in a liberal democratic state necessarily applies universally, to all immigrants and ethnic minorities. Hence an effective programme of anti-discrimination legislation threatens to clash with the needs of sections of capital for a low-wage labour force. The only possible reconciliation of these two aims involves the introduction of inconsistencies at the heart of state intervention which threaten to render it ineffective. This I shall argue in the remainder of this paper explains the failure, and contradictory nature, of the sixties legislation.

Immigration control and racial integration

Let us assume that state intervention in the form of the sixties legislation had been successful in achieving a qualitative reduction in racial prejudice and discrimination. What would have been the consequences?

The absence of discrimination, coupled with the increasing socialisation of immigrant workers, would have laid the basis for a strengthening of trade-union organisation and industrial militancy among immigrant workers which would have threatened to undermine low-wage labour in sectors dependent upon immigrant labour to maintain such conditions. It might be argued that the weakness of trade-union organisation in sectors with a high proportion of immigrant workers would have in any case been perpetuated by rising unemployment as economic stagnation set in at the beginning of the seventies. However, it is unlikely that this would have been the case. From the strike at Woolf's in Southall in 1965, through the spate of actions in the East Midlands' textile industry in 1972–3, including the well known Mansfield Hosiery strike, up to the recent struggle for trade-union recognition by immigrant workers at Grunwick's in North London, it has been demonstrated that immigrant workers exhibit a capacity for industrial militancy often well in advance of those native workers remaining in employment in the same sectors. Immigrant workers in a number of cases have taken the lead in fighting to establish branches of the stronger industrial unions in areas where union organisation has been weak or non-existent. An effective state-enforced mechanism for the dismantling of racial discrimination would have given a strong reinforcement to these tendencies. Furthermore, in an environment of declining racial discrimination and prejudice immigrant workers would begin to behave more like the majority of native workers and increasingly reject jobs offering low wages, unsocial hours, shiftwork and heavy work intensity, even under conditions of rising unemployment.

The task confronting the state was thus to attempt a reconciliation of the immediate concerns of capital for cheap labour, on the one hand, and the wider problem of deteriorating urban social conditions with the attendant threat of racial conflict, on the other. At first sight it seems that the solution embodied in the sixties legislation ignored the concerns of those sections of capital to which cheap immigrant labour was important. The programme of racial integration and anti-discrimination legislation threatened to weaken social control over immigrant workers, and immigration controls, held to be a necessary prerequisite for successful integration, threatened to end the supply of cheap labour. The latter conflict – between immigration controls and cheap labour – never materialised, as it had shown signs of doing in some European countries in the early seventies (cf. Power, 1975, pp. 338–40), by virtue of the slower rate of expansion of the British economy during the sixties.

As we have seen, the conceptions in terms of which the sixties legislation was formulated and explained stipulated a regulation of immigrant numbers as essential to successful integration. Critics of such measures generally attacked them in the first instance as unnecessary: first, because immigration was essentially self-regulating by means of the balance of supply and demand in the labour market, and, second, that the numbers of immigrants were too small to affect to any significant extent the housing shortage or the strain on social resources. Indeed, an important piece of research conducted in the mid-sixties showed that immigrants generally claimed less from social-service benefits than the indigenous population.[4]

However, this was not the only consideration in terms of which immigration control was seen as necessary to successful integration policies, as the White Paper preceding the 1965 legislation made clear: 'It must be recognised that the presence in this country of nearly one million immigrants from the Commonwealth with different cultural and social backgrounds raises a number of problems and creates various social tensions in those areas where they have concentrated' (HMSO, 1965, note 9).

Again, if the problem was cultural antagonism between immigrants and the native population, immigrant controls in no way assist in the alleviation of such conflict. It is not the numbers of immigrants *per se* but the availability of racism as an ideology which is instrumental in presenting deteriorating social conditions in the inner cities as rooted in the presence of immigrants. Indeed, in this respect immigration controls have positively hindered racial integration through their general ideological effect, ably transmitted and magnified by the media, in locating the immigrant as the source of the urban crisis.

Immigration controls, however, have from the outset of the sixties legislation been concerned with more than simple restrictions upon numbers. A closer look at the legislation reveals that, in addition to this function, it has, up to and including the Immigration Act 1971, consistently expanded the control and surveillance functions of the state in relation to immigrants. This has taken in three main areas:

1. Control at the point of entry, through the necessity for all new immigrant workers (since the coming into force of the 1971 Act) who are neither EEC nationals nor 'patrials' under the terms of the Act to secure work permits; the necessity for the dependents of resident immigrants to secure entry certificates (under 1969 legislation), the percentage of refusals of which have been increasing in recent years; and through the power of the immigration officer at the port of entry to refuse admission, on occasion in excess of powers derived from legislation. [5]
2. The power of deportation from Britain for indictable offences, or if the Home Secretary considers such to be required by the 'public good', or for illegal entry. The last, while it may in theory concern only a small minority of immigrants, in fact creates, in the form of search for illegal residents, a widening of the areas of state intrusion into the personal lives of wide sections of the immigrant community. In this context the formation of the Home Office National Immigration Intelligence Unit in 1973 exemplifies a general trend towards the development of techniques of mass surveillance by the state.
3. Control by the employer of the immigrant worker is intensified under the 1971 Act during the initial period of residence through the consent necessary by the employer for the annual renewal of work permits.

The process of tightening up surveillance and control of immigrants at the same time as a full-scale programme of racial integration was allegedly under way seems at first sight to be contradictory. At one level of course it was and is. Without doubt the strengthening of immigration controls has been a major factor in the general alienation of the immigrant community from a more positive view of the role of the state in race relations, an attitude that it was a major aim of the integration programme to create. On what level, then, does the immigration control aspect of the sixties legislation become part of a coherent strategy?

The immigrant population already resident in the UK was largely, irrespective of the original intentions of the migrants, a settled community. As such it was producing a second generation which, having passed through the education system, was not only better equipped for and more vociferous in demanding a spectrum of job opportunities identical with that of working-class youth in general, but was increasingly unwilling to tolerate the type of working conditions and levels of pay that its parents accepted. The avoidance of increasing frustration, tension and conflict in the inner cities thus clearly dictated that an integration programme be inaugurated during the sixties. However, a state onslaught on racial discrimination and prejudice would be necessarily universalistic in character and would apply to all minorities now and in the future. It would thus undermine the basis of cheap labour for sections of both capital and state employment itself. The maintenance of a labour force available for low-wage and intensive working conditions in an environment of absent or weakening racial prejudice and discrimination required the elaboration of some formal legal criteria whereby a section of the immigrant work force could be excluded from the effects of racial integration. There was only one sphere in which this could be done without openly conflicting with not only the integration programme itself but with liberal democratic values in general. The development of liberal democracy has not only paralleled but has been integrally related to the rise of the nation state. It is not surprising therefore that the one area in which a high degree of supervision and control, at times approaching the arbitrary, is acceptable to a liberal democracy is in the crossing of the boundaries of the nation state. Such control in this area is also advantageously out of sight of the citizenry at large.

Far from racial integration requiring as one of its prerequisites the control of immigration to limit numbers, racial integration requires, if it is not to disrupt certain sectors of the socio-economic structure, immigration controls as a form of social discipline to insulate, through the minimisation of civil rights, at least a section of the immigrant work force from the effects of the integration programme. This process of insulation reached its conclusion in the form of the Immigration Act 1971, which completed the process of eliminating the effects of the special status of Commonwealth citizenship begun in 1962. Long before this process was completed in 1971, however, there was a marked tendency in the recruitment of immigrant labour after 1962 to shift to the recruitment of immigrants from outside the New Commonwealth, who fell automatically under the Aliens legislation and the rigours of the work-permit system. This is

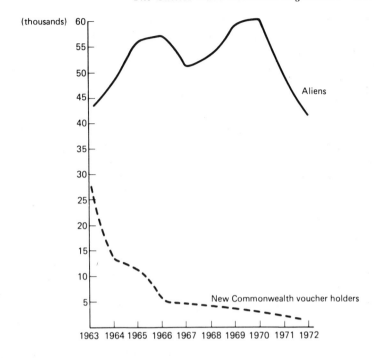

SOURCE   Based on Department of Employment, *The Role of Immigrants in the Labour market* (London: HMSO, 1976) tables B7, B13.

FIGURE 5.2   *The relationship between employment voucher holders under the Commonwealth Immigration and Aliens Acts admitted to the UK*

illustrated in Figure 5.2. Again it is clear from these figures that the effect of the 1962 Act was not simply to regulate numbers but to permit a shift in the structure of immigration in the direction of an immigrant labour force amenable to control and supervision.

This relation between immigration control and racial integration is uneasy, as we have said. We have mentioned the political effect of controls both in alienating the immigrant community and focusing on the black community as a scapegoat for social problems. In addition, from the viewpoint of those sections of capital dependent upon a cheap labour force, the surveillance and control effects of immigration legislation apply, except for the spread effects in the field of surveillance, only to new immigrants in a period in which, owing to economic stagnation, little new immigration is to be expected, or, in aggregate, required by capital. Thus the strengthening of immigration controls only partially solved the problem of the reconciliation of racial integration with cheap labour.

The machinery of racial integration

When we turn, therefore, to consider the machinery and legislation established during the sixties for the purposes of racial integration, instead of discovering a coherent single-mindedness, as we might have been led to expect from a study of the conceptual scheme in terms of which such legislation was articulated, we find weaknesses and contradictions which point in the direction of an attempt to embrace within the mechanism of racial integration itself the conflicting objectives I have mentioned above. By far the most important example of this was the seeming determination of the sixties legislation to avoid at all costs any intrusion in the labour market. There are two aspects to this: first, the orientation of the anti-discrimination legislation towards the question of refusal to employ, or to allow access to resources rather than to the conditions under which access to employment, housing etc. was granted; and, second, the choice of the community rather than the labour market as the arena in which the major thrust of the integration machinery was to be directed.

The reluctance of the state to allow integration policies to interfere with the operation of the labour market is shown perhaps in the studious avoidance of the area in the 1965 Act. Even the 1968 Act, which made discrimination illegal in employment, exempted actions taken by employers 'in good faith' to maintain a 'racial balance' in a work-place. However, at this level it can of course be argued that it was a combination of public opinion, together with the opposition of the TUC and the Confederation of British Industries to any further extension of state interference in the company and the work-place, which delayed and then ensured the weakness of legislation in this area.

More fruitful, therefore, is to look not so much at the delay and weakening of legislation applying to the labour market but at its underlying structure, its conception of the problem to be eliminated. It is clear that the problem of discrimination in the labour market is defined as the problem of the refusal to hire. The adoption of this perspective ensured that the eyes of the state were focused primarily on the higher wage employer who refused black labour rather than on the low-wage employer who relied on the exploitation of black and immigrant workers. The latter, in fact, was not defined as a problem.

Of course, in theory, if the discrimination against black workers and other immigrants in higher paid jobs were eliminated, low-wage employers would have to raise wages and improve working conditions to retain their labour force. As I have argued above, it was to avoid just such a development that immigration controls were an essential accompaniment to racial integration. But the very attempt to eliminate discrimination by focusing on refusal of access meant that discrimination was to be dealt with as it applied to individuals: by the reporting of individual cases of discrimination to the Race Relations Board. Yet such manifestations of discrimination are notoriously difficult to identify, let alone prove in a court of law.

One method of assessing the existence of individual cases of discrimination used by the PEP research has been the 'actor test', in which applicants of different ethnic backgrounds but identical in other respects are sent to apply for the same vacancy. Smith makes the following point: 'As they stand and by themselves the tests would probably fail [as evidence in law] because there is no detailed background information about the firm and because nothing is known about the intentions of the discriminators (under the present law there must be proof of intent)'[6] (Smith, 1977, p. 115).

Referring to the fact that in 1973 the Race Relations Board dealt with 150 complaints regarding employment discrimination and confirmed discrimination in all but 16 per cent of them, Smith estimates that in the sphere of unskilled employment alone, assuming accuracy on the part of the actor tests as indicators of percentages of cases in which job applications will be met with discrimination, there must be about 6,000 cases of discrimination a year in this sector alone. It is hardly necessary to add that the ordinary individual applicant is in an even weaker position as regards the identification of discrimination than the participants in the actor tests.

Thus the functions of immigrant labour as cheap labour, and labour available for working conditions which the majority of workers would reject, are in fact protected by the anti-discrimination legislation. Any other policy – for example, that of outlawing directly the use of immigrants or any other category of workers as low-wage labour – would have stood in direct conflict with the conditions necessary to the survival of important sections of the economy.

Such legislation is, however, logically possible. Indeed regulation of working conditions has been a constant feature of reforms under industrial capitalism from the nineteenth century. An example of such legislation preventing the super-exploitation of 'minority-group' workers is, for example, the prevention of night-shift work by women. However, the prohibition of female night work was precisely the obstacle to the intensive use of labour which led employers in the textile industry to switch increasingly from female to. immigrant labour from the mid-fifties onwards. The passing of similar legislation to regulate shifts, rates of pay and work intensity would defeat the very purpose for which immigrant labour was recruited in the first place.[7]

Community relations

One of the few writers on race relations to have noted the significance of the institutional structure created by the sixties legislation is Ira Katznelson:

> In the critical period of the migration of Third World people to Britain, the most critical structural decision made was the establishment of national and local institutions outside of the traditional political arenas to deal with the issues of race. The structural arrangements . . . did not integrate the Third World immigrants into the politics of institutionalised class conflict that characterise the liberal collectivist age, but rather set up alternative political structures to deflect the politics of race from Westminster to the National Committee for Commonwealth Immigrants, and from local political arenas to the voluntary liaison committees (Katznelson, 1973, p. 150).

The result was that 'the Third World population has been institutionally separated from the society-wide, largely class-based network of political institutions and associations, and has been unable to compete effectively for the scarce resource of political power' (Katznelson, 1973, p. 178).[8]

Thus the avoidance of a strong attack on racial discrimination in the labour market and the work-place is paralleled by a similar avoidance in these areas in that part of the state initiative concerned with the elimination of prejudiced attitudes. It might be thought that, having declared discrimination in the labour market and the work-place illegal (under the 1968 Act), it was only natural that the state machinery aimed at encouraging racial tolerance, cultural pluralism, and the breakdown of prejudice, should have concentrated its attention on the community at large rather than the specific areas of the labour market and the work-place. This is because only a section of the potentially racially prejudiced native population is included in trade-union and work-place organisation, because labour-market and work-place discrimination is only one manifestation of racial discrimination, and finally because with growing unemployment, especially in the inner urban areas, the traditional institutions of the labour market are becoming less relevant for the population of these areas when viewed as mechanisms of social integration.

There are, in fact, two distinct questions here. First, the fundamental role of employment as the key to the elimination of racial prejudice does not lie simply in the number of workers, immigrant and native, who are employed or in trade unions, but in the fact that conflict over employment, wages and the geographical distribution of jobs are (1) crucial factors themselves in sustaining racial prejudice and (2) have a determining influence over other conflicts generative of prejudice, such as access to housing.

However, there is a second sense in which the avoidance of the labour market and work-place as the most important terrains for the elimination of racial prejudice is crucial in determining the nature and functions of the sixties legislation. Granted that anti-discrimination intervention by the state leaves the position of immigrant workers in the labour market virtually intact, then an intervention aimed at the elimination of prejudice which concentrates on the community as its terrain of operation cannot but metamorphose into a strategy of containment and stabilisation of the immigrant population. In this context the question of employment takes on a precise significance. To the extent that a high rate of unemployment generally among immigrant workers is directly related to their position in the labour market as part of the unskilled/semi-skilled low-wage labour force, highly vulnerable to fluctuations in the demand for labour, then the state indeed exhibits a rational response in focusing its attention on the community at large rather than on the labour market. It is precisely in the former area that mechanisms of social control appropriate to the supervision of a section of the labour force highly vulnerable to unemployment must be located in order to be effective.

The machinery established under the 1965 and 1968 Acts was thus primarily, quite irrespective of intention, an apparatus of social control and not one designed to assist immigrants to mobilise against racial discrimination. The National Committee for Commonwealth Immigrants' guidelines on the formation of local voluntary liaison committees in 1967 expressly warned that 'it should be emphasised at every stage that this is not a committee to serve the interests of one section of the community but a committee to promote racial harmony. It is therefore beneficial to all'.[9]

In conditions in which the basic sources of racial inequalities remained largely undisturbed such a conception of 'racial harmony' could not but become a conception of social control and stabilisation. Such a function dictated that the machinery of 'racial harmony' remain firmly under the control of the central state apparatus through the careful selection of its leadership. This was achieved from the outset.[10] At the local level the voluntary liaison committees and later the local community relations committees, as they became under the 1968 Act, were staffed by predominantly middle-class elements from within the immigrant community itself.[11] Any articulate working-class, or politically radical, leadership would have threatened to line up a local committee too closely with immigrant grievances and class issues to maintain the 'beneficial to all' functions of local committees.

How far has this apparatus of social control over the immigrant community succeeded? According to Sivanandan, the Community Relations Commission, which replaced the National Committee for Commonwealth Immigrants in 1968,

> . . . took up the black cause and killed it. With the help of its 'black' staff and 'black' experts, with the help of an old colonial elite and through the creation of a new one, it financed, assisted, and helped to set up black self-help groups, youth clubs, supplementary schools, cultural centres, houses and hostels . . . it has together with the [Race Relations] Board created a black bourgeoisie, especially West Indian (the Asian bourgeoisie was already in the wings) to which the state can now hand over control of black dissidents in general and black youth in particular. In terms of the larger picture, what has been achieved in half a decade is the accommodation of West Indian militant politics within the framework of social democracy. The Asians had already settled into the cultural pluralist set-up ordained for them by the state as far back as a decade ago. They had their own TV and radio

programmes, their Mosques and their Temples, their shops and cinemas, and social centres. More importantly they had thrown up leaders who spoke to and worked with the state (Sivanandan, 1976, pp. 364–5).

It is important to distinguish, however, between the existence of a black middle class – made up of small-business and white-collar professional elements – and the ability of such a group to act independently in such a way as to gain a degree of political hegemony over the black community. The initial experiment in this direction was abortive. The establishment of a new state machinery of integration/stabilisation required a reformist civil-rights movement within the immigrant community with which a dialogue could be established linking the black community to the state. The most important initiative in this direction was the founding of the Campaign against Racial Discrimination (CARD) in 1965 as an umbrella organisation to bring the existing immigrant political and community groups into a closer dialogue with the state. Eventually two major immigrant organisations – the West Indian Standing Conference, and the National Federation of Pakistani Organisations – affiliated to CARD, but the important Indian Workers Association could see no purpose in affiliation. A year later the West Indian and Pakistani organisations left CARD, when two members of its national committee took up offers to serve on the National Committee for Commonwealth Immigrants. This action of CARD leaders was sufficient to precipitate a break-up of the organisation (see Heineman, 1972), revealing clearly the weakness of the black middle class and its lack of hegemony over the black community as a whole.

After the CARD experience the state machinery itself was strengthened. Under the 1968 Act the National Committee for Commonwealth Immigrants, which had been a voluntary body, was replaced by the Community Relations Commission, an organ fully integrated into the state apparatus and responsible to the Home Office. It was clear that a black middle class existed. What was not clear, however, was its capacity to provide leadership. Every leadership in a class, community, or other grouping has to establish its hegemony on the basis of some gains which it can be seen to have achieved for its constituency. Only by having achieved leadership by such means can it then turn to exercise a function of restraint and control. The leadership of the trade-union movement, for example, has been able in the recent period to call for large sacrifices from working-class people on questions such as wage restraint. Its success is by no means guaranteed, but its ability even to attempt such a role lies in the fact that it represents a political tradition that has, in the past, achieved real reforms for working-class people.

By contrast, the essential dilemma of leadership in the black community is this: unable to permit the integration of the immigrant workers on a class basis, the state was faced with the task of creating a leadership in the immigrant community under conditions in which any real gains for immigrants in terms of the elimination of racial discrimination or a significant degree of occupational and social mobility were not possible. Indeed, had they been possible, then integration of immigrants on a class basis would have proceeded ahead in any case.

After the collapse of CARD it was clear that a credible black middle class would have to have state finance placed at its disposal if it was to show any gains for the community. The machinery for this existed in the Urban Programme initiated by the Local Government Grants (Social Needs) Act 1969, which allowed funds to be directed to immigrant organisations especially aimed at youth and community work, and 'self-help' in deprived areas. During the early seventies this was attempted. However, quite apart from the smallness of the funds available, such urban aid has not and indeed cannot focus on the most important single factor in the success or failure of the black middle class to establish its leadership, namely, the amelioration of the growing unemployment affecting second-generation black youth, who now consist of growing proportions of the respective black communities[12] and face a disproportionate level of unemployment.[13] The Department of Employment project report of November 1976 noted that many black youth 'have rejected what they see as the low status, menial jobs accepted by their parents and in some instances have effectively dropped out of the labour market' (Department of Employment, 1976, p. 79). The report noted that 'a number of the employers and industrial training boards visited during the Unit's project referred to considerable difficulties in attracting school leavers, whatever their ethnic origins into the less popular unskilled and semi-skilled jobs'. The report concluded that 'it may therefore become more and more difficult to rely on immigrants and their descendants as a source of labour for jobs other workers find unattractive' (Department of Employment, 1976, p. 84).

A combination of disproportionately high unemployment at the same time as increasing difficulty in forcing black youth into low-wage jobs suggests that black youth are refusing the latter not because of increasing opportunities elsewhere derived from economic expansion but because of their socialisation and adoption consequently of the same spectrum of aspirations as that of working-class youth in general. The hegemony of the black middle class thus becomes predicated on the provision of gains which are just not possible in conditions of economic stagnation. Now that black youth are rejecting a role as cheap labour, on their own initiative, there is even less that the middle class can do to control them. The result, in the form of growing frustration and simmering anger among black youth, signals the failure of the sixties legislation to have provided a coherent framework for the stabilisation of race relations from the standpoint of capital, let alone a coherent strategy for genuine racial integration.

Conclusion

To conclude, I shall summarise the hypothesis that this chapter has attempted to elaborate. The use of immigrant labour, by capital, as a particular type of labour force – one which accepts wages and working conditions that few indigenous workers would tolerate – poses, under conditions of organised mass industrial trade unionism, particular problems of social control for capital. On the one hand, to preserve the cheap labour function of immigrants, it is in the interests of capital, particularly those sections immediately concerned, to prevent immigrants as far as possible from coming to exercise the organisational and bargaining strength characteristic of the working class as a whole. On the other hand, immigrants, by virtue of their employment, become concentrated in areas of high economic and social deprivation. If the intensification of racial antagonism and conflict in these areas is to be minimised, and it is surely in the interests of capital to minimise such social instability, then a policy of racial integration is called for. Such a policy, however, threatens to undermine the very cheap labour function of immigrants.

The solution adopted by governments in Britain and embedded in the legislation of the sixties has been to combine the racial integration of the settled community of immigrants with a system of increasing legal control over further immigrants to prevent the latter benefiting from the hoped-for atmosphere of harmonious race relations. However, the economic downturn during the sixties meant that despite a considerable switch from New Commonwealth immigrants (who, owing to the anachronisms of a colonial past, arrived possessed of citizenship) to controllable non-Commonwealth immigrants, the settled black immigrant community still had a role to play as cheap labour. Because of this the conflicting principles of integration and control were built into the machinery for racial integration itself, transforming it into a machinery for social control. The consequence is that racial integration has failed. But, perhaps more important from the viewpoint of capital, so has social control. The plausibility of a scenario in which a conformist black middle class exercises a pacifying hegemony over the ghettos of the inner city has steadily declined throughout the seventies, with the worsening of the economic crisis and the changing aspirations of black youth.

6
Ghettos of Freedom

An examination of permissiveness

Victoria Greenwood and Jock Young

Nostalgia is in vogue; myths die hard; amidst the crisis of the seventies, with all its restrictive and repressive overtones, we reflect and reminisce on the golden past of the swinging sixties. Prey to romanticism, we depict an era of liberalism and permissiveness, when the limits and restrictions of post-war Britain were torn asunder by a new morality of freedom and when an enlightened Parliament endorsed the move into a progressive era. What are the truths behind such a cultural revolution? We have chosen four areas where the new morality would supposedly have its greatest impact: prostitution, homosexuality, drugs and abortion.[1] We propose to examine the legislation of this period with an eye to significant change – to test the myth of permissiveness.

At the outset we confront two puzzles when we examine these areas. Firstly, these activities have in common that, although they occur between consenting partners and have no direct victims in the outside world, they all generate an extraordinary degree of public hysteria and moral outrage. These 'crimes without victims' have a grim fascination for the mass media and public, often comparable with the concern over crimes with obvious victims, such as burglary and mugging. The problem, then, is what is the social basis of the legislation in these supposedly victimless areas. What is behind the common distinction between the control of crime and of morality. In particular, it is strange that if the sixties involved a gradual rationalisation and liberalisation in these areas, it was also characterised by a series of moral panics over permissiveness. On the most overt level the Profumo affair, the arrest of Mick Jagger on drugs charges, the tales of Britain as an 'Abortion Mecca', and the constant theme of Youth as the enemy, from Mods and Rockers to Hippies, scarcely suggest a non-ambivalent mood of permissiveness.

The second puzzle is that existing attempts to describe the trends in legislation in Britain give rise to seemingly contradictory assessments.

1. There are those who see the sixties as a period of increasing liberalisation of legal control. Acts which were once subject to sanctions become decriminalised, and the individuals concerned are integrated into the spectrum of normal human behaviour. Let us call this process *normalisation*.

2. There are those who see an increasing use of scientific techniques in the deployment of reaction to deviance. Decriminalisation occurs, but where we once had the wilful perpetrator of evil deeds (who must be punished), we now have the sick deviant, a victim of his or her own under-socialisation (who must be treated rather than punished). Let us call this process the *medicalisation* of social problems. By this we include the whole gamut of therapeutic approaches to the 'cure' of deviancy, ranging from drug therapy through psychotherapy to the use of therapeutic communities.

3. There are others who view Britain as becoming increasingly coercive. The caring welfare state of the sixties is seen, in the seventies, to progressively discard its liberal rhetoric and actively criminalise new areas of behaviour whilst becoming increasingly punitive against existing crimes. This is simple *criminalisation*.

Now whereas the myth of the sixties would suggest that normalisation occurred in these areas, the most perfunctory examination of the period suggests otherwise. Some prostitutes suffer extreme legal harassment, other financially flourish; some homosexuals are legally ignored whilst others are seen as suitable cases for treatment; and in the drugs field 'pushers' are subject to longer sentences whereas the majority of cannabis smokers become of little interest to the police. Processes of normalisation, medicalisation and criminalisation would seem to occur coincidentally within these areas. Our concern is whether such processes are arbitrary or if they betray an underlying moral logic; for both puzzles relate to the same theme – how moral hysteria can exist side by side with permissiveness and how decriminalisation and criminalisation can exist as legislative bedfellows.

The interventionist state

To understand these contradictory assessments of the period one must examine the nature of the dominant ethos. The ideology of this period involves particular conceptions of human nature, social order and the state. Centrally it invokes the notion of capitalism with a human face: able to provide the goods, to bind its citizenry into a social contract of high productivity and high consumption, to build a progressive affluent society where the state intervenes to iron out any problems which occur within the social order. The discipline of the Protestant ethic, stressing work as an end in itself, coupled with the threat of poverty and coercive control for the recalcitrant, is replaced by the conception of a free society where the rewards of leisure are sufficient to justify the sacrifices of work. This is a Keynesian ethos, where the demands of a high-production, high-consumption economy are embraced by all citizens and where the state intervenes on an unprecedented scale to balance out both the economic and the moral order.

Such an interventionist social philosophy[2] holds specific beliefs as to the nature of human normality and deviance. It views the vast majority of its citizens as possessed of the capacity of free will and choice, whether it is in the area of employment, marriage, voting, leisure or consumption – this being the political underpinning for a free democratic society. Possessed of this magical attribute of free will, the overwhelming mass of the population all choose to act in the same way. That is, they agree on what activities are praiseworthy and which condemnable, and embrace a consensus as to what is normal and what is deviant behaviour. They agree further that, on the whole, the system is just and that merit is commensurably rewarded and lack of merit appropriately punished. They have a common definition of reality and accept a social contract of justice which states within the two major institutional areas of society – the economic and the sexual – that the national interest is a meaningful concept and best served by a mixed capitalist economy, and that sexuality finds its optimum expression within the nuclear family. Freedom is not merely seen as an attribute of such a rational citizenry, it is exhorted as an ideal whether it be in the competitive context of work, the spiralling aspirations for consumer goods within the home, or the rising expectations of sexual satisfaction within marriage. Competitive individualism – the struggle for the good life, for the satisfying leisure, for the successful marriage – becomes the major ideal.[3]

But why then, in such a rational order, do certain people deviate from this consensus? Why do people find themselves unable to enter the social contract of work and leisure, reject the fruits of such abundance, or pursue illicit pleasures outside the world of work, leisure and sexual 'normality'?

The first level of explanation within interventionist ideology is that there is at the margins of society a small minority of individuals who lack free will, who are beset by determinations whether genetic, physiological, psychological or social. These people are the in-adequates; they do not choose to be deviant, they are impelled in that direction by forces beyond their control. Such a consensual model is above all concerned with justice: it states emphatically that normality is rewarded and deviancy punished. Thus initially there is a bifurcation of the world and human nature into the following:

1. the normal, rational, average citizen who shares common values, and displays a well-deserved happiness – he or she is part of the vast majority;
2. the tiny minority of inadequates whose actions are determined by their affliction. Their deviancy has an in-built punishment: they are unhappy because of their deviancy; normality is seen to be rewarded and deviance punished. The underlying message is simple: the rational is the pleasurable, is the handsomely rewarded, is the freely chosen, is the meaningful, is the non-deviant; the non-rational is the painful, is the punished, is the determined, is the meaningless, is the deviant.

But repeatedly such a simple bifurcation of the world encounters problems, for often large numbers of individuals engage in activities which are palpably deviant, e.g. strikes, the rising abortion rate, and the spread of marijuana-smoking amongst the young. The simple consensual model would not seem to fit this; for the 'normal' young person, the 'normal' working-class individual, the 'normal' woman, etc., must of necessity embrace the consensus. And if simple inadequacy were so widespread, the social order itself must be at fault. A significant elaboration of the consensual myth is therefore necessary in order to deal with large-scale deviation and avoid such a presumption. Thus it is argued that there exists a body of innocents within society who are corrupted by normal people that are wicked

and seek to gain from their fellows' weakness. Thus the simple
bifurcation of the social universe becomes a four-fold social
categorisation:[4]

1. the inadequate (who cannot help it),
2. the innorent (who are corrupted),
3. the wicked (who corrupt),
4. the reduced number of the normal.

The social universe is thus viewed as composed of various social
categories, and social reaction towards a person is dependent on how
he or she is categorised. The role of the interventionist state is to
bring about justice. The sick are seen to have an in-built punishment
mechanism: they must be treated by the benign state and brought
back into the consensus. The innocent must be protected from the
corrupter. The wicked, who corrupt, must be punished to ensure
justice. The normal must be congratulated and rewarded.

The roots of interventionism in moral indignation

We are now in a position to turn to our first problem: why 'crimes
without victims' are the focus of enormous moral consternation. To
understand this it is necessary to examine the way in which the
ideology of interventionism is attractive to the mass of the people.
Intervention involves a mythology of the average man and the
deviant – within which Mr Average is seen to prosper and be content
in his universe of hard work and industrious consumption whilst the
deviant is portrayed as being beset by forces which lead to ineluctable
misfortune. But the real world outside this spectacle differs radically;
for often the worker doubts the fairness of his rewards, the housewife
surveys her ideal home with ambivalence, the teenager is dismayed
by the abyss of work discipline which lies before him. It is on this base
that interventionist ideology finds its mark, for there exists widespread suspicion that the sacrifices made are not worth the rewards
received. This is the basis for what Albert Cohen calls moral
indignation. Thus he writes:

> The dedicated pursuit of culturally approved goals, the adherence
> to normatively sanctioned means – these imply a certain self
> restraint, effort, discipline, inhibition. What is the effect of others
> who, though their activitives do not manifestly damage our own

interests, are morally undisciplined, who give themselves up to idleness, self-indulgence, or forbidden vices? What effect does the propinquity of the wicked have upon the peace of mind of the virtuous? (Cohen, 1965, pp. 5–14).

What Cohen is arguing is that deviant activities, even though they may have no direct effect on the interests of those who observe them, may be condemned because they represent concrete examples of individuals dodging the rules. If a person lives by a code of conduct which forbids certain pleasures and which involves the deferring of gratification in certain areas, it is hardly surprising that he will react strongly against those people perceived to be taking short cuts.

Thus, the ideology is attractive because it purveys a sense of a just world and due deserts, in a system where in fact the equation between reward and sacrifice is riddled with doubt and uncertainty. Short cuts to accepted rewards or, more potently, the pursuit of illicit pleasures outside the normal patterns of reward, threaten this justice mechanism. Most of the commonly called 'crimes without victims' are potent activators of anxiety about justice: they demand intervention in order to allay doubts about the sanity of the 'taken for granted' world. This is why the distinction between the legislation of crime and morality does not in fact reflect separate judicial spheres, for both involve the notion of the state intervening to ensure 'fair play' in the balance of social merit and acceptable reward.

Britain from the late fifties through the sixties was a society where old disciplines had been loosened by change and competitive individualism, and where arose both grass-roots movements for personal liberation, which pushed beyond the parameters of the interventionist ethos, and a backlash of moral indignation against the new morality. Containment theories of the sixties, which bemoaned the incorporation of people within the consensus and their enslavement to personal consumerism, only encapsulated one side of the dialectic of rising aspirations. The immediate post-war period presented a crisis for capitalism: people returned from the war demanding social justice and to some extent such aspirations were channelled by the subsequent boom.

But the resulting ethos of affluence, with its emphasis on individual freedom and reward for merit, did in the long run contain dissension. People took its injunctions seriously, pushing to the boundaries of the ethos and in many cases beyond. Thus workers questioned the balance of the equation a fair day's work for a fair day's pay, women resented the domestic limits set to their liberation, gays demanded sexual equality, bohemians denied the validity of consumer rewards, and significant sections of youth developed their own leisure culture separate from and disdainful of work. The lid was off the pressure cooker and the state was faced with the problem of setting the parameters to the permissive society. In this role interventionism found ready sources of political support; for side by side with rising aspirations was the backlash of moral anxiety. As the authors of *Policing the Crisis* put it:

> It seemed clear that consensus, affluence and consumerism had produced, not the pacification of worry and anxiety – their dissolution in the flux of money, goods and fashion – but their reverse: a profound, disquieting sense of moral unease . . . Significant social groups in society felt abandoned by the scramble of some for the affluent, 'progressive' middle ground and threatened by rising materialism below; amidst the 'never had it so good society', they yearned for a finer moral purpose. They provided the backbone for the entrepreneurs of moral indignation. (Hall *et al.*, 1978, pp. 233–4).

The sacrifices made in past, more austere times – both at work and in marriage – began to look foolish now; the existence of hedonistic pop cultures of youth, of the new bohemia, of women's liberation, of the gay movement, goaded many into deep resentment and suspicion. The very belief in the affluent society of success in a world which was in reality unequal and where affluence was inequitably distributed added fuel to these flames. Further, we must emphasise that the roots of moral indignation are not necessarily negative and backward-looking. The power of the notion of social justice in interventionist ideology lies in the fact that it takes genuine desires for justice and order within the working class and fixes them on spurious targets.[5] For example, it is not property speculators who become the enemy but squatters, not the unemployment endemic under capitalism but the social security recipient.

An amalgam of resentment occurs between the fact that past sacrifices, both in work and marriage, are threatened by any change in social relations, and the fact that a more genuine disgust has arisen at the exploitative nature of new *mores*. This is particularly true in the moral arena of 'crimes without victims', where dislike of the sexual marketplace becomes transmuted into hatred of the prostitute, where the defence of adolescent sexuality against exploitation becomes fear of the homosexual, where dismay at a world where women are economically unable to have the children they desire becomes transfixed on limiting access to abortion, where fear of the degradation which certain drug use can lead to becomes an attack on bohemian drugtaking. Both the negative movement of resentment, in which people actively oppose any breakdown in the chains which enslave them, and the positive movement of dismay at the brutality of the modern world are tightly interwoven.

The debate with J. S. Mill

It is no accident, then, that public discussion centring around these moral areas was concerned with drawing the lines between freedom and licence. Interventionism on the one hand celebrated the freedom of competitive individualism, whilst, on the other, it aimed to control the excesses which such an ethos engendered. Hence the stress on J. S. Mill in all the documents of this period. The *Wootton Report* exemplifies this well:

13. The great majority of the restrictions currently imposed upon an individual's freedom in this country are defended on the ground that they are necessary for the safety or well-being of others . . .
14. Much more controversial, however, is the question whether, and if so, how far, it is justifiable for the law to restrict a man's freedom in what is presumed to be his own interest. On that issue there is considerable support today for J. S. Mill's dictum that 'the only purpose for which power can rightly be exercised over any member of a civilised community against his will is to prevent harm to others. His own good, either physical or moral, is not a sufficient warrant'. It was, indeed, on this very ground that the Wolfenden Committee put forward a recommendation, which Parliament subsequently accepted, that homosexual acts committed in private between two consenting adults should no longer be criminal; and it can be argued that by similar reasoning the use or sale of drugs in general, and of cannabis in particular, ought not to be the subject of criminal proceedings. Adult men and women, it is said, ought to be free to make their own decisions, in accordance with their personal tastes, and their own moral judgements, as to what substances they think it proper to consume. Added weight is, moreover, given to this argument by the multiplicity of restrictions

on individual liberty which in any modern complex society are incontestably necessary for the common good. The greater the number and variety of unavoidable limitations on personal freedom, the more pressing, it may be said, is the urgency of preserving freedom of choice in what are matters of purely individual concern.

15. While we appreciate the force of this argument, it has to be recognised that no hard and fast line can be drawn between actions that are purely self-regarding, and those that involve wider social consequences . . .

16. Every proposal to restrict the freedom of the individual in his own supposed interests must, therefore, be decided on merits, in the light of the probable severity of any damage that he may inflict upon himself, and of the risk that in damaging himself he may also involuntarily be the cause of injury to others (HMSO, 1968, paras 13–16).

Such a liberal position takes no account of moral indignation; although no obvious infringements of the public interest in these terms may be present, public anxieties are nonetheless aggravated by seeming attempts to despise and reject accepted *mores*. Nor does it take into account the role of an interventionist state, which must preside over the allocation of reward and punishment, and will, of necessity, intervene when sacred institutions are challenged. The recurrent problem for liberalism is that if we start with a Millian definition of liberty, there is never sufficient factual ground to exert control in these areas of 'crimes without victims'. The liberal rhetoric of interventionism contradicts with its desire to maintain the 'nature' and 'just' order of the mixed economy and the nuclear family – its espousal of freedom falters at these parameters. This is the basis of the constant lacuna in logic that one finds in the Government reports of this period.

Ideology and praxis: the problems of the interventionist state

The interventionist state faces two types of problem in the control of deviant behaviour:

1. *Ideological.* Why, in a just social order, do free individuals persist in acting deviantly? We would argue that, following the moral logic of interventionism, these individuals are viewed as having

lost their freedom either because they are basically inadequate and/or they have been corrupted by unscrupulous individuals. It is here that the problem of explaining the phenomenon meshes well with the justification for intervention; for talk of 'inadequates', 'corruption of the innocent', etc., removes these activities from the category of the rational pursuit of freedom, whilst providing the rationale for the 'benign' state to intervene in their amelioration.

2. *Practical.* The immediate practical problems which confront the state are the size and propinquity of a deviant phenomenon, and the cost and degree of efficiency of existing techniques of control.

Size creates not only ideological but also practical problems. A common method of achieving practicable control is to bifurcate the phenomenon. That is, a large part of it may be deemed to pose a lesser threat than the problem of the remaining recalcitrant minority. Propinquity creates obvious problems in that it exacerbates moral indignation and points to palpable weaknesses in the social order. A common solution to a sizeable and blatant deviant problem is to remove it from direct public view – what we shall term ghettoisation. Bifurcation and ghettoisation frequently accompany each other: they occur as part of the process of medicalisation.

The practical problems of medicalisation are inherent in the theory of medicalisation itself. To believe that prostitutes go on the street, homosexuals prefer their own sex, people take drugs or women seek abortions because of their own personal inadequacies, viewed in a social vacuum, is ideology of the first order. It is to take for granted that such activities are pathological, that they are caused by individual failings and are unrelated to the structure of the society we live in. If prostitutes make a living by selling their bodies, then we must find the roots in the sexist nature of our society; if women have abortions because they cannot afford to have another child, then we must look to the economic problems which capitalism engenders. If, on the other hand, people are persecuted for following their sexual inclinations without harm to others, if women are prevented from controlling their own fertility, and if cannabis users are constantly harassed by the law – then we must look to the irrationality of the social order, not the inadequacy of the individual.

We would argue that, in the first instance, social evils are directly caused by the structure of our society, whilst, in the second category, certain activities which are in themselves innocuous are transformed into social problems merely by the irrational reaction of authority. In both cases medicalisation smokescreens failings in the social order by attributing them to personal weaknesses. Now this does not imply that we would deny that certain individuals are, in fact, rationally inadequate. But this inadequacy is not a psychological attribute detached from their situation; rather, in those cases where failings in rationality occur, it is a direct function of the brutalising nature of the social order.

However, because medicalisation reduces social evils to personal failings, it provides a theory which cannot solve individual problems – rather, it obfuscates and bedevils them. Medicalisation, in practice, is doomed to failure from the start. Given sufficient financial outlay, it can fool the 'patient' into believing that he is inadequate, and it can effect 'cures' where all the material forces which have beset him are temporarily held in obeyance. But seldom is sufficient financial largesse forthcoming to achieve this, especially when the deviant population is large. The practical solution, then, to the problems of efficacy, cost and size, is a quasi-medical one – ghettoisation. It is either the attempt to quieten a population in order to make them more manageable (e.g. the use of tranquillisers in mental hospitals), or the creation of private twilight worlds of permitted inadequacy removed from direct public view. In neither case is the stated aim of medicalisation – to 'cure' the deviant – carried out.

But there will always be a part of the deviant phenomenon which is considered too dangerous or recalcitrant for ghettoisation. Bifurcation then occurs between the 'dangerous' minority and the 'innocuous' majority. The minority are then subject to criminal sanctions, which are justified, in part, to ensure their treatment. It is this minority, as we shall see, who are most vulnerable to direct medicalisation; and what is considered humanitarian by the interventionists is, of course, often correctly viewed as coercive by the deviants themselves.

We shall now turn to an examination of sixties legislation in the moral arena, and analyse how such ideological and practical problems were specifically resolved.

Prostitution

The 1957 Wolfenden Committee was concerned not so much with the rise in prostitution, which it doubted, but with its blatancy. The

committee's problem was to assuage the moral indignation generated by the propinquity of prostitutes, especially in residential areas,
and yet to maintain the freedom of consenting adults. Thus there was
a classic conflict between moral indignation and liberalism, as
follows:

> It is not the duty of the law to concern itself with immorality as
> such. If it were the law's intention to punish prostitution *per se*, on
> the ground that it is immoral conduct, then it would be right that it
> should provide for the punishment of the man as well as the
> woman. But that is not the function of the law. It should confine
> itself to those activities which offend against public order and
> decency or expose the ordinary citizen to what is offensive or
> injurious; and the simple fact is that prostitutes do parade
> themselves more habitually and openly than their prospective
> customers, and do by their continual presence affront the sense of
> decency of the ordinary citizen. In doing so they create a nuisance
> which, in our view, the law is entitled to recognise and deal with
> (HMSO, 1957, para. 257).

The legal tools to achieve the removal of such a public nuisance
were as follows (Street Offences Act 1959):

1. it was no longer necessary to prove public annoyance, a police
    officer's testimony being sufficient;
2. fines were increased from a maximum of £2 to a rising scale (first
    offence maximum £10, second offence maximum £25, third
    offence £25 and/or imprisonment for a maximum of 3 months);
3. length of imprisonment rose from a maximum of 14 days
    to 3 months;
4. a system of cautioning for public soliciting was formalised.

The Street Offences Act in practice

Number of convictions

In the years prior to 1959 the conviction rates for prostitution had
steadily risen from 6,843 in 1950 to 19,536 in 1958. The effect of the
Act was a drastic drop in convictions: for example, 2,726 in 1960 and
1,652 in 1970. Given that the problem of proving annoyance had
been removed and that conviction was, if anything, technically

easier, this is remarkable. What had happened was that prostitution had been driven off the streets. This is not to suggest that there was a decline in prostitution. *The Working Party on Vagrancy and Street Offences* (1974) is candid enough about this:

> Since the passing of the Street Offences Act, soliciting by prostitutes in the streets has visibly been greatly reduced. This was the agreed view of those whom we consulted, including some with a thorough and longstanding knowledge of the problem. However, the majority of police forces whom we consulted were agreed that this did not mean that the amount of prostitution had decreased. In some areas prostitutes have resorted to a peripatetic mode of life so as to avoid prosecution following a second caution. Other means of attracting clients have also been developed (HMSO, 1974, para. 230).

So, in fact, by forcing prostitution out of public visibility the Act achieved a considerable measure of decriminalisation.

Sentencing

The increase in the punitive nature of sentencing was immediately apparent. Whereas before the Act, in 1958, 0.8 per cent of prostitutes were imprisoned, in 1960 this had risen to 16.3 per cent. In 1958 1 per cent of those imprisoned received a sentence of greater than 2 months, but in 1961 this had risen to 69 per cent. The average number of prison convictions in the 5-year period 1954 to 1958 was 90, whereas in the 5-year period 1960 to 1964 it was 354. Of these, convictions involving a greater than 2-month sentence rose in the same period from an average of two to 148: Thus, for prostitutes remaining on the street, a remarkable rise in criminalisation had occurred. Such criminalisation was justified on the grounds of increasing the likelihood of treatment but, in reality, no such techniques of rehabilitation existed.

Thus, overall, we have the ghettoisation of the majority of prostitutes, and, given the remarkable decline in convictions, a situation of virtual decriminalisation occurred. For the remaining minority, however, a rapid escalation of criminalisation occurred. Moreover, it was by the continual coercion of this minority that the invisible majority were socially controlled, that is, prevented from returning to the streets.

The Wolfenden Committee, faced with the ideological problem of explaining why women should, in a supposedly affluent society, resort to prostitution, plumped for an explanation in terms of the women's psychological inadequacy. Such an inadequacy, of course, contradicted the manifest economic rationality of many prostitutes.[6] Consequently, the result of the Street Offences Act had both self-fulfilling and self-negating components.

The self-fulfilling prophecy

The young girl, the working-class woman with little money, social expertise or connections, the woman whose brutalised position engendered rational inadequacy, all were rendered more vulnerable by the Street Offences Act. Thus the more inadequate prostitutes were left on the streets, and their inadequacy was exacerbated by the punitive harassment which they encountered. The stereotype of the prostitute was thus fulfilled.

The self-negating prophecy

The Wolfenden Committee recognised that removing girls from the streets would not eliminate prostitution – this was not the Committee's concern – but would result in the growth of organised call-girl agencies. Such a mode of prostitution is virtually free from arrest, it has much less social stigmatisation associated with it, it involves a high level of business adequacy, and it reaps very high financial gains. It is, of course, a violation of the ideological explanation of prostitution utilised by Wolfenden, for what has been created is a career characterised by adequacy and economic rationality. It involves a more regular clientele, which, furthermore, violates the stereotype of the transient client. But, given the lack of propinquity of such prostitution, not only is elimination impossible but public disquiet at such transgressions is minimised.

Homosexuality

The change in the laws regarding homosexuality between consenting adults is often seen as the highlight of progressive legislation during the sixties. Let us examine the reality behind this legislation. The Wolfenden Committee was faced with several problems – why homosexuality existed, why it was in their mind on the increase, and what right the state had to intervene in such a consensual activity.

Homosexuality, according to the Committee, was undoubtedly a serious problem, though a problem of a minority. Its causes lay in inadequate socialisation. Leo Abse, the doyen of homosexuality reform, put it as follows when introducing the second reading of the Sexual Offences Bill in the House of Commons:

> Surely, what we should be preoccupied with is the question of how we can, if it is possible, reduce the number of faulty males in the community. How can we diminish the number of those who grow up to have men's bodies but feminine souls?
>
> It is clear from the number of homosexuals who are about that, unfortunately, little boys do not automatically grow up to be men. Manhood and fatherhood have to be taught. Manhood has to be learnt. The only way for it to be taught is by example. It is true that there are dangers to a boy – a sophisticated House knows it – if an over-possessive mother ties her son to her with a silver cord so that the boy is enveloped in a feminine aura out of which he is never able to break and assert his masculine independence. We know that this happens. But, equally, it is certain from all the research that has been done that there is particular vulnerability for those who have had jealous or loveless fathers, for those with inadequate fathers, and for those – these are in the greatest danger of all – who are fatherless either by death or desertion. These have no father substitute with whom they can learn to identify.
>
> We often hear about mothercraft. We do not hear a great deal about fathercraft. The children of parttime parents, the children of the ambitious executive returning home after the boy is abed, perhaps, too, the children of over-busy Members of Parliament who work very hard from early in the morning till late at night and who sometimes say their children grow up without their knowing them – all these young people who, in effect, become de facto fatherless children, are hostages to fortune. In order to become men they need fathers with whom they can identify, not shadowy fathers, not hostile fathers, but fathers with whom they can learn, play, and discuss things, fathers from whom they can have proper attention. Boys need more than pocketmoney fathers who send them out to the cinema. They need real fathers (Hansard 19 December 1966, cols 1086–70).

Why then was homosexuality supposedly on the increase? The

prime reasons were seen as broken homes, coupled with the increased permissiveness of modern society. The existence of broken homes did not, in itself, threaten an interventionist conception of the world because such occurrences could be viewed as a random breakdown likely in a minority of families within any social order.

As with prostitution, the Wolfenden Committee faced the dilemma of stemming moral indignation as to the public occurrence of homosexuality yet maintaining the liberty of consenting adults. As homosexuals were 'inadequates', the Committee had, of course, a prima facie justification for intervention on humanitarian grounds. But the problem here was that there was no known medical treatment that could 'cure' such inadequacy and, more importantly, the existing laws served to make matters worse. Firstly, the laws were increasingly seen to be practically unenforceable; secondly, they gave rise to the scandal of blackmail accusation; thirdly, and more sophisticatedly, by placing homosexuals 'outside of the community' it increased their 'anti-social manner' (Leo Abse, at the second reading of the Sexual Offences Bill 1966). Indeed, the Wolfenden Committee suggested that if adult homosexuals were allowed to relate in private, this would positively protect minors, for the majority would prefer to remain within legal possibilities. Here the Committee introduced a bifurcation between types of homosexuals – the vast majority who preferred adult company and a minority of pederasts whose sexual orientation was towards minors. As far as the first group was concerned there was little damage in them relating together, for their inadequate personalities had already been cast. Thus a law which granted them permission to engage in private sexual activities had the virtue of both decreasing public visibility and concern, and diminishing the chances of public proselytisation. Like prostitution, it provided a tolerated ghetto for 'inadequates'. However, there remained the minority of pederasts, and those adults who persisted in public display. For these individuals, prison was justifiable, firstly, because as adult males they had the power to control themselves – homosexuality was, as the Committee succinctly put it, like a 'controllable cough', – and, secondly, because prison offered the possibility of medicalisation. They admitted that medicalisation could not change the homosexual propensity. Indeed, even castration was of little use:

> We are aware that in some countries castration is practised, with the consent of the offender. We understand, however, that there is

no guarantee that this operation removes either the desires or the ability to fulfil them: it would clearly have no effect, in the latter respect, in the case of the man who is addicted to the passive role of acts of buggery, or to other forms of homosexual behaviour not involving the use of his own genitalia. For many reasons, we do not believe that this operation would commend itself in this country (HMSO, 1957, para. 195).

However, although treatment may not change behaviour, it could be used to quiesce homosexuality:

Treatment may have yet another purpose. It may be directed simply towards making the man more discreet or continent in his behaviour, without attempting any other change in his nature. This is not to be despised as an objective, for if it is successful such treatment will reduce the number of homosexual offences and offenders. It is here that the use of oestrogens, to which we refer later, has its place.

As we have said earlier, we see little likelihood of any 'cure' of homosexuality in the sense of changing the nature and object of a man's sexual desires; it is possible in some cases to diminish the strength of these desires by physical means. The strength of a man's desires may well be an important factor in his behaviour, and if the strength of the desire can be diminished it 'is not unreasonable to suppose that the disposition to commit offences will be correspondingly lessened. In this connection we have given some consideration to the possible use of hormones (oestrogens), which affect the strength, though not the direction, of the sexual desire or libido, in the treatment of convicted homosexual offenders. At present, the use of oestrogens is forbiden in prisons in England and Wales (though not, we understand, in Scotland) even where the prisoner himself expresses a desire for oestrogen treatment (HMSO, 1957, para. 209).

Wolfenden went on to recommend that such a ban be lifted.

Thus the Wolfenden Committee's recommendations, which were implemented in the Sexual Offences Act 1967, involved:

1. the decriminalisation of the majority of consenting adults;
2. a criminalisation of the remaining few, coupled with

3.   medicalisation in order to quiesce rather than change aberrant homosexual behaviour.

Effects of the Act

The 'progressive' legislators on homosexuality started from a base that homosexuals were a small minority of inadequates. Their ideology contradicted reality; for they could not see that the problem of homosexuality was the problem of a sexist society, that inadequacy where it occurred was a product of social reaction and legal oppression, and that the numbers of homosexuals are large and the potential number enormous.

Decriminalisation of homosexuality between consenting adults spurred a large number of people to 'come out of the closets', to venture out of the ghettos; it permitted the pronouncement of gayness as normal behaviour; it effected greater proselytisation precisely because of the limited freedom granted. But in order to make contacts, public interaction was necessary, as in hetrosexual relationships, and thus the segregation and distancing of homosexuals which was the aim of the Act was stymied by the grass-roots intervention of gays themselves. The limited decriminalisation of the Act was fought against, yet a backlash of control persisted. The conviction rate thus remained high; in fact, as the Homosexual Law Reform Society argues:

> The actual operation of the Sexual Offences Act 1967 has had some puzzling results. From the annual volumes of *Criminal Statistics*, for both buggery and attempted buggery (two of the three categories of conduct to which the Act applies), the number of offences given as 'known to the police' and 'cleared up' declined during the years 1967–72. So did the number of those convicted of those offences. By contrast, offences of indecency between males – the third category – increased over the same period, from 840 to 1,069 'known to the police' (in the 1972 volume, just published, this formula was altered to 'recorded as known to the police'), and from 817 to 1,039 'cleared up', while the number of those convicted of this offence increased from 444 in 1967 to 1,137 in 1971, an increase of no less than 160 per cent. Even allowing for a slight reversal of this trend to 1,079 convictions in 1972, the overall rate of increase was very sharp indeed, compared with that for any other offence in the criminal calendar, and that during a period

when the 1967 Act might have been expected to produce precisely the opposite result in the case of indecency between males (Tom Harper, *The Listener*, 27 September, 1973).

The Wootton Report 1968

The Wootton Committee was faced with the ideological problem of explaining why large numbers of young people were smoking cannabis, and the practicalities of enforcing the drug laws in this area. The members of the Committee were reluctant to argue that such a large section of youth could be inadequate. In interventionist terms such an admission would suggest either that there must be major problems in the social order to produce so many inadequate young people, which was inadmissible, or that the smokers were corrupted by drug-pushers and thus embarked upon an irrational course of behaviour. But to plump for irrationality would demand proof that the use of cannabis was indeed a dangerous and deleterious activity. No such evidence was forthcoming; the Committee failed to find any concrete evidence of correlation between the use of marijuana and escalation to heroin, physiological addiction, crime or violence. Thus they were unable to justify the intervention demanded by moral indignation. Here, then, was a large section of youth incorporated in bohemian cultures which manifestly provoked moral panics,[7] yet there was insufficient evidence to overcome the J. S. Mill parameters of non-intervention.

The Wootton Committee, therefore, took a course which was the opposite of the treatment of homosexuals, prostitutes or women seeking abortion. It argued that the majority of cannabis users were a normal cross-section of the community, and productive at that. The productive smoker became a hallmark of the normalisation of cannabis-use:

The 'professional' group, for example, was described to us as fundamentally law-abiding; discriminating in the use of cannabis for introspection and elation as well as for social relaxation; 'involved in life' often to the point of social protest; not much interested in experiments with LSD; generally disinclined to take amphetamines or alcohol (which was regarded as much more damaging than cannabis); and tending to stop the use of cannabis on marriage, or when the risk of prosecution was felt to be inimical to career prospects. The 'unskilled' group was said to be similarly industrious and law-abiding and to see nothing wrong or harmful in its use of cannabis (HMSO, 1968, para. 41).

But, in a typical interventionist fashion, they separated out a small minority of inadequates who were, in contrast, disturbed and work-shy.

> There appears to be a particular group of emotionally deprived, disturbed personalities who have tried most of the illegal drugs (including cannabis) before becoming heroin addicts. In fact most heroin addicts are multiple drug-users and have the emotionally impoverished family background not infrequently found in other delinquent groups, such as high incidence of broken homes, poor school record, police record, unemployment and work-shyness. Cannabis-users with similar personalities and backgrounds may have a predisposition to heroin, amphetamines and other illegal drugs. It is the personality of the user, rather than the properties of the drug, that is likely to cause progression to other drugs (HMSO, 1968; para. 50).

The boundaries of illicit drug use were, therefore, redrawn by the Committee. Faced by a large-scale social problem, interventionism once again bifurcates the phenomenon into a majority category which is more or less innocuous, and a minority category where the residual essence of the problem is seen to lie. This ideologically obviates the problem of explaining its size, and practically renders the problem more manageable.

Overall, this approach would suggest the normilisation of cannabis use, accompanied by the medicalisation or criminalisation of multi-drug use. But the Committee, surely aware of the political storm it was about to create, was too cautious for this, despite its partial obeisance to the principles of J. S. Mill. There was, in its view, insufficient evidence for legalisation as yet; instead, they recommended a reduction of fines for possession of small amounts of cannabis; the reduction of prison sentences, which were to be used only in exceptional circumstances; and a reduction in sentences for sale. But the Committee's caution and timidity were insufficient: both press and Parliament refused to accept this step towards normalisation. They flatly maintained that there was evidence of the harmful effects of cannabis. The Committee's recommendations were variously termed by the press 'A Junkie's Charter', opening 'the gates of servitude to countless thousands', and like 'Russian Roulette – with a fully loaded revolver'. It was stridently reiterated that the evidence showed cannabis to be directly linked with heroin addiction and anti-social behaviour. Cannabis use thus being irrational and deleterious could only be explained by reaffirming the corrupter – corrupted dichotomy. In this vein James Callaghan, then Home Secretary, stood out against what he termed the 'rising tide of permissiveness', and the subsequent Misuse of Drugs Bill 1971 was grounded in the interventionist categories of the pusher (corrupter) and the smoker (victim). Penalties for sale increased (the increased criminalisation of the dealer), while sentences for possession were reduced (the partial decriminalisation of the user). Thus the forces of moral indignation won over the liberal resort to factual evidence. As Lady Wootton was to remark later:

> The causes of the hysteria are familiar to the student of social psychology. They occur in other connections as well, particularly in relation to sexual crimes, and they are always liable to recur when the public senses some critical and objective study threatens to block an outlet for indulgence in the pleasure of moral indignation (*The Times*, Parliamentary Report, 27 March 1969).

Abortion law reform[8]

Before 1967 the main practical problem of control was that existing legislation was unfair, unenforceable and legally dubious. The widespread use of back-street abortions was seen as a direct function of the criminalisation of abortion. The 1967 Act, which aimed to eliminate these abuses, was phrased entirely in interventionist categories. It was argued that the demand for abortion stemmed from the margins of society (those women who were physically, psychologically or socially unfit to form a family, too young to form a family or to whom an extra child would threaten their already large family). Abortion allowed the judicious intervention of the state in those problem families which were seen as perpetuating 'the cycle of deprivation', with its corollary of high delinquency rates and mental disorder. At no point was 'abortion on demand' deemed feasible or desirable, for this would be to suggest that 'normal', non-marginal women desired abortions, and this, in turn, would indicate that not all was well in the economy in general (i.e. women could not afford to have an extra child) or in the nuclear family (i.e. married women were rebelling against their supposedly natural propensity to bear children). As a result, the Act aimed to decriminalise abortion for women in the marginal categories. Further, as interventionist premises suggested that such women were inadequate (either in a physical, psychological or social sense), the obvious adjudicators of the right to abortion were members of the medical profession. This was underlined by the powerful medical lobby, which sought to ensure that decisions on surgical operations remained within its own domain. Thus we have selective decriminalisation through medicalisation.

As the demand for abortion was perceived as small and emanating from marginal categories of women, no special provisions were made in the National Health Service for abortion. Thus the ideological categorisation of those in need of abortion had the practical corollary of medical control and limited provision.

But interventionist categories are not the real world, although their practical implementation results in real and contradictory changes in society. The actual demand for abortion was high, stemming from the widespread desire of large sections of women to regulate their own fertility. In this, women were aided by an administrative loophole in the law. The medical profession, stressing the indispensability of its skills, had maintained that abortion was a dangerous operation. The architects of the Act fixed on this as a useful criterion for restricting access to abortion, and inserted the clause which stated that abortion would be permitted if 'the continuance of pregnancy would involve risk to the life of the pregnant woman, or of injury to the physical or mental health of the pregnant woman . . . greater than if the pregnancy were terminated (Abortion Act 1969, Clause 1[a]).

This 'greater risk' clause proved their downfall, for, as the number of abortion operations soared, medical proficiency increased, and it was soon possible to argue that the abortion mortality rate was lower than that of the maternal mortality rate. It was here that liberal general practitioners innovated in a manner which transformed the Act, for, unlike the higher echelons of the medical profession, they daily faced the realities of their patients' lives being devastated by unwanted pregnancies. Thus, many were willing to reinterpret the 'greater risk' clause as justifying a near 'abortion on demand' situation.

The number of abortions soared as a consequence, far outstripping the NHS facilities. The consequences of this were a rise in the proportion of private agencies dealing with abortions, and by 1972 the number of abortions under the NHS had declined to 50 of the total. In a situation where supply does not meet demand, women with the know-how and money have greater control of the market. The result was that abortion facilities became more easily available to precisely those 'normal' women whom the Act had taken pains to exclude and not to the marginals that were its target population. Further, accusations of touting and commercialisation began to abound.

By 1975 the interventionists were faced with two problems: ideologically how to explain the high demand from 'normal' women, and practically how to reverse this situation of what they saw as 'abortion on demand' and provide for marginal women only. Here we see the fashion in which social categorisation determines the differential social reaction to the various actors involved. It was impossible, in interventionist terms, to blame 'normal' women for the occurrence. But women, and pregnant women in particular, were tailor-made for the 'innocent' corruptible category. But who were the corrupters? It was not permissible to blame general practitioners in general, for they, like policemen or solicitors, are a pre-eminent part of the 'normal' world. Thus the analysis focused on 'black sheep' doctors variously described by the Parliamentarians involved as 'psychopathic', 'ideologically motivated' and 'bad apples' within the medical profession. These men were seen to have caused the rise in abortion through touting and abuse of their medical status. They were the 'corrupters' in the moral scenario. The attempt to solve the practical problem occurred in two Private Members Bills which aimed to resurrect the spirit of the 1967 Act: the 1975 James White Bill, and that of William Benyon in 1977. The suggested legislation included a reaffirmation of the right to abortion in marginal cases, a tightening of the medical permission needed to obtain abortion, police access to records on abortion operations and an increase in the fine from £100 to £1000 for doctors committing an unlawful abortion. Whilst these Bills failed to become statutory, a series of administrative measures virtually achieved the remedicalisation of abortion, while public pressure made doctors fearful of providing abortion services.

The stages through which abortion law reform passed, therefore, were from decriminalisation through medicalisation, in 1967, to the drift towards real decriminalisation (i.e. normalisation) in the years that follow. The reaction to this was a reaffirmation of the principle of the medicalisation of marginal cases, combined with an increasing threat of punitive recriminalisation of abortion outside this category, directly aimed at aberrant members of the medical profession.

Thus processes of medicalisation, normalisation and criminalisation are all to be found in the recent history of abortion law reform. Their deployment is not arbitrary but relates to the interventionist categorisation of the social world and the ideological and practical problems to which this gives rise.

*   *   *

We have shown in the foregoing examples the recurrent ideological and practical problems of control. The problem must be explained, intervention justified, moral indignation assuaged, and legal tools fashioned to cope with the size and propinquity of the phenomenon. Furthermore, both ideological explanation and practical resolution are dependent upon the moral logic emanating from the social categorisation of the actors involved. We are now at a position to summarise the basic themes of such interventionist 'permissiveness':

1. *Bifurcation.* In order to explain an act of deviancy, the deviant is bifurcated from the normal in terms of his or her inadequacy, and thus intervention is justified.[9] 'Normal' women are contrasted to the 'inadequate' prostitutes, and the 'adequate' client (being male and heterosexual) is contrasted with his 'consenting' female partner. The 'adequate' adult male is compared to the 'inadequate' homosexual, and then further bifurcation occurs between the stable discreet male homosexual and a small minority of proselytising pederasts. In abortion 'normal' women do not desire or need it: only the marginal woman does. In drugs, according to the *Wootton Report*, the cannabis user is in profile little different from normal youth – it is the multi-drug user who is inadequate. By the time of the Misuse of Drugs Act 1971, however, all drugtaking youth had become inadequate.

2. *Medicalisation.* The deviant thus categorised as inadequate is a candidate for medicalisation. But, despite repeated reference to treatment, the reality of the high cost and low effectiveness of existing techniques ensures that thoroughgoing medicalisation is rare.[10] In prostitution and homosexuality, where the problem of propinquity was foremost, a compromise was arrived at: if the 'inadequates' stay within their ghettos, out of public view, they are subject neither to medicalisation nor criminalisation. But to

coerce them into this position, strong legal sanctions are engendered against those who stray beyond the limits. These, of course, are justified under the rubric of making it more likely that incarceration will allow treatment, but in reality what occurs is the criminalisation and coercion of those who break the barriers of their ghetto. In abortion, attempts are made to tighten the criminal law so as to prevent 'normal' women from obtaining abortions; 'marginal' women are granted facilities, but as a means of ameliorating their inadequacy rather than to 'cure' it. In the case of drugs the inadequate cannabis user is increasingly tolerated, provided he offers a law public profile and does not sell to others.

3. *Criminalisation.* The concept of permitted inadequates, of course, gave some room to manoeuvre for deviant populations. But it was accompanied by the increased criminalisation of a recalcitrant minority in order to maintain the boundaries of the ghetto, and by the criminalisation of what we might term the 'causal scapegoats' of the moral scenario; for in every instance where it is necessary for interventionism to explain how inadequate or innocent people embark on deviant careers, a corrupter becomes the causal link and thus a candidate for criminalisation. Thus we have the pimp, the proselytising homosexual, the black-sheep doctor, and the drug-pusher – the particular candidate set up as villain of the piece depending on the moral logic of interventionism in each case.

4. *Normalisation.* Only in the *Wootton Report* was a cautious move towards normalisation hazarded as a legal measure from above – an argument dependent on the fiction of the productive smoker – a stance which was speedily dismembered by the Misuse of Drugs Act 1971. Real gains in terms of normalisation occur as grass-roots phenomena, the most spectacular example being the exploitation of the loophole in the Abortion Act 1967 by women and sympathetic GPs.

We have examined four legislative areas which are often said to be characteristic of the 'progressive' sixties. Yet precisely how 'permissive' was the legislation? How much did it reflect the actions of a Government bent on endorsing a new morality?

Even a cursory examination of these legislative areas throws doubt on the extent to which the encouragement of permissiveness was ever a concern of Government in this period. Rather, intervention was necessary to delineate the parameters to permissiveness, and to solve the problem of an ideology dedicated to competitive individualism. Millian discussions of freedom were frequent, but the removal of coercion where it occurred was justified by the use of a medical rhetoric. The arch of liberation was supported by the twin pillars of inadequacy and expediency. As such it represented a gain for sections of the deviant population that were previously more directly harassed and persecuted. But, compared, for example, to arguments based on human rights, such a gain is always easily rescinded. We have seen how such a process occurred in abortion reform. Constantly the real issues were obfuscated. No one bemoaned the plight of the prostitute as a victim of a sexist society, no one talked of the problem of homosexuality as being a problem of moral indignation, no legislator argued for the freedom of all women to control their fertility, and our backward drug laws remained backward despite all factual evidence. The gains that were made were either a function of grass-roots pressures against the existing law, or the control strategies necessary for an interventionist state to counter, more effectively, the size and propinquity of morally threatening behaviour whilst continuing to support an ideology of individualism.

Permissiveness and control became two sides of the same coin, for in not one case was normalisation an intention of the legislation; rather, interventionism created ghettos of 'inadequates' surrounded by a ring of coercion. Permissiveness was a product of individuals taking the ideology of freedom seriously; the role of Government was to curb 'excesses', to manoeuvre policy in a way which would make control more practicable, to pursue the ideal of individual freedom whilst obeying all the restraints of moral indignation. It is in such a climate that criminalisation and decriminalisation become a unity: two moments in the politics of interventionism.

Notes on Organisations

National Deviancy Conference

To receive information about the NDC, send £2 mailing list subscription (cheques payable to NDC) to Mike Fitzgerald, Faculty of Social Science, Open University, Milton Keynes MK7 6AA.

European Group for the Study of Deviance and Social Control

The NDC is affiliated to the European Group for the Study of Deviance and Social Control, which holds an annual conference in one of the member countries. Details can be obtained from the Secretary, Dietlinde Gipser, European Group for the Study of Deviance and Social Control, Hinterm Horn 48, D–2050 Hamburg 80, West Germany.

Crime and Social Justice

The Crime and Social Justice Collective publishes the magazine *Crime and Social Justice*. The address is Crime and Social Justice, PO Box 4373, Berkeley, California 94704, USA. It is published twice a year, and the annual airmail subscription rate for individuals is $11.

Notes

Chapter 1

1. For some early formulations of arguments in this paper, I am especially indebted to John Clarke and Tony Jefferson: for some later ones, to Catherine Hall.
2. See 'Social Policy and the Drugtaker', in Young (1971).
3. For an analysis of the turn towards authoritarianism and 'law and order' in the seventies, see Hall *et al.* (1978).
4. The most comprehensive analysis of this aspect of the legislation is Richards (1970). See also Alderman (1966).
5. See especially *The Enforcement of Morals* by (Lord) Patrick Devlin (1965), which reprints his famous 1958 Maccabean Lecture in Jurisprudence to the British Academy; and Hart (1963).
6. An early survey of party opinion on 'ideological' issues is reported in Finer, Berrington, *et al.* (1961). It is more fully examined in Richards (1970) and Pym (1974). The case that, though a 'liberal' fringe exists within the Conservative Party, it is Labour which is the 'party of reform' on these issues, is argued in Jenkins (1959). The analysis of the voting on these issues, presented in Richards (1970), is based on the work of Margaret Fuller.
7. Cf. Grey, in Frost (1975), Hyde (1972), and Weeks (1977). Though the Abortion Law Reform Society experienced a remarkable revival of activity in this period, it was originally founded as early as 1936 at the time of the Birkitt Committee. See Hindell and Simms (1968 and 1971).
8. On the differences between the Homosexual Law Reform Society and the Gay Liberation Front, see Weeks (1977).
9. The embedded quote from Pollock is from the *Essays In Jurisprudence and Ethics* (London: Macmillan, 1882).
10. His position was argued out in *The Right to Live* (1963).
11. The Society for the Protection of the Unborn Child was formed in 1967 specifically to fight the Steel Abortion Bill. For 'Clean Up TV' and NVALA, see Whitehouse (1967 and 1971).

12. Opinion in the 1945 Attlee administration appears to have hardened against abolition. Their proposed amendments to the criminal law did not, as at first expected, include an abolition clause. They permitted a clause to be moved at the report stage, but would not allow ministers to vote 'by conscience'. The Silverman amendment, voted on in April 1948, was carried, the most senior ministers voting against (but forty-six ministers failed to vote). Cf. Richards (1970) pp. 39–42, and Christoph (1962).

13. Attested to by Wolfenden (1976), by Butler (1971), and by the general tone of many of the interventions in the House of Commons debate on Wolfenden. See Hansard (Commons Debates), vols 596ff. (26 November 1958).

14. For example, with respect to prostitution, the section on 'The Extent of the Problem', *Wolfenden Report* (1957) pp. 229–32; and with respect to homosexuality, a similar entitled section (pp. 37–47), including 'Inadequacy of Statistical Information'.

15. See the intervention by Walter Edwards, Labour MP for Stepney, in Hansard, (Commons Debates), vol. 596, 26 November 1958.

16. Wildeblood wrote his own account of the 'Montague affair', which was also a passionate and cogent attack on the law and its implementation by the police, in *Against the Law* (Wildeblood, 1955 and 1957).

17. On the 'to do' which followed the publication of the *Report*, see Wolfenden (1976) pp. 140ff.

18. For a similar point with respect to legislation on pornography and obscenity, cf. National Council of Civil Liberties (1972) and Cox (1976).

19. See, *inter alia*, Greenwood and Young, elsewhere in this volume, and in *Abortion in Demand* (1976).

20. The Labouchere amendment to Section II of the Criminal Law Amendment Act 1885 provided for 'Any male person, who, in public or private, commits or is party to the commission of, or procures or attempts to procure the commission by any male person of any act of gross indecency with another male person, shall be guilty of a misdemeanour . . .'

21. The *Wolfenden Report* only glanced at this possibility in passing: 'We think it possible, indeed probable, that there will be an extension of the 'call-girl' system . . .' (HMSO, 1957, p. 96).

22. Some remarks by Althusser on the 'purely juridical' basis of this distinction in bourgeois society could be read in this way. Clearly, it *does* 'matter' where and how the line is drawn at any time, for the distinction has pertinent effects. Cf. Althusser (1971) p. 137. For a critical discussion on this point, cf. Hall, Lumley and McLennan (1978).

23. Despite differences in approach, the similarities between the French and English approaches are striking. They will only surprise the epistemological purists who are determined to divide knowledge into rival encampments.

24. See also Foucault (1972, p. 207) but see also the ambiguous hope held out on p. 208.

25. About the 18th century, Foucault argues: 'This explains why the "reform" did not have a single origin . . . However, this general principle defined an overall strategy that covered many different struggles . . . Throughout the eighteenth century, inside and outside the legal apparatus, in both everyday penal practice and the criticism of institutions, one sees the emergence of a new strategy for the exercise of the power to punish . . . And "reform", in the strict sense, as it was formulated in the theories of law or as it was outlined in the various projects, was the political or philosophical resumption of this strategy' (Foucault, 1978, pp. 81–2).

26. 'The interest of the State in marriage comes from two different sources. The first is general: it has an interest in monogamy as an institution. The second is particular: it has an interest in the welfare of any children of the marriage' (Devlin, 1965, p. 76).

27. 'Most ordinary contracts are of no concern to the public. Nevertheless, there has to be a law of contract to provide a basis on which the parties can impose their particular arrangement . . . Moreover, the terms of a marriage are not of purely private concern' (Devlin, 1965, p. 63).

28. The strategy of 'exemption' is crucial, for it allowed the law to 'give over' certain aspects of conduct from the 'juridical' to the 'contractual' regime, without thereby positively conferring moral approval. As Devlin argued: 'A man and a woman who live together outside marriage are not prosecuted under the law but they are not protected by it. They are outside the law . . . English law has from the earliest times refused to enforce certain classes of contracts as being against public policy. Irregular sexual unions constitute one of those classes . . . It is enough that the restraint should not be imposed unless it serves some important social purpose. The decision whether it does or not is a political not a moral one' (Devlin, 1965, pp. 77–8).

29. In this respect, as in so many others – as J. A. and O. Banks (1974), discussing family planning and the position of women observe – 'It has become a commonplace to refer to the 1870s as "a watershed in English life"'.

30. That is to say, it undermines the notion that there is a fixed and inevitable 'correspondence' between capitalism, in all its phases, and Puritanism, in all its variants. This does not mean, as has sometimes recently been argued, that the two domains are wholly autonomous of each other; nor does it prove that there are no tendencies, in specific conjunctures, to 'conform' the two structures. This approach has sometimes been described as 'neo-Gramscian'. It does indeed follow some of the fruitful formulations of this sort of problem by Gramsci. This retains the notion of a social formation as 'articulated as a complex unity', while refusing any tendency to an economic reductionism.

31. For a similar argument, and an examination of alternative approaches –
    in this instance, with respect to education and schooling – cf. Hall
    (1977).
32. There is a good deal of research now in progress on the position of
    women in the fifties. Cf. especially Wilson (1977).
33. See the quote and an extended discussion of the *Beveridge Report*'s
    relation to the quantitative and qualitative reproduction of labour
    power in Bland, McCabe and Mort (1978).
34. For the purposes of discussing the reproduction of labour power, Marx
    recognised a historical determinacy as to both the 'number and extent of
    his [the worker's] so-called necessary wants' and 'the modes of satisfying
    them' – the 'historical moral element' in determining the value of the
    reproduction of labour power, which 'are themselves the product of
    historical development'. Recent marxist feminist theory has shown just
    what a 'history' is hidden within this unexamined promise.
35. How these elements are balanced out would require a more extensive
    analysis of the ideological structures of the literature and ideologies of
    'motherhood' and 'the family' in the psychological and welfare literature
    of the period – and their increasing interpenetration.
36. Winship (1978) makes this point, and gives an extended analysis of
    women's magazines of the period.
37. For a detailed analysis of advertising imagery of women, which shifts the
    accent towards the erotic and narcissistic pole, cf. Millum (1975) and
    Winship (1978).
38. One of the best, but unjustly neglected, studies of post-war
    Conservativism.
39. Hobsbawm (1968) p. 224. Hobsbawm's discussion on the internal shifts
    within the class structure as a result of 'affluence', though brief, is
    exemplary. At the time, everything was declared to have changed:
    classes abolished, the working class 'embourgeoisified'. Since then, in
    reaction to this gross ideological over-simplification, it has become
    fashionable to argue that nothing changed. Both views are woefully
    inadequate as historical generalisations.
40. *The Labour Case*, was prepared by Roy Jenkins as a Penguin Special for
    the 1959 election, and *Why Conservative?*, by Timothy Raison, as a
    Penguin Special for the 1964 election.
41. In addition to earlier references cited, cf. 'The Labour Party in
    Opposition' in Bogdanor (1970).
42. The growing interpenetration of the state and big capital (international
    and national) is often spoken of as if (a) it happened overnight, (b) its
    installation was unproblematic, (c) the identification of this phase of
    modern capitalist development accounts, in a simple way, for all its
    variant combinations, (d) the consequent transformation of the state,
    the political structures, civil society and culture presented no problems.
    This left–functionalism arises, in part, through a basic theoretical

confusion about the levels of abstraction in the analysis of social formations. The identification of a general, 'sub-epochal' shift within the capitalist mode only provides us with a broad framework for the analysis of particular conjectures. In opposition to this generalised function-alism, we would argue that, in general, such a historical shift represents the attempt, by capital, to overcome certain internal contradictions or barriers to its expansion; and that such shifts are, as always, limited by the relations of class forces – this is, by the class struggle. This means, in detail, that (a) we are analysing a historical process, not an overnight transformation (this phase has been 'in process' since the last decades of the 19th century, and is still nowhere near its 'completion'); (b) its installation has proved extremely problematic, especially – though not exclusively – in Britain; (c) we have seen successive attempts to instal different variants of the state–capital combination (each 'mix' has required its own political and ideological 'work', each has encountered its own contradictions, and each 'mix' has had specific and pertinent 'effects'); (d) the securing of the political and ideological conditions of existence for the reproduction of this phase of the mode has provoked moments of contestation and resistance – and these have dictated the pace, rhythm and direction of post-war struggles, especially in the politics and ideological fields. The success of the Tory 'radical right' in mobilising a powerful 'anti-state-big-capital' alliance shows how in-securely, as yet, has been the state's attempts to raise or found a new 'level of civilisation' appropriate to the new modes of capital accumu-lation and realisation.

43. Laclau has make a powerful argument for the necessity of a non-reductionist theory of ideology within Marxism. The strategy of argument in this paper has been extensively influenced by Laclau's formulations. Cf. Laclau (1977). Laclau, however, appears to argue that the Gramscian requirement, to identify the strategic class fractions and their 'representations' in specific political and ideological social forces, is itself a complex form of 'class reductionism'. But this appears to confine 'class struggle' and class formations exclusively to the economic level. In this chapter we have held to the premise, outlined by Gramsci in his work, that the identification of the strategic fractions and combinations of specific 'historical blocs' is a necessary phase in the analysis of ideological conjunctures. This should not be taken as arguing that specific ideological discourses are ascribed to these class fractions as their origin or 'subjects'; nor that these discouses are given an unproblematic or universal 'class belongingness'. We believe that there remains, in Gramsci, the basis for a non-class-reductionist, 'class' analysis of ideological struggle.

44. This formulation attempts to circumvent the simple counter-position, in the analysis of the 'welfare reforms' of the 1945 Labour Government, between 'real advances for the working class' and 'successful social

control of the working class' through welfare. We believe that the welfare reforms – gains and limits – represented the outcome of a protracted class struggle. They were, at one and the same time, 'real, if limited gains', made by the class against capital, *and*, of course (since they took place within the structures of capitalism and a capitalist state), new forms of 'social control'. In the process of 'recuperation' of the 'welfare state' to the dynamic of private capital, we would argue that the absorption and modes of containment instituted under the Tory hegemony of 1951–64, on the back of an extensive but selective capitalist 'boom', is a critical phase in the story of its active containment. It was out of the results of this process of recuperation that the Conservative hegemony of the fifties was constructed. On this point, cf. Corrigan (1977). For a critique of the concept of 'social control', see Jones (1977).

45. Gamble's perceptive analysis has considerably informed my argument at this point.

46. The 'exhaustion of consent' and the 'construction of a "soft" law-and-order society' are more fully examined in Hall, Clarke, *et al.* (1978).

47. *The Times*, Parliamentary Report, 28 January 1969. For this quote, and extensive discussion of the *Wootton Report* and its public reception, cf. Young (1971) pp. 198ff.

48. 'Classification and Framing of Educational Knowledge', Bernstein (1975) pp. 88–9.

49. In the succeeding essay, 'Class and Pedagogies: Visible and Invisible', Bernstein (1975).

50. For a more general model of these processes, see Bourdieu and Passeron (1971). For an analysis of the shifts in style and taste associated with the 'progressive middle classes', cf. the study of 'haute couture et haute culture', by Bourdieu and Delsaut (1975).

Chapter 2

1. This article will focus upon a particular way in which youth unemployment, a structural and public problem, may be translated into private troubles. The particular form of individualisation of structural problems discussed here is termed a 'pathologisation' of working-class youth, because it involves the characterisation of members of that group as suffering from individual developmental problems so severe as to merit public anxiety and preventive and curative management. But this is only one of several possible forms of individualisation of structural problems. And these problems may also be translated into the language of failure of intermediate institutions: failure in the educational system ('The Great Debate'), failure in the welfare system (encouraging 'scrounging'), or failure in the family or in local community leadership may also be put forward as explanations.

2. This discussion is drawn from a more complete study, in progress (paper presented at 5th Conference of the European Group for Deviance and Social Control, Barcelona, 1977). See also Adams (1972), Musto (1973), Johnson (1975), and Room (1976).

3. Figure 2.1 represents an over-simplification of the situation, but one that may be useful for initial orientation. A more adequate theorisation would have to acknowledge the triangular relationship between youth and parental and control cultures, and also the interactions between control institutions (e.g. between welfare agencies, the courts, the professions and the press).

4. I do not discuss the details of recent court cases and legislative changes caused by a 'loophole' in the 1971 Act that resulted in short-term uncertainty about the exact legal status of cannabis leaves. That uncertainty was resolved in 1977 by Parliament, replacing leaves in the same legal category as cannabis resin, and echoing the intention of the 1971 Act. It is notable that cannabis law reform groups were apparently unable to capitalise upon that brief period of uncertainty. But, if the arguments here are correct, future conditions may favour them more.

5. As yet lacking such research, I have not been able in this paper to discuss working-class responses to the problems posed by contemporary control solutions. The Alcohol and Teenage Culture Project, funded by the Health Education Council and carried out by the Evaluation Research Unit of ISDD, is designed to generate this research and to contribute to the reform of health education practice. I would like to acknowledge the encouragement of Victoria Greenwood, John Auld and Steve Butters, and the editorial suggestions of Jock Young, with the usual disclaimers.

Chapter 3

1. This chapter is essentially a working paper which is part of a larger study of the English juvenile court. I am grateful to Stuart Hall, Richard Johnson, Roisin McDonough, Paul Corrigan and Hilary Walker for their help in a variety of ways with its preparation.

2. Thus, there are implications that failure to pay rent, for example, is caused by poor budgeting, incompetence, recklessness, and so on.

3. Though, in reverse, the *practice* of casework should not itself be taken to be unidimensionally psychotherapeutic, simply because this forms the dominant professional and training conception. Given this, it is not difficult to see that there are important resonances between these proposals and the emergent social work agencies.

4. This point might be expressed in a different way. The emphasis in Labour strategy on 'scientific' industrial management, and the development of a higher education programme better adapted to the demands of a technological capitalism in this period, can lead us to forget that this is accompanied by the development of the science of human relations, and

the growing importance of 'man management'. It is also, of course, the period of expansion in the humanities and social sciences in higher education, aimed at delivering skilled and sensitive people to both the state 'personal' sectors and to the commercial sectors of capital – advertising, marketing, the media and so on.

5. There is no actual overlap of membership between these groups, though Alice Bacon, a member of the Study Group, had, in responding as Shadow Under-Secretary for the Home Office to the Children and Young Persons Bill 1963, drawn extensively on the second of the Fabian pamphlets.

6. These paragraphs are a very abbreviated account of complex arguments. For more detailed analyses, see CSE (1976), RCG (1976) and Wilson (1977).

7. This point is further emphasised in the section of the Longford Group's report on women criminals, in which they are dealt with solely as mothers and potential mothers, and reforms are aimed to help them be better mothers.

Chapter 5

1. This paper is indebted to previous attempts to develop a general analysis of British race relations policy, notably those of Katznelson (1973) and Sivanandan (1976). Any weaknesses of the present paper are in no way traceable to these authors.

2. For the relationship between capital restructuring and the use of immigrant labour in the textile industry, see Cohen and Jenner (1968).

3. The conception of racial prejudice as part of a cyclical process of 'cumulative causation' was first developed by Myrdal (1944).

4. The best known calculations were those produced by the National Institute for Economic and Social Research in August 1967.

5. For an invaluable account of control at the point of entry, see Moore and Wallace (1975).

6. The Race Relations Act 1976 removed the necessity to prove intent.

7. Thus, although the size of the labour force in wool textiles, for example, fell from 174,016 in 1953 to 59,917 in 1975, the percentage of that declining labour force consisting of Indian and Pakistani workers has risen from 1.5 per cent in 1957 to 13.1 per cent in 1973. At the same time, the percentage of shiftworkers as a proportion of all workers engaged in textile employment as a whole has risen from 11.1 per cent in 1954 to 24.8 per cent in 1968. See Department of Employment (1976) tables F4 and H.1).

8. Katznelson sees the race relations apparatus as consisting of 'buffer institutions, replicating key features of traditional colonial relationships' (Katznelson, 1973, p. 178). This is an important insight, though he then tends to suggest that the source of 'racial buffering' lay in an

attempt to depoliticise race. Thus 'The issues of race for British politicians were incoherent and anomic. This central feature of domestic racial politics produced a political consensus that strictly controlled Third World migration and that – in the key structural decision of the period – linked the immigrants to the polity indirectly – through quasi-colonial buffer institutions' (Katznelson, 1973, p. 185). In my argument the issues of race were anything but 'incoherent and anomic'.

9. National Council for Commonwealth Immigrants, 'Notes on the formation of a voluntary liaison committee', April 1967, quoted in Katznelson (1973) p. 177.

10. For a lively account of the overwhelming white middle-class composition of the race relations machinery, cf. Mullard (1973) part 3.

11. Hill and Issacharoff (1971), in their study of the working of eight local community relations committees, found the following social composition of the immigrant members of the executive committees (in percentages):

Professional, executive, managerial	46
Routine non-manual	12
Skilled manual	16
Semi-skilled/unskilled	26

12. The following table gives the percentage age structure for youth in the black communities and the total population:

Age group	New Commonwealth America	India	Pakistan	Total Population
0–14	51	36	34	24
15–24	11	18	20	15

Source Gillian Lomas (1973).

13. For example, at the time of the 1971 census 16.2 per cent of West Indian males aged 16–20 were unemployed, compared with 8.1 per cent of the total male population of that age group.

Chapter 6

1. Such an investigation is part of a larger work in preparation, covering the areas of abortion, homosexuality, pornography, prostitution and rape, to be entitled *Crimes of Sex*. Limitations of space in this chapter allow us merely to touch upon the arguments regarding interventionist depictions of homosexuality and prostitution.

2. In this chapter we discuss interventionism as a general feature of the centrist politics of the period. In Greenwood and Young (1976) we focus

on the social democratic variant of this, namely reformism.

3. Limitations of space do not permit us to expand on the manner in which male and female roles are defined in interventionism – such distinctions have direct bearing on explanations of prostitution, homosexuality and abortion during this period.

4. For a use of such categorisation in analysing mass media imagery, see J. Young (forthcoming).

5. For a discussion of the ideological harnessing of moral indignation in terms of crime in general, see J. Young (1975).

6. In the *Wolfenden Report* prostitutes are depicted as inadequates who in turn corrupt the client. The pimp was a psychological prop who shored up her inadequacy. This was discarded in the Street Offences Act, wherein the pimp once more regained his position as the corrupter of the prostitute.

7. For a discussion of bohemian culture, drug use and moral panics see J. Young (1973).

8. A general account of the politics of abortion occurs in Greenwood and Young (1976).

9. Similar processes of bifurcation involving liberalisation, on the one hand, and a hardening of reaction, on the other, occurred throughout the legislation of this period – e.g. Children and Young Persons Act 1969, *Mountbatten Report*, 1967, Criminal Justice Act 1967.

10. It is noteworthy that thoroughgoing positivist techniques aimed at changing behaviour are rarely used in the process of medicalisation. Instead, positivism is more usually co-opted and its methods debased in order to quiesce, pacify and make deviant populations more manageable.

Bibliography

Adams, L. (1972) 'The Historical Setting of Asia's Profitable Plague', appended to A. McCoy, *The Politics of Heroin in S.E. Asia* (London: Harper and Row).

Alderman, R. K. (1966) 'The Conscience Clause of the Parliamentary Labour Party', *Parliamentary Affairs*, vol. XIX, pp. 224–32.

Althusser, L. (1969) *For Marx* (London: Allen Lane).

Althusser, L. (1971) *Lenin and Philosophy and Other Essays* (London: New Left Books).

Andy, O. J. (1970) 'Thalamotomy in hyperactive and aggressive behaviour', *Confinia Neurologica*, vol. 32, pp. 320–7.

Balch, R. W. (1975) 'The medical model of delinquency', *Crime and Delinquency*, vol. 21.

Baldwin, H. *et al.* (1968) 'The relationship of allergy to cerebral dysfunction', *Southern Medical Journal*, vol. 61, pp. 1037–40.

Banks, J. A. and O. (1974) *Feminism and Family Planning* (Liverpool University Press).

Bax, M. (1972) 'The active and overactive school child', *Development Medicine and Child Neurology*, vol. 14, pp. 83–6.

Baxley, G. B. and LeBlanc, J. M. (1975) 'The hyperactive child: characteristics, treatment, and evaluation of research design', *Child Development*, vol. 8.

Bean, P. (1974). *Social Control of Drugs* (London: Martin Robertson).

Beechey, V. (1977) 'Some Notes on Female Wage Labour in Capital Production', *Capital and Class*, no. 3 (Autumn).

Bell, R. Q. (1968) 'A reinterpretation of the direction of effects in studies of socialization', *Psychological Review*, vol. 75, pp. 81–95.

Bernstein, B. (1975) 'Classification and Framing of Educational Knowledge' and 'Class and Pedagogies: Visible and Invisible', in *Class, Codes and Control*, vol. 3 (London: Routledge).

Beveridge Report, see HMSO (1942).

Blacker, C. (1952) Introduction to *Problem Families, Five Enquiries* (London: Eugenics Society).

Bland, L., McCabe, T. and Mort, F. (1978) Unpublished paper to the BSA 1978 Conference, Cultural Studies, University of Birmingham (mimeo).

Bogdanor, V. (1970) 'The Labour Party in Opposition', in V. Bogdanor and R. Skidelsky (eds), *Age of Affluence* (London: Macmillan).

Bogdanor, V. and Skidelsky, R. (eds) (1970) *Age of Affluence* (London: Macmillan).

Bottoms, A. (1975) 'On the Decriminalisation of English Juvenile Courts', in R. Hood (ed.), *Crime, Criminology and Public Policy* (London: Heinemann).

Bourdieu, P. and Delsaut, Y. (1975) 'Le Couturier et sa Griffe: Contribution à une Théorie de la Magie', *Actes*, No. 1 (Paris).

Bourdieu, P. and Passeron, J-C. (1971) *Reproduction in Education, Society and Culture* (New York: Sage).

Box, S. (1977) 'Hyperactivity: a scandalous silence', *New Society* (1 December).

Box, S. (forthcoming) *Eaten by the Locust: systems of therapeutic control in industrialised societies* (London: Macmillan).

Breggin, P. R. (1972) 'The return of lobotomy and psycho-surgery', *Congressional Record* (24 February) pp. 5567–74.

British Medical Journal (1973) 'Hyperactive Children' (10 February) pp. 305–6.

British Medical Journal (1975) 'Hyperactivity in Children' (18 October) pp. 123–4.

Brittan, S. (1969) *Steering the Economy* (London: Secker and Warburg).

Broudy, H. S. (1975) 'Ideological, political and moral considerations in the use of drugs in hyperkinetic therapy', in J. Bosco and S. S. Robin (eds), *The Hyperactive Child and Stimulant Drugs* (Chicago University Press) pp. 43–60.

Butler, R. A. (1971) *The Art of the Possible* (London: Hamish Hamilton).

Cantwell, D. (1977) 'The hyperkinetic syndrome', in M. Rutter and L. Hersov (eds), *Child Psychiatry* (London: Blackwell Scientific Books).

Carmen, J. S. and Tucker L. S. (1973) 'Benztropine in childhood hyperkinesis', *Lancet* (8 December) pp. 1337–8.

Christoph, J. O. (1962) *Capital Punishment in British Politics* (London: Allen and Unwin).

Clarke, J. (1975) 'The Three R's; Repression, Rescue and Rehabilitation', CCCS stencilled paper.

Cloward, R. A. and Ohlin, L. E. (1960) *Delinquency and Opportunity* (New York: Free Press).

Coates, D. (1975) *The Labour Party and the Struggle for Socialism* (Cambridge University Press).

Cockett, R. (1971) *Drug Abuse and Personality in Young Offencers* (London: Butterworth).

Cohen, A. K. (1955) *Delinquent Boys* (New York: Free Press).

Cohen, A. K. (1965) 'The Sociology of the Deviant Act', *American Sociological Review*, vol. 30.

Cohen, B. (1971) 'The Demographic and Statistical Background', in S. Abbott (ed.), *The Prevention of Racial Discrimination in Britain* (Oxford University Press).

Cohen, B. and Jenner, P. (1968) 'The Employment of Immigrants: a case study in the Wool Industry', *Race*, vol. x, No. 1 (July).

Cole, S. H. (1975) Hyperkinetic Children: the use of stimulant drugs evaluated', *American Journal of Orthopsychiatry*, vol. 45, No. 1, pp. 28–37.

Conrad, P. (1975) 'The discovery of hyperkinesis: notes on the medicalisation of deviant behaviour', *Social Problems*, vol. 23, No. 1, pp. 12–21.

Conrad, P. (1976) *Identifying Hyperactive Children* (Mass: Lexington Books).

Corrigan, P. (1977) 'The Welfare State as an Arena of Class Struggle', *Marxism Today* (March).

Cox, B. (1959) *Civil Liberties in Britain* (Harmondsworth: Penguin).

Cressey, D. R. (1969) *Theft of the Nation* (New York: Harper and Row).

Crosland, C. A. R. (1962) *The Conservative Enemy* (London: Cape).

Crosland, C. A. R. (1963) *The Future of Socialism* (London: Cape).

CSE (1976) *On the Political Economy of Women* (London: Stage One).

Curran, C. (1962) 'The New Model Bourgeoisie', *Crossbow*, 21.

David, O. *et al.* (1972) 'Lead and hyperactivity', *Lancet*, vol. 2, pp. 900–3.

Davies, C. (1975) *Permissive Britain* (London: Pitman).

Deakin, N. and Ungerson, C. (1973) 'Beyond the Ghetto: the Illusion of Choice', in D. Donnison and D. Eversley (eds), *London: Urban Patterns, Problems and Policies* (London: Heinemann).

Department of Employment (1976) *The Role of Immigrants in the Labour Market* (London: HMSO).

Devlin, (Lord) Patrick (1965) *The Enforcement of Morals* (Oxford University Press).

Dickson, D. (1968) 'Bureaucracy and Morality', *Social Problems*, vol. 16, pp. 143–56.

Donnison, D. and Stewart, M. (1958) *The Child and the Social Services*, Fabian pamphlet (London: Fabian Society).

Donnison, D., Jay, P. and Stewart, M. (1962) *The Ingleby Report; Three Critical Essays*, Fabian pamphlet (London: Fabian Society).

Dorn, N. (1977) *Teaching Decision-making Skills about Legal and Illegal Drugs* (London: ISDD and HEC).

Drug Abuse Council (1975) *Survey of Marijuana Use and Attitudes, State of Oregon* – press release (Washington, December).

Drugs and Therapeutics Bulletin (1977) 'Stimulant Drugs for Hyperactive Children', vol. 15, No. 6, pp. 22–4.

Ellis, N. R. and Pryer, R. S. (1959) 'Quantification of gross bodily activity in children with severe neuropathology', *American Journal of Mental Deficiency*, vol. 63, pp. 1034–7.

Engels, F. (1968) 'Ludwig Feuerbach and the end of Classical German Philosophy', in *Marx and Engels: Selected Works* (London: Lawrence and Wishart).

Finer, S. (1958) *The Anonymous Empire* (London: Pall Mall).

Finer, S., Berrington, H. *et al.* (1961) *Backbench Opinion in the House of Commons* (Oxford University Press).

Finn, D., Grant, N. and Johnson, R. (1978) 'Social Democracy, Education and the Crisis', in Centre for Contemporary Cultural Studies, *On Ideology* (London: Hutchinson).

Foucault, M. (1978) *Discipline and Punish* (London: Allen Lane).

Foucault, M. (1972) *Archaeology of Knowledge* (London: Tavistock).

Gamble, A. (1974) *The Conservative Nation* (London: Routledge).

Giller, H. and Morris, A. (1976) 'Children Who Offend: care, control, or confusion?', *Criminal Law Review*, pp. 655–66.

Gramsci, A. (1971) 'The State and Civil Society', in *Prison Notebooks* (London: Lawrence and Wishart).

Greenwood, V. and Young, J. (1976) *Abortion in Demand* (London: Pluto Press).

Grey, A. (1975) 'Homosexual Law Reform', in B. Frost (ed.), *The Tactics of Pressure* (London: Stainer and Bell).

Grinspoon, L. and Hedblom, P. (1975) *The Speed Culture* (London: Harvard University Press).

Hall, S. (1977) 'Review of the Course', Open University Course E 202, *Schooling and Society*, Unit 32.

Hall, S. *et al.* (1978) *Policing the Crisis* (London: Macmillan).

Hall, S., Lumley, B. and McLennan, G. (1978) 'Politics and Ideology in Gramsci', in CCCS, *On Ideology* (London: Centre for Cultural Studies and Hutchinson).

Halliday, J. and Fuller, P. (1977) *The Psychology of Gambling* (Harmondsworth: Penguin).

Hart, H. L. A. (1963) *Law, Liberty and Morality* (Oxford University Press).

Hay, D., Linebaugh, P. and Thompson, E. P. (1975) *Albion's Fatal Tree* (London: Allen Lane).

Heineman, B. W. (1972) *The Politics of the Powerless: a Study of the Campaign against Racial Discrimination* (Oxford University Press).

Hill, M. and Issacharoff, R. (1971) *Community Action and Race Relations* (Oxford University Press).

Hindell, K. and Simms, M. (1968) 'How the Abortion Lobby Worked', *Political Quarterly*, vol. 39.

Hindell, K. and Simms, M. (1971) *Abortion Law Reformed* (London: Peter Owen).

HMSO (1942) *Social Insurance and Allied Services* (Beveridge Report), Cmd. 7321 (London: HMSO).

HMSO (1957) *Report of the Committee on Homosexual Offences and Prostitution* (Wolfenden Report), Cmnd. 257 (London: HMSO).

HMSO (1965) *Immigration from the Commonwealth*, Cmnd. 2739 (London: HMSO).

HMSO (1965a) *The Child, the Family and the Young Offender*, Cmnd. 2742 (London: HMSO).

HMSO (1968) *Report of the Advisory Committee on Drug Dependence* (*Wootton Report*) (London: HMSO).

HMSO (1968a) *Children in Trouble*, Cmnd. 3601 (London: HMSO).

HMSO (1974) *The Working Party on Vagrancy and Street Offences*, Working Paper (London: HMSO).

Hobsbawm, E. (1968) *Industry and Empire* (London: Weidenfeld and Nicolson).

Howell, D. (1976) *British Social Democracy* (London: Croom Helm).

Hyde, H. Montgomery (1972) *The Other Love* (London: Heinemann).

ISDD (1976) 'Seeing Glue Through Heroin Spectacles' and 'Solvent Sniffing: Coverage in the Press', *Druglink*, vol. 2, No. 3, pp. 1–5.

Jenkins, R. (1959) *The Labour Case* (Harmondsworth: Penguin Special).

Jephcott, P. and Carter, M. P. (1954) *The Social Background of Delinquency* (Nottingham University Press).

Johnson, B. (1975) 'Righteousness Before Revenue: the Forgotten Moral Crusade against the Indo-Chinese Opium Trade', *Journal of Drug Issues*, vol. 5, No. 4, pp. 304–26.

Jones, G. Stedman (1977) 'Class Expression versus Social Control', *History Workshop*, No. 4 (Autumn).

Katznelson, I. (1973) *Black Men, White Cities* (Oxford University Press).

Kittrie, N. H. (1971) *The Right to be Different* (Baltimore Maryland: Johns Hopkins Press).

Klein, M. W. (1971) *Street Gangs and Street Workers*, (Englewood Cliffs, N.J.: Prentice-Hall).

Kolvin, I. (1976) 'Maladjusted Pupils in Ordinary Schools', *Special Education*, vol. 3, No. 3, pp. 15–20.

Krager, J. M. and Safer, D. J. (1974) 'Type and Prevalence of Medication used in the Treatment of Hyperactive Children', *New England Journal of Medicine*, vol. 291, pp. 1118–20.

Laclau, E. (1977) *Politics and Ideology in Marxist Theory* (London: New Left Books).

Lanuette, W. (1972) *Legislative Control of Cannabis*, unpublished Ph D thesis, University of London.

Lerman, P. (1975) *Community Treatment and Social Control* (University of Chicago Press).

Lewis, M. A. (1973) *Hyperactivity and Variations in Prevalence Rates for Assignment to Special Classes Among Black, White and Spanish Surnamed*

Students in Twenty-Five Urban and Suburban School Districts in New Jersey, Unpublished Ed D, Rutgers University, New Jersey.

Linsky, A. S. (1970) 'Theories of Behaviour and the Image of the Alcoholic in Popular Magazines: 1900–1966', *Public Opinion Quarterly*, vol. 34, No. 4.

Lomas, G. (1973) *The Coloured Population of Great Britain* (London: Runnymede Trust).

Longford Study Group (1966) *Crime: a challenge to us all* (London: Labour Party).

McFarland, J. N. *et al.* (1966) 'Mental Retardation and activity level in rats and children', *American Journal of Mental Deficiency*, vol. 71, pp. 381–6.

McGregor, O. R. (1958) *Divorce in England* (London: Heinemann).

Mark, V., Sweet, W. and Ervin, R. (1967) 'Role of brain disease in riots and urban violence', *Journal of the American Medical Association*, vol. 222, p. 363.

Marx, K. (1857) Introduction to the *Grundrisse* (Harmondsworth: Pelican, 1973).

Marx, K. (1961) *Capital*, vol. ı (London: Lawrence and Wishart).

Marx, K. (1967) *Capital*, vol. ı (Moscow: Foreign Languages Publishing House).

Mathieson, T. (1974) *The Politics of Abolition* (London: Martin Robertson).

Matza, D. (1964) *Delinquency and Drift* (New York: Wiley).

Menkes, M., Rowe, J. and Menkes, J. (1967) 'A twenty-five-year follow-up study of the hyperkinetic child with minimal brain dysfunction', *Pediatrics*, vol. 39, pp. 393–9.

Miliband, R. (1961) *Parliamentary Socialism* (London: Allen and Unwin).

Miller, W. (1958) 'Lower-class culture as a generating milieu of gang delinquency', *Journal of Social Issues*, vol. 15, pp. 5–19.

Miller, W. (1962) 'Preventive Work with Street Corner Groups', *Annals*, p. 324.

Mills, C. W. (1959) *The Sociological Imagination* (Oxford University Press).

Millum, T. (1975) *Images of Women* (London: Chatto and Windus).

Montagu, J. D. and Swarbrick, L. (1975) 'Effect of amphetamines in hyperactive children: Stimulant or sedative? a pilot study', *Developmental Medicine and Child Neurology*, vol 17, pp. 293–8.

Moodie, G. and Studdert Kennedy, G. (1969) *Opinions, Publics and Pressure Groups* (London: Allen and Unwin).

Moore, R. and Wallace, T. (1975) *Slamming the Door: The Administration of Immigration Control* (London: Martin Robertson).

Moyer, K. E. (1975) 'Allergy and aggression: the physiology of violence', *Psychology Today*, vol. 9, pp. 76–9.

Mullard, C. (1973) *Black Britain* (London: Allen and Unwin).

Musto, D. (1973) *The American Disease: Origins of Narcotic Control* (New Haven, Conn.: Yale University Press).

Myrdal, G. (1944) *An American Dilemma* (New York: McGraw-Hill, 1964).

National Council for Civil Liberties (1972) *Against Censorship* (London: NCCL).

NCCDE (1977) 'Medical Therapy, Legalisation Issues Debated at Marijuana Reform Conference', *National Drug Reporter*, vol. 7, No. 1 (January).

Neville, R. (1972) 'Never Trust Anyone Over Thirty', *Oz*, vol. 40, p. 5.

Omenn, G. S. (1973) 'Genetic issues in the syndrome of minimal brain damage', *Seminars in Psychiatry*, vol. 5, pp. 5–17.

Oppenheimer, P. (1970) 'Muddling Through: the Economy 1951–64', in V. Bogdanor and R. Skidelsky (eds), *Age of Affluence* (London: Macmillan).

Pinto-Duchinsky, M. (1970) 'Bread and Circuses: the Conservatives in Office, 1951–64', in V. Bogdanor and R. Skidelsky (eds), *Age of Affluence* (London: Macmillan).

Platt, A. (1969) *The Child Savers* (University of Chicago Press).

Power, J. (1975) 'Europe's Army of Immigrants', *International Affairs*, vol. 51, No. 3.

Prescott, J. W. (1968) 'Early social deprivation', in D. B. Linksley and A. H. Ricset (eds), *Perspectives on Human Deprivation* (Bethesda, Md.: National Institutes of Child Health and Human Development).

Prescott, J. W. (1970) 'A development psychophysiological theory of autistic depressive and violent–aggressive behaviours', *Psychophysiology*, vol. 6, pp. 628–9.

Pym, B. (1974) *Pressure Groups and the Permissive Society* (Newton Abbot: David and Charles).

Raison, T. (1964) *Why Conservative?* (Harmondsworth: Penguin Special).

RCG (1976) 'Women's Oppression under Capitalism', *Revolutionary Communist*, vol. 5.

Richards, P. G. (1970) *Parliament and Conscience* (London: Allen and Unwin).

Roberts, G. K. (1970) *Political Parties and Pressure Groups in Britain* (London: Weidenfeld and Nicolson).

Room, R. (1976) 'The Political Economy of Alcohol and Drug Problems' (conference report), *Drinking and Drug Practices Surveyor*, vol. 12 (December).

Rose, E. J. B. *et al.* (1969) *Colour and Citizenship* (Oxford University Press).

Ross, D. M. and Ross, S. A. (1976) *Hyperactivity: Research, Theory and Action* (New York: Wiley).

Ryan, W. (1971) *Blaming the Victim* (London: Orbach and Chambers).

St John-Stevas, N. (1963) *The Right to Live* (London: Eyre and Spottiswoode).

Sandoval, J. *et al.* (1976) 'Current medical practice and hyperactive children', *American Journal of Orthopsychiatry*, vol. 46, No. 2, pp. 323–4.

Schain, R. J. and Reynard, C. L. (1975) 'Observations on effects of a central stimulant drug (methylphenidate) in children with hyperactive behaviour', *Pediatrics*, vol. 55, pp. 709–16.

Schenkman, J. (1976) 'Why They Call Us White Trash', *High Times*, vol 16 (December) pp. 109–11.

Schrag, P. and Divoky, D. (1975) *The Myth of the Hyperactive Child* (New York: Pantheon Books).

Schulman, J. L. and Reisman, J. M. (1959) 'An objective measure of hyperactivity', *American Journal of Mental Deficiency*, vol. 64, pp. 455–6.

Schur, E. (1973) *Radical Non-Intervention* (Englewood Cliffs, N.J.: Prentice-Hall).

Scottish Office (1964) *Children and Young Persons: Scotland*, Cmnd. 2306 (London: HMSO).

Scull, A. T. (1975) 'From madness to mental illness: medical men as moral entrepreneurs', *European Journal of Sociology*, vol 16, pp. 218–61.

Shaw, C. and McKay, H. (1942) *Juvenile Delinquency and Urban Areas* (University of Chicago Press).

Shevitz, S. A. (1976) 'Psychosurgery: some current observations', *American Journal of Psychiatry*, 133:3, pp. 266–70.

Simon, G. B. (1974) 'A Teachers' Guide to "Drugs" ', *Special Education*, vol. 1, pp. 25–7.

Sivanandan, A. (1976) *Race, Class and the State: the Black Experience in Britain*, Race and Class Pamphlet No. 1 (London: Institute of Race Relations).

Smart, R. (1976) *The New Drinkers* (Toronto: Addiction Research Foundation).

Smith, D. J. (1977) *Racial Disadvantage in Britain* (Harmondsworth: Penguin).

Sollenberger, R. T. (1968) 'Chinese-American child-rearing practices and juvenile delinquency', *Journal of Social Psychology*, vol. 74, pp. 13–23.

Spencer, D. A. (1970) 'Ronyl (Pemoline) in Overactive Mentally Subnormal Children', *British Journal of Psychiatry*, vol. 120, pp. 239–40.

Spitzer, S. (1975) 'Toward a Marxian theory of deviance', *Social Problems*, vol. 22, p. 638–51.

Sprague, R. L. and Toppe, L. K. (1966) 'Relationship between activity level and delay of reinforcement in the retarded', *Journal of Experimental Child Psychology*, vol. 3, pp. 390–7.

Szasz, T. (1963) *Law, Liberty and Psychiatry* (New York: Macmillan).

Szasz, T. (1977) *Schizophrenia* (New York: Basic Books).

Taylor, I. and Taylor, L. (eds) (1973) *Politics and Deviance*, (Harmondsworth: Penguin).

Taylor, I., Walton, P. and Young, J. (eds) (1975) *Critical Criminology* (London: Routledge).

Thompson, E. P. (1975) *Whigs and Hunters* (London: Allen Lane).

Timms, N. (1964) *Psychiatric Social Work in Great Britain* (London: Routledge).

Triantafillow, M. (1972) 'Pemoline in Overactive Mentally Handicapped Children', *British Journal of Psychiatry*, vol. 121, p. 577.

Tuttle, E. O. (1961) *The Crusade against Capital Punishment in Great Britain* (London: Stevens).

UK Government (1975) *Report to the U.N. by H. M. Government in the UK of Great Britain and Northern Ireland on the Working of the International Treaties on Narcotic Drugs* (London: Home Office).

Walkland, S. A. (1963) *The Legislative Process in Great Britain* (London: Allen and Unwin).

Weeks, J. (1977) *Coming Out* (London: Quartet).

Werry, J. (1968) 'Studies on the hyperactive child IV. an empirical analysis of the minimal brain dysfunction syndrome', *Archives of General Psychiatry*, vol. 19, pp. 9–16.

Werry, J. S. and Sprague, R. L. (1970) 'Hyperactivity', in Costello, C. G. (ed.), *Symptoms of Psychopathology* (New York: Wiley).

Whitehouse, M. (1967) *Cleaning Up TV* (London: Blandford Press).

Whitehouse, M. (1971) *Who Does She Think She Is?* (London: New English Library).

Wiener, G. (1970) 'Varying psychological sequelae of lead ingestion in children', *Public Health Reports*, vol. 85, pp. 19–24.

Wildeblood, P. (1955 and 1957) *Against the Law* (London: Weidenfeld and Nicolson, 1955; Harmondsworth: Penguin, 1957).

Wilson, E. (1977) *Women and the Welfare State* (London: Tavistock).

Wilson, J. Q. (1975) *Thinking about Crime* (New York: Basic Books).

Winship, J. (1978) 'A Woman's World: *Woman* – an Ideology of Femininity', in *Women Take Issue* (London: Women's Studies Group, Centre for Cultural Studies and Hutchinson).

Witter, C. (1971) 'Drugging and Schooling', *Transactions*, vol. 8, nos 9–10 (July/August) pp. 30–4.

Wolfenden, (Lord) J. (1971) *Memoirs* (London: Bodley Head).

Wolfenden, (Lord) J. (1976) *Turning Points* (London: Bodley Head).

Wolfenden Report, see HMSO (1957).

Wood, A. (1969) *Pot or Not, a Plain Guide to Drug Dependence* (London: BMA Family Doctor Publications).

Wootton Report, see HMSO (1968).

Young, J. (1971) *The Drugtakers* (London: MacGibbon and Kee).

Young, J. (1973) 'The Hippie Solution', in I. Taylor and L. Taylor (eds), *Politics and Deviance* (Harmondsworth: Penguin).

Young, J. (1974) 'Drugs, Deviance and the Mass Media', in P. Rock and M. McIntosh (eds), *Deviance and Social Control* (London: Tavistock).

Young, J. (1975) 'Working Class Criminology', in I. Taylor, P. Walton and J. Young (eds), *Critical Criminology* (London: Routledge).

Young, J. (forthcoming) *Media as Myth* (London: Macmillan).

Zentall, S. (1975) 'Optimal stimulation as theoretical basis of hyperactivity', *American Journal of Orthopsychiatry*, vol. 45, pp. 549–63.

Zola, I. (1972) 'Medicine as an institution of social control', *Sociological Review*, vol. 20, pp. 487–504.

Index

abortion   5, 24, 156, 158, 170,
   173–4; legislation on   15–17,
   169–72
acquisitive society   82, 89
affluent society   36–7, 151, 154–5
alcohol   49, 58–9, 61–3, 68

behavioural therapy   105, 119
Benthamism   14
Bernstein, Basil   40–2
bifurcation   164, 168, 172
birth rate, falling   22
Butler, R. A.   1, 26, 28–9, 37, 125

Callaghan, J.   38–9, 58, 169
cannabis   56–71, 158; ambiguous
   position of   64–5, 150; commercialisation of   66, 68; conservatism of, debate on   44–71;
   decriminalisation of   66–8;
   immigrants' use of   52–3; law
   reform   44–8, 49, 59, 63–8, 71;
   Wootton Report   58, 167–9
capitalism   30, 32, 36–8, 155, 158,
   179–80n; immigrant workers and
   123–4, 132, 134–6, 138–41,
   146–8; problem groups under
   115–16; reformed   39, 88, 151;
   state   36, 38, 94
capitalist reproduction and delinquency   90, 92, 94–5
castration   164–5
categorisation, social   153, 169–71,
   172; delinquents   47–8, 79, 87,
   88; drugs   47–8
children: measurement of behaviour of
   103–4; naughty   85, 91, 96–121;
   see also hyperactivity; schoolchildren

Children and Young Persons Act 1969
   72, 86, 94, 113–14
Church of England   5
class discrimination   82–3, 84–5,
   127
community relations   142–7; black
   middle class and   144–8; committees   144
Community Relations Commission
   126, 144–5
community studies   73–4
Conservative Party   26–31, 32, 36,
   74, 95
contraception   24
corruption and permissiveness   58,
   171, 173
crime: causation of   81–2; without
   victims   148, 154, 155, 157
criminal problems   9–10
criminalisation   150, 161, 165, 173
Crosland, C. A. R.   32–4, 36
Crossbow   30
Curtis Committee   73

death penalty   1, 3, 7
decriminalisation   66–8, 150, 161,
   165–6, 170, 171
delinquency: deprivation and   73,
   78–9, 81, 84, 88–9, 116; drugs
   and   55, 105–21; gang
   116–17; Labour and Fabian views
   on   72–4, 76–7, 79–90, 93–5;
   White Papers   86–7
delinquents: categorisation of   79, 87,
   88; drug therapy for   105–21;
   parents of   76–9, 86; residential
   care   77, 85–6; social democratic
   thinking on   72–95

deprivation and delinquency 73,
78–9, 81, 84, 88–9, 116
determinism, biological 117
deviancy 152–6, 157–8; control of
158–9, 168, 172–4; as hyperactivity 104, 118–19
Devlin, Patrick (Lord) 2, 5, 14, 20,
29
divorce 15–16
drug therapy 119, 159; for hyperactive children 105–15, 118–21
drugs 46, 156, 174; control of
47–59, 66–8; definition of 63,
67; delinquency and 55, 105–21;
education on 68–70; middle class
use of 54–7, 67–8, 69; Misuse of
Drugs Act 1971 1, 49, 58–9,
169, 172; pushers 57–8, 59, 107,
150, 169, 173; social categories of
47–8; social problems of 48–51;
unemployment and 60, 63–4;
Wootton Report 1, 38–9, 58,
167–9, 172–3; youth problems
46, 49, 52–7, 60–4, 67–71; *see
also* cannabis; glue-sniffing
drugtakers 47, 62, 65, 168, 172

education: on drugs 68–70; reform
in 28, 38, 41, 83
educational knowledge, classification
and framing of 40–3
equality of opportunity 126–8, 130,
132–4

Fabian Society 72, 74; family service
plan 74–81, 84; views on delinquency 72, 74, 76–7, 81–9, 93
families, problem 73, 76–7, 78–9,
169
family: councils 86; courts 86;
service plan 74–81, 84, 88–9,
91–2; state and 90–2
Family Planning Act 1967 15
femininity, reconstruction of 21–6
freedom of choice 151, 156–7

gambling 25–6
gangs, youth 116–17
ghetto children, hyperactive 98, 101,
105, 108
ghettoisation 158, 159, 161, 164,
172–4
ghettos of freedom 149–74
glue-sniffing 44, 49, 61–2, 68

handicapped children 99
heroin 47, 52, 59, 168
High Times 62
Homosexual Law Reform Society 4,
166–7
homosexuality 163, 172, 174;
incidence of 8, 163–4, 166;
legislation on 7, 15, 20, 162–7;
privatisation of 12–13, 164;
treatment of 165; *Wolfenden
Report* on 11, 15, 156, 162,
164–5
homosexuals 150, 156
Howard League 3
hyperactivity in schoolchildren
97–121; brain surgery for 105;
causes of 102; as deviancy 104;
diagnosis of 103–4; drug therapy
for 105–15, 118–21; incidence
of 101–2, 111; naughtiness as
104–19

immigrants 122–3; as cheap labour
123–4, 132, 134–6, 138–41,
146–8; drug use by 52–3;
geographic concentration of
130–2; industrial militancy 135;
organisations 145–6; second
generation 138, 146–7; socio-
economic distribution of
129–34; unemployed 146; work
permit system and 138–9; *see
also* community relations; race;
racial
immigration control 124–6,
135–40, 148
individualism: competitive 151–2,
154, 156, 174; economic 28–30,
32, 34, 35
inequality of opportunity 130; self-
reinforcing 127–8

Jenkins, Roy 1, 7, 30, 35, 38, 125,
126
juvenile court 72–4, 86, 111–12,
114; reform proposals 78–9, 82,
84–5, 89
juveniles *see* delinquency; delinquents; schoolchildren

Labour Party: delinquency and
72–4, 79, 82, 86–9, 94; drugs and
57, 69; policy on social services
80–6, 93–5; reformism 7, 26–8;
revisionism 31–6, 38, 80

legislation: of consent   1, 17–18, 27,
   33; moral regulation and   12–21,
   149–50; organisation of   3–9;
   permissive   173–4
Liberal Party   48
lobby organisations   3–6, 39
Longford Group   81–6, 88–9, 91,
   92, 93

Macmillan, Harold   26, 28, 36–7
maladjusted children   98–9, 104–6
marriage   16–18
medical profession   108–9, 111,
   113–14, 119–21, 170, 171
medicalisation of social problems
   96–7, 99, 115, 117–18, 121, 150,
   158–9, 166, 170–3
mental hospitals, children admitted to
   99–100
mental illness   96–7, 99–100, 114,
   115, 120
middle class   29, 36, 37–8, 41, 63;
   black   144–8; use of drugs by
   54–7, 67–9
Mill, J. S.   156–7, 167
minors and homosexuality   11, 163
moral conduct, classification and
   framing of   40–3
moral indignation   153–8, 160, 164,
   169, 174
moral panic   8, 149, 150
moral reformism   37–40
moral regulation   17–18, 151;
   legislative   12–21, 149–50;
   politics and   30–4, 37–8;
   Wolfenden Report and   9–12
morality: public and private   20–1;
   self-regulating   11–12, 14

National Committee for Commonwealth Immigrants   126, 142, 144,
   145
naughtiness   85, 91; as hyperactivity
   104–19; *see also* schoolchildren
normalisation   150, 168, 171, 173–4

Obscene Publications Acts   1, 20
opium trade   47–8

parents: of delinquents   76–9, 86;
   drug therapy and   109–10, 115
permissiveness   34, 35, 149–74; in
   education   41; interventionist
   172–4; liquidation of   38–9,
   58, 153–6

pharmaceutical companies   107–9,
   111, 115
pleasure   33–4
politics, reformism in   26–40
poor, urban, drugs and   120–1
positivism   116–17
privatisation   34; of homosexuality
   12–13, 164; of prostitution
   12–13, 24, 160–1; regulation and
   12–21
prostitution   150, 155, 158, 172,
   174; call-girl agencies   162;
   commercialisation of   13;
   incidence of   8, 160–1; privatisation of   12–13, 24, 160–1;
   sentences for   161–2; Street
   Offences Act   1, 160–2;
   Wolfenden Report on 9–11
psychiatric social work   113–15
psychopathy and hyperactivity   100
psychotherapy   105
psychotics   99
Puritanism   25–6, 31, 33

race and drugs   52–3, 101, 111, 118
Race Relations Board   126, 141, 144
race relations legislation   122–48;
   ideological framework of   122–9;
   see also immigrants; immigration
racial discrimination   125, 142–3;
   Campaign against (CARD)   145,
   146; in housing   124, 126; in
   labour market   123–4, 126–9,
   131–4, 140–1, 143
racial integration   125–8, 146;
   failure of   129–35, 147;
   immigration control and   135–40;
   machinery of   140–2; in USA
   118; *see also* community relations
racial prejudice   126–9, 131, 136,
   143
racism, institutional value of   118
reform: churches' influence on   4–6;
   lobbies   3–6
reformism   1–3; character of
   26–34; contradictory nature of
   18; legislation of consent and
   1–43; progressive, fate of   35–40;
   social democratic   27; Victorian
   9–10
regulation and privatisation   12–21
religion: fundamentalist   6; influence
   of, on reform   4–6, 20, 25–6

remoralisation 89
residential care 77, 85–6
rock press 69–70
Roman Catholic Church 6
Royal Commissions 3

schoolchildren: attitudes to school
  system 111; drug therapy for
  105–15, 118–20; handicapped
  99; maladjusted 98–9, 104–6;
  see also hyperactivity
sexual conduct, regulation of 15,
  20–1; *see also* homosexuality;
  prostitution
sexual valorisation in advertising 25
Smith, D. J. 130–3, 141
social control 144, 147–8
social services, personal 74–5, 78, 84
social democratic delinquents and
  Fabian families 72–95
spy scandals 8
squatters 155
state: capitalism 36, 38, 94; family
  and 90–2; interventionist
  151–9, 164, 167, 169, 170–4;
  welfare 87–9, 93
street gangs 116–17
Street Offences Act 1959 1, 160–2

teachers, drug therapy and 107,
  110–11, 115
trade unions 135, 145–7
truancy 114, 116

unemployment 59–60, 116, 143,
  146, 155; impact on youth drug
  problem 60–4, 120
United States of America 112,
  117–18; hyperactivity in 97–8,
  101, 113–14
utilitarianism 14, 16, 26, 35–6

welfare state 80, 87–9, 93
welfare-statisation of criminal problems 9–10
Wolfenden Report 8–16, 39, 156,
  159–60, 162, 164–5
women 20–3, 142; *see also*
  femininity
Wootton Report 1, 38–9, 58,
  156–7, 167–9, 172–3
working class 83, 92; teenage drug
  use in 54–6, 60–1, 63, 67–71

youth problems: alcohol 59; drugs
  46, 49, 52–7, 60–4, 67–71, 120;
  homosexuality 11, 163; gangs
  116–17; unemployment 59–64